I0816675

STRIPPED DOWN

Bunnie XO

STRIPPED DOWN

UNFILTERED AND UNAPOLOGETIC

DEYST.

An Imprint of William Morrow

Some names and identifying details of the individuals discussed in this book have been changed to protect their privacy

All insert photographs are courtesy of the author.

HarperCollins books may be purchased for educational, business, or sales promotional use. For information, please email the Special Markets Department at SPsales@harpercollins.com.

hc.com

FIRST EDITION

Designed by Alison Bloomer

Library of Congress Cataloging-in-Publication Data has been applied for.

ISBN 978-0-06-344519-2

26 27 28 29 30 LBC 11 10 9 8 7

To the people who protected me and loved me
when they didn't have to, thank you.
Y'all are my chosen family, and I'll forever be in debt to you.

To the people who tried to break me—
I've got one thing to say to you.

I changed your names to protect my peace. Not yours.

CONTENTS

STRIPPED DOWN

1 STILL HERE

THE THING ABOUT ME IS THAT I SHOULD BE DEAD.

But in those last few minutes before it all went dark, I was riding high, my girl Tamra behind the wheel of my Cadillac Escalade EXT, blasting music and screaming at the top of our lungs. I lay my head down on the edge of the door, letting the cool breeze tingle across my skin through the open window.

I wasn't thinking about the man waiting at home for me, or how Tamra and I had constructed an alibi so I could get some damn breathing room. He thought we were with a client, and there was no reason for him to know the truth. I don't let people drive. I *need* to be in the driver's seat. The one in control. But even I could feel I was too far gone, and she was completely sober. So I gave her the keys and stopped thinking.

I didn't think about the F-250 barreling down the other side of the highway, getting closer. I didn't think about anything but the bright, sparkling lights of the Strip, growing fainter as Tamra drove us home.

When it hit us at seventy miles per hour, my brain went to the crackling static between radio stations. All six thousand pounds of the Escalade flipped into the air, and everything slowed down. Without a seat belt to keep me in place, I arced through the car in slow motion. I swear you could have played a classical concerto as I was tossed around like a rag doll. Metal crunching, windows shattering. Then finally, *crack*. I hit the windshield face-first. My legs whipped up behind me like a scorpion. *Crunch.*

I came down hard in the driver's seat, twisted metal and broken glass everywhere. I couldn't get my bearings and finally clocked Tamra hanging over me by her seat belt.

"Tamra. You okay?" I asked. I couldn't see her face, just her body gone limp.

"Yeah, I'm okay." *Thank God.*

I smelled gas, and I knew we had to get the fuck out. I unhooked her seat belt, and her dead weight slammed on top of me. The entire front windshield was crushed, but somehow the driver's-side window was still intact. Smoke filled the car, so I kicked the window out. It was only a matter of time before a fire would start. Dazed, I pulled myself and then Tamra out. I still had my phone on me. I called Eric and told him we flipped my truck, and I needed him to come and get me before the cops came.

"You're a lying bitch," he said. "You didn't get in a wreck. You sound *way* too calm." Going silent and eerily calm in the face of a crisis is a textbook trauma response, but it would be years before I'd even begin to understand how much I needed to heal. Out on the road with broken glass all around us, I hung up the phone. *Fuck this motherfucker. I'll get you back later, bud.* The cops pulled up, and everything started to go black. I did the only thing I could think to do. I took off running like a bat out of hell.

"Why are you running?" the cop screamed after me.

"I don't talk to police!" I screamed back.

"You're in shock!" he yelled. "You need to sit the fuck down!" But I kept going, one foot in front of the other, running for my life. Or maybe I was trying to run *from* my life—to outrun everything that had come before.

I put my whole body into running, but lit as I was, I must not have gotten very far. The cops caught up with me easily. Hell, maybe I was even running in place. Someone strapped me to a gurney.

Lights out.

XO

I'M GOING TO BE REALLY honest with you. I've spent most of my life trying to get up and get out—to run as fast as I could to escape the pain and the trauma and the past. Whether I was bombed out of my mind on drugs and booze, slipping from one toxic relationship into another, creating drama and reveling in the chaos, packing up to change my life and start fresh, or trying to save people because it made me feel like I was a better person, I was an absolute expert at flooding my bloodstream with numbing agents. But I've got news for you: None of that shit works, at least not in the long run. Eventually, I had to get healthy and get therapy and get *honest.* I had to start seeing myself as worthy of healing and protecting. It's been a process. It still is a process. I'm not done.

I'm blessed that my husband and I found each other, but that wasn't all Cinderella and Prince Charming from the jump. We both tried to dip a time or two—but time, maturity, twisted wisdom, and true fucking connection has brought us to where we are now. I'm blessed that I get to parent our daughter and watch her grow up surrounded by love, but our happy family didn't come easily. I'm blessed to find so much recognition among the flawed, imperfect, beautiful humans out here trying to heal and grow, who find me online or at shows or listen to every single podcast and make me feel less alone. I'm blessed to finally be at peace with myself.

The life I have now wouldn't be possible without acknowledging that I had to stop doing what I was doing. Running away into the arms of a man, into the embrace of a high, or into my own destruction wasn't leading me anywhere good.

I had to find and keep real love—especially for myself. I had to learn how to stay put—to sit still in the pain, to stop pushing away the trauma, and let this body heal. God never left me, and I had to learn how to accept His blessings by showing up for myself like He always had. I had to face death many times over, to look the Grim Reaper in the eye and tell him I wasn't ready to go with him just yet.

Writing this book is part of the healing. I'm not perfect, and my story isn't always pretty. It's a testimony of the many, many failed hits on my life, and an honest excavation of the times when I was the one to try to pull the trigger. It's living proof that when the darkness seems like it's going to pull you under, we're still all worth saving—you and me.

I'm still here, living and breathing and feeling. Thank God.

2 UNHOLY MATRIMONY

BEFORE I WAS BUNNIE, BEFORE THE DRUGS, THE MEN, and the money, and before everything I am today, I was just a bouncy little brunette baby girl named Alisa in Houston, Texas.

My pops was a musician—and a great one at that. Bill Carter was the lead guitarist and lead singer in a big Texas band called BC and Company. He lived the rocker life, and all the clichés of sex, drugs, and rock 'n' roll were Bill's legacy—like when he stole the lead singer of ZZ Top's girlfriend and found himself facing down bullets through the sunroof of his limo. Dad played the circuits, and he was even supposed to sing "The Gambler," but the higher-ups at United Artists gave it to Kenny Rogers instead. You know Bill held a grudge. We weren't allowed to even mention Kenny's name in our household, and whatever Dad said went.

My pops was born in Queens, New York, to my Brazilian grandmother, Zenaide, and his father, Bill senior. It wasn't an ideal home for any kid. His father was a vice president of Valvoline oil company, and my Vovo was an immigrant, which didn't leave her very many career choices, so she became a stay-at-home mom. That woman hung my moon and my stars. When I think of the model of fierce feminine energy and love from my childhood, it's her.

But she didn't show Bill the same love she showed to me. My dad's father ended up leaving Zenaide for his mistress, who he also had children with—and it just broke her. In return, she abused my father mentally, verbally, physically, and emotionally. I've heard from random family members that she was the meanest woman they'd ever met. But for some reason, with me, she never once raised her voice or hands. She only told my father that she loved him one time in his whole life. My heart breaks for the little boy in him who never healed.

Bill attended a college prep school—where he learned that musicians seemed to get all the ladies, so he taught himself how to play guitar and sing. He had a voice like Sting. Bill soon discovered that he could find the love his mother never gave him in the different women he would meet. And until the day he passed, he chose abusive women who never deserved him, replaying the dynamic he had with his mom over and over again.

Bill caused me no end of trauma, but we did have some good moments too, and those I will cherish for the rest of my life. We bonded over music—it was our thing. I'd listen with him for hours in our home studio, watching him sing and play guitar. Sometimes, he'd call on me to be his backup singer. Billy Ocean never saw us coming! My dad would play Billy's tracks and replace Billy's vocals with his own over a microphone blasting through our studio, and I was his backup, ready to sing my heart out with my own mic in hand. If we were really into it, I'd do a backup-singer shimmy like the girls I saw on MTV. He always encouraged me to get out in front as the star of the show, and when people came to visit, he had no problem hyping me up and letting me perform a full production with mics and background music. Those memories will forever make me smile.

Mom was a stripper, and they met at the club. Bill was thirty-three when I was born and Vanessa was, apparently, twenty-two, but she liked to say that Dad made her lie about her age on my birth certificate. Dad always liked his girls young. Their relationship was the typical stripper-musician toxic love affair. Mom was a drug addict and a paranoid schizophrenic, so lies were her only means of communication, and most of Dad's relationship with her was trying to sift through what was real and what was in her head. It was all partying, lying, screaming, and Dad eventually wound up in the hospital with hepatitis from shooting blow. (They lied to me for years and said it was from food, but Bill later confirmed it was drug-related.) While Dad recovered, Mom left me in a car seat on some stranger's doorstep and ran off with the organ player in Dad's band. Going to the lengths I am now to have a child of my own, I could never imagine abandoning my baby and not having a care in the world about what happened to her. Some women just weren't meant to be mothers. Dad got out of the hospital and hunted me down. I was locked in a closet on the other side of town when he found me. He divorced Mom and sued for full custody of me—and honestly, rightfully so.

Again. What the fuck, Vanessa?

Mom didn't put up a fight, and Dad became my sole parent. She wouldn't reenter the scene until one night on AOL Instant Messenger when I was twenty-two. I wouldn't physically hug my mom until I was thirty-six. When she left, I was three months old.

XO

AFTER MOM RAN OUT AND she and Dad divorced, it was just me, Bill, and his group of best friends. I called them all my uncles, and they'd take toddler-me to bars, sit me up on the pinball machine, and let me watch the flashing lights for hours. Some kids have toys—I had three men and a barmaid. Babies in bars—what a time to be alive. Dad said it was his fault I've always been attracted to bright lights and glittery things. It all began on that pinball machine.

My job was to be the comic relief. All I wanted was to make him laugh, especially when things got hard. If I could get Bill to crack a smile, the world would be okay. Even until his last days, I was just trying to make the man laugh. I never cried in front of him. I couldn't let my guard down that way. I'd rather fight back tears than let him see me be weak.

He was a rocker raising a little girl, and it definitely wasn't three meals a day for me. He used to feed me cheese and raw hot dogs, which he kept in his jacket pocket. Years later, I had to break the habit of eating raw hot dogs once I finally started taking care of myself. I love those fucking things. And Vienna sausages. Don't judge me.

There were always women around, coming in and out of our place. I saw everything. Bill had a bad habit of bringing women home and doing the deed right in front of me when I was a young child—literally in the living room where I was supposed to be sleeping. I may have been only two or three, and maybe he thought I wouldn't notice or understand. Or that I wouldn't remember. But those memories are forever burned in my brain. I've seen women passed out on our couch, and I've seen them stay the same age as he got older. None of them stuck around for long, and there were always more of them for Bill to choose from.

This went on until one day when I was five years old and Mindy entered the picture. Everything was about to change.

XO

I WAS A TINY KID sitting on a big motorcycle with Dad when Mindy came up to me and introduced herself.

"I'm Mindy," she said. "I'm gonna be your new mom." Instantly, my defenses went up. *My new mom? Is this woman insane? Does she not know the line of women my pops has going? Get a grip, lady.*

Right off the bat, I sensed that she wasn't a good person. I was only five, but I could see right through her facade. Reading people's energy came early for me, and there was a sinister power just radiating off her. It pulsed stronger as she flashed me a fake smile.

To her irritation, I didn't reply right away. I kept looking down, tinkering with the keys in the ignition on the bike. I had a thousand thoughts running through my head.

Bill could tell I wanted to leave, but he told me, "Be nice, Alisa." I managed to smile at her and giggle, but I knew this shit show was about to start. It went from that conversation right into unholy matrimony. I begged him not to marry her. I screamed and pleaded. I knew what my life would look like with her, and she proved me right the minute she came home with us. Screaming. Dragging me by the arm until I thought my shoulder might come loose. She didn't raise a hand to me yet, but I knew it was coming. But Bill didn't listen to me. He never listened to me.

Come two months later, I was a flower girl in their wedding. Terrified and furious, I sulked through the entire ceremony. My life was blowing up, and I was losing my dad to the Wicked Witch of the South. I wasn't going down in this unholy union without a fight. I did everything I could to make the wedding miserable for everyone.

She had picked the most hideous powder-blue bridesmaid

dresses, the fluffy, frilly 1980s frocks from hell. I was so mad I was being forced to even be in this clown show that I ripped the shit out of my dress. I tore it to shreds. To this day, I can't wear blue clothes or even blue eyeshadow because of that blue dream scene they chose for a wedding. Barf. They had to throw me in a stairwell to scream it out alone, and without anyone watching me, I ran up and down the stairs, hell on wheels, absolutely losing my shit. Pretending to be Alice in Wonderland and escaping from my reality. Finally, the ceremony was over.

"Do you want to call me Mindy or Mommy?" she asked immediately after they said "I do." I looked up at her like *What the fuck? Lady, you have been married for an hour and you're already trying to assert power.*

"Mindy," I said flatly. I could tell it bothered her, but I didn't care. Mindy used to play a manipulative, dramatic game where she'd pretend her feelings were hurt to get what she wanted. She'd curl her bottom lip and make her eyes tear up. It was hideous. You guessed it—the waterworks started. So Dad came over to investigate.

"She won't call me Mom," Mindy said.

"Alisa. You don't have a mom. Just call her Mom," he said, trying to be the hero for his new bride. I gritted my teeth and balled my fists. Rage also came early for me. But he was my pops and the only person I respected. I did what he said. Reluctantly, I started calling Mindy Mom.

They held the reception at a bar in an old train caboose. We were all there—family, Mindy's friends, Dad's crew of uncles, partying like crazy. I was still pissed and spent the event running around like a wild banshee.

What a sight to see. The misery I felt came across loud and clear. My dress was torn, and my face was puffy from crying. I went into the bathroom to sob my eyes out some more, and when

I looked up, I saw the most beautiful woman I'd ever seen. She had thick, jet-black hair and sparkly blue eyes. She leaned down so she was face-to-face with me. I'll never forget the way I felt when I looked at her face. I'd never seen someone so beautiful, and I was transfixed.

My disdain for Mindy must have been seeping through my pores.

"You're not happy your dad married her, huh?" I shook my head. This lady *knew* me! I felt seen! We were connected. She was an angel sent from above.

"She's mean to you, isn't she?" My eyes went wide, and my jaw dropped to the floor. *How did she know about that? How did she know how Mindy already talked to me like I was lower than dirt? That she'd already raised her voice to me and threatened her hands and then sweetly pretended nothing had happened? How did this stranger know what I'd already intuited: that once Mindy and Bill were married, she was only going to get unimaginably worse?* I nodded.

"Do you want to come home with me?" she sweetly asked.

"Yes," I said. I was a kid, and she was so beautiful and warm. I just needed someone to be nice to me and to take care of me. I had never felt that kind of motherly love. She felt like that. And she was a way out. An escape. *Fuck yeah, I'm going with you.*

My new mom took my hand and we walked out into the bar. There was a back kitchen with an exit door, and she started leading me in that direction. This was it! Home free, fuck you Mindy—*yank!*

Someone grabbed my new mom by her hair so hard her feet flew off the damn ground. The next thing I knew, Mindy picked up a wineglass and smashed it over the beautiful lady's face. Blood poured everywhere, and Mindy beat the living shit out of her.

Knowing how Bill operated, I'm guessing that beautiful, nice lady was one of his ex-girlfriends or side chicks who was just as pissed as I was about the new nuptials. Putting two and two together all these years later, it's clear that she was trying to use me as some kind of pawn against my dad, the prettiest, gentlest kidnapper you ever saw. But till the day he died, Bill still swore he didn't know who that woman was. He said she was just some random lady at the bar. *Sure.*

I don't ever think about what would have happened if we'd made it out the door. God wanted me to have *this* life. But in the bar that night, I was scared and angry and hurt. Mindy was kicking that woman's ass, everyone was fucked up and rowdy, and Dad scooped me up, took me outside, and threw me in the car.

We ended the night running like hell from the cops, and when we got home, Bill spanked me to hell and back and grounded me. Knowing what I know now, it was the perfect start to our new life together as a family.

XO

BILL HAD A KNACK FOR marrying jealous women, and he didn't do much to make them trust him. Mindy hated that I was from another one of Dad's relationships, and so she tried to separate us as much as possible. It went from just Dad and me against the world, to Mindy lying about things I'd done to get me in trouble and drive a wedge between me and the only parent I'd ever known. Her parenting style was less Mary Poppins and more Mommy Dearest. She was five ten, platinum blond, and meaner than a junkyard dog.

The abuse started early, and it started with Mindy. She'd go on to introduce me to her sister, who joined in on the abuse, but we'll get there. And the line continued from there: I, too, was abusive and picked one abusive man after the other—whether it was emotional, mental, or physical. And if my man wasn't already abusive, I made him abusive. Eventually, I got to the unholy grail of vile men, the final wannabe boss who almost ended my life. But it all began with Mindy.

If I knew Mindy was evil from the start, she must have thought the same thing about me, even though I was just a kid. Remember, I was five. Right away, she put me to work. Anything she wanted done around the house was my job. She screamed all the fucking time and ruled with her fists. *Was this motherly love? No, thanks.* But she was the only mother figure I'd ever had, and even though I feared her, I looked up to her in a twisted way. She taught me that love meant violence. And like the men who would put their hands on me later, she would always come crawling back after hurting me and say she was sorry.

But looking up to Mindy made things confusing, and as much hell as she put me through, she also taught me how to be a woman. Every morning—even when she wasn't working—she would get up, do her hair, and do her makeup. I would sit and watch her.

"Every morning that you get up is a new day," she'd say. "You make sure you do your hair. Do your make up. No matter what happens throughout the day, you'll feel good."

She taught me to cross my legs when I sat, something I'd teach our daughter when we got custody of her years later. Mindy would put books on my head and make me walk so I learned to stand up straight. She taught me to be poised. She taught me how to keep a house. She taught me how to keep a man. For those things, I'm grateful. I guess if she was going to make my life a living hell, the least she could do was teach me to be "the perfect wife."

XO

MINDY WAS BEAUTIFUL. SHE WAS a busty blond cowgirl with a Southern drawl. But she was also seventeen when she married Dad. He was thirty-seven. Like I said, he liked his girls young. Insert side-eye right here. Her chemical engineer dad and over-the-top beautiful mom sent lavish gifts, held money over their kids' heads, and pretty much hung them out to dry. The fact they let a seventeen -year-old child marry a thirty-seven-year-old man speaks volumes.

She came from a severely abusive home, and I saw that first-hand. I know what type of hell Mindy came from. And I feel for her, ironically, because she brought that same hell to me.

Years later, Mindy apologized.

"I was a child raising a child," she said. "I didn't know any better." I know there's truth to that. She was so fucking young. But the years of abuse she inflicted on me made it damn near impossible to trust a word she was saying. I still can't help but wonder if she only asked for forgiveness because she knew that I was becoming someone worth a damn, someone who got out of the life she made for me. I wonder if she saw my star rising and figured she better get right with me. I forgave her—for myself. But I never forgot.

I'll never forget the first time Mindy really flipped out on me. She had taken me with her to a doctor's office visit, and somehow in the middle of the waiting room, some old man picked me up and put me on his knee. Now, why the fuck we're letting strange men hold our daughters I'll never understand. He asked me if I had a favorite song, and of course I did! Madonna raised me. And then he asked me in front of everyone in the waiting room to sing it to him. So I did.

Ahem. I cleared my throat.

"Like a virginnnnn, touched for the very first timeeeee. Like a virrrrriiiiirrrrrginnnnn—"

"ALISA ANDREA!" Mindy shrieked, yanking me off the old man's lap and smacking my ass right there in the waiting room. I had no idea what I'd done wrong. I was six at the time. I had no idea what the hell a virgin was. I just knew it was a jam. The entire way home, she slapped me across my legs. *How dare I humiliate her like that?* It didn't matter to her that *I'd* been humiliated—picked up onto some strange man's lap and then having my ass beat in front of everyone for doing something I didn't understand.

But as much as Mindy ruled with an iron fist, she protected me too. Talk about confusing. If a boy came around who she didn't like, she'd go get the shotgun. If someone talked shit about me, she'd fight them without a second thought—even if she'd punish me for her trouble with closed fists when we were back home. Over the next twenty years, I'd confuse that kind of fierceness with love. I hated her, but I respected her. And I'm grateful to her too. If it weren't for her, I'd still be eating those raw hot dogs from Dad's coat pocket.

But as much of a monster as Mindy was, she was nothing compared to her sister.

3 NOT A FUCKING DISNEY MOVIE

ANDI WAS MINDY'S YOUNGEST SISTER, AND SHE WAS model gorgeous. I swear to God, she stood six feet tall with the most perfect, beachy blond hair and the longest legs—all natural. She had big brown eyes that looked straight out of a magazine, and when seventeen-year-old Mindy became my stepmom, Andi had just become a teenager. But to my child's brain, she didn't seem like a young kid. She seemed like a full-grown adult with all the power.

I'd watch her put her makeup on and brush her long, perfect hair as she got ready for dates. All the boys lined up for her, and she knew she had that *it* factor they all wanted.

Growing up in the same household Mindy grew up in, Andi experienced the same abuse. A lot of it.

Being a survivor of abuse herself, it was only natural that she'd inflict her pain on someone else—isn't that how pain works? You bleed on the people who didn't cut you? I know what she found with me: a way to feel some kind of control. He abused her, so she'd abuse me. It was all she knew. She'd been taught that love hurts, so she taught me the same lesson.

Andi would come to Mindy and Bill's house to babysit me while they were out at work or partying, and we had a routine. She'd pour some of my parents' cheap boxed wine into one of our many crystal wineglasses and hand it to me. My parents made sure we always had a fully stocked bar wherever we lived.

"Drink," she'd say, and I'd take a sip, even if it tasted like rubbing alcohol and burned my mouth. Even if I was only barely five years old. Then she'd put me on the couch and smirk.

"Okay, Lizard," she'd say sarcastically, using the nickname my father so lovingly gave me. "Let's watch a Disney movie." I knew she wasn't talking about fucking *Cinderella*. We'd been through this plenty of times.

I'd keep sipping my wine, and she'd put on the movie. It was always porn, usually lesbian porn with women not too much older than her. Nowadays I wonder if she was experimenting with something, or if she had some kind of deep hatred of men after what her dad did to her and didn't want to watch them get off. But back then, I didn't understand what I was watching. I didn't know shit about sex or lesbians. I just knew this wasn't a fucking Disney movie. I knew something was wrong, and that it made me feel funny. I wanted it to stop.

I don't remember Andi ever molesting me. She didn't touch me like that. That's not to say she didn't lay a hand on me—she definitely did. I didn't say a word about the porn to Bill or Mindy, because Andi threatened to beat my ass like she had over and over since the day we met. She would also threaten me while hanging me upside down by my Achilles tendons on both ankles. It was torture. And she did it all the time.

But when she'd put on those Disney movies, we'd just sit on the couch next to each other, watching, like she was showing me her favorite movie and I was drinking Hi-C in my sippy cup. It was our thing we did together. *I guess this is what families do?* When my parents got home from wherever they were, I'd lie and say we'd watched the Fairy Godmother turn Cinderella into a princess.

Andi would beat the dog shit out of me when she was bored or angry or frustrated. It didn't take much. And then she'd love on me like nothing had happened. Mindy was the same way: They'd hurt you and then flip the switch to turn on the Southern charm. *Oh honey. You know I love you, right?*

I couldn't wait to get out of that fucking family of two-faced fakers. To this day, I can't stand fake people. Be real or don't talk to me.

XO

IF I DO THE MATH, Mindy was probably pretty damn pregnant with my little sister, Baby Sis, when she married Bill. This chubby-cheeked cherub we later would lovingly call Burger showed up in August 1985, and I was officially a big sister. I was excited to be a big sister, but Mindy made it clear that I was no longer a part of the family. I wasn't worth shit, she told me, because my own mom was a stripper who showed her titties to men in clubs. It didn't bother me at all that my mom danced. I didn't think there was anything wrong with it. Sounds like she was just like one of the women in the movies her sister made me watch. It even sounded fun.

But Mindy said we were trash, and in the family of Mindy, Bill, and Baby Sis, I was the wicked stepchild who was a constant reminder that there were women before her.

XO

I WAS FIVE WHEN THE son of a family friend who was visiting got into bed with me and started me down the path of sexual trauma.

He was so much older—about sixteen or seventeen. For some unknown reason, my parents thought it would be a great idea to let him sleep in my Strawberry Shortcake–themed bedroom. They even let him sleep in my bed, and I had to sleep on the floor.

I was a water baby. If it was summertime, I had a bathing suit on—especially my aqua one with ruffles. I'd played my heart out that day at a family barbecue and must have just passed out in this bathing suit. Suddenly, I snapped awake. Someone was tugging at my bathing suit from the bottom. He slid it to the side, and I felt fingers on my vagina and someone spreading my lips open. I opened my eyes just a little bit. I was too scared to react, but I saw who was touching me.

As he poked and prodded around, all that was flashing in my mind were the porn videos Aunt Andi had shown me. *This is what they do? Why does it feel so scary? Surely the people in the video don't feel like this?*

He flipped me on my stomach, and as I pretended I was still asleep, he spread my cheeks open and ran his fingers over my asshole. Fury started building up inside me. *Why is everyone so fucked up?*

Remember how I've said God has always divinely protected me? He didn't let me down this time either.

Suddenly, my ear burst into pain. It felt like my ear drum had popped. I screamed so loud that it scared the shit out of him, and he got back into bed. I ran to my parents' room, hollering from the pain. And in front of Bill and Mindy, I was so focused on my ear and wanting the pain to stop that I didn't tell them what he'd done. To this day, I regret keeping quiet, because years later I found out that he had been violently raping his own sister. He did it to her for years. It broke my heart when she and I got closer later in life and shared our traumas. Mine was nothing near what she'd gone through. I wish I could have saved her.

XO

IN TEXAS, WE LIVED IN a duplex with a huge front yard, and Bill and Mindy used to throw me outside and lock the door so they could party, drink, do drugs—whatever they wanted. Baby Sis was just a baby and got to stay inside, but they left me to entertain myself for hours on end.

We had a boat out on the side of the house, and I could kill a whole afternoon alone out there sailing the high seas. My imagination was my best friend as a child, and I always made my own fun—even as lonely as I was. I didn't think about whether or not I was safe outside. With Andi's weird antics, that fucking family friend, and Mindy's temper, I wasn't safe around anyone older than me. Alone outside, I felt free.

But it's not surprising that some sick, twisted men saw an opportunity when they came across a little girl like me all alone. It doesn't take much to tell that a kid is vulnerable and easy prey. It's exactly what happened at Bill and Mindy's wedding with that beautiful, dark-haired woman. I guess I was an easy target.

When a rusty brown van pulled up and two guys got out, they pulled the same thing.

"Do you wanna come play with us?" one of them asked. I can't remember what they looked like, just that they made me queasy with anxiety.

"You look like you need a friend," the other said, as they stalked closer to me. I remember the fear as clearly as if it were happening right this very moment. *They're going to take me away. They're going to hurt me.* Like I said, my gift is seeing people for who they are. It was the kind of fear that's so intense, you feel like your feet have been lifted up off the ground. Something inside me said *run*.

I took off sprinting toward my parents' house. The door was locked like always, and I could hear their loud music from inside. I pounded on the door with my little hands, terrified the men were right behind me. Someone finally answered and I fell inside, but when I told them men had tried to take me, Bill and Mindy didn't believe me. They rolled their eyes and went back to whatever they were doing.

They kept on locking me outside, and now I was scared. I got back in the damn boat and played my games. There just weren't any other options, so I was going to make it work.

One afternoon on the boat, a crusty old bearded man came up and knocked on the deck. I eyed him and stood back, disgusted by his sick smile.

"Do you wanna play milk-the-snake?" he asked.

"What's milk-the-snake?" I asked. I must have been about six, and I guess first grade hadn't covered milking snakes yet.

"Milk this snake," he said, stepping back from the boat and showing me his dick. "Have you ever milked a snake?"

I'd never seen a penis in real life before, only in the pornos Dad watched and the ones Andi showed me, but it absolutely repulsed me. He was jerking off—not like I knew what that even was—and when he came, my whole body rebelled. I started screaming my head off, and the dude pulled up his pants and ran. I screamed and screamed and ran back to the locked door and pounded again, and this time Mindy actually believed me when I described what happened. She must have figured *someone* had made me scream like that. And how would I know what ejaculation looked like? Mindy let me stay inside that day, but come the next morning, I was out in the boat with the door locked behind me.

Over the next few years, they'd put me to work more and more. It would become my job to pick up the dog shit in our yard, but they wouldn't let me use a shovel, because the whole point was to keep me occupied and out of the house. Mindy gave me barbecue tongs, and I had to pick up one tiny piece at a time over an acre of land. Yup, you heard that right. BBQ tongs that flip chicken. Did I mention we had thirteen dogs? Those cocker spaniels wouldn't stop fucking each other. If I so much as looked at a shovel, I'd get in trouble. I was like any kid, and I wanted to be normal. I wanted to go play. But I had jobs to do, so I started making all my chores into a game or a challenge in my head. *How fast can I get this done?* Then after that, it was off to weed and mow the lawn. I swear they thought I was their servant.

While I was outside tweezering dog shit, my dad would sit on his computer all day every day. He had two screens going, and he'd pretend to be trading stocks, but I know he had a secret online life of chat rooms and weird shit. He was obsessed with porn, and he even watched it on our living-room TV. I'll never forget the time I saw him sitting at the damn dining-room table, craning his neck at the TV in the living room. From my own room, I could see the TV and the naked women getting plowed. I told Mindy what I'd seen the next day, and you better believe Bill grounded me for snitching him out. I don't know what he was doing at the dining-room table, and I sure as hell don't want to know.

Those early years were a fast track to adulthood. There weren't any moments of just being a kid—those weren't allowed.

Plus, who was going to clean the house? Who was going to make sure Bill and Mindy didn't kill each other? Being a child just wasn't in my cards, and it affects me to this day. I struggle to relax or do the things I wished I could have done as a kid. I'm not programmed to have fun. I'm programmed to work. It's all I've ever known.

4

"HEY GOD, IS THAT YOU?"

"PUT A DAMN DRESS ON. WE'RE GOING TO CHURCH," Mindy said. *What the fuck?* Our family didn't go to church. We were a rock 'n' roll family with drugs, sex, porn, and liquor, and I couldn't imagine setting foot in God's house.

We'd just packed up and moved from Houston to Las Vegas, allegedly because of Bill's job. And this might be pure speculation on my part, but it seemed obvious to me even then that Bill was having an affair. I'd hear Bill and Mindy scream at each other all night long, and it wasn't hard to catch the gist. One thing Bill was gonna do was *Bill*—no matter who it hurt.

All they ever did was fight, and I learned to tune most of it out. Mindy didn't speak below a level 9, and to this day I can still hear her screams in my head. It's probably why I'm such a soft-spoken person these days. When your house is a war zone, you learn to sleep through the battle. Even today, if my husband is on a business call and asks for my opinion, I always tell him I didn't hear a damn thing and he's going to have to bring me up to speed. You learn never to eavesdrop and to mind your own business. It's safer that way. But in fleeting moments I did catch a few things: other women, lying and cheating, *go to fucking hell.*

Instead of hell, we went to Vegas's fiery inferno. We had to get away from it all, and it was time for a new start without the lying, cheating, good-for-nothing version of Bill in Texas. And just to be sure the change of location worked, Mindy needed *some* way to keep Bill in check, something that could take up all of Bill's time and focus, leaving no room for him to wind up in another woman's bed. The Pentecostal Church would do the job.

By then, I was about nine, and being as young as I was, I had no other choice but to convert like my parents. Life changed overnight. I'd grown up with Pops's band practicing across from my room with the bass at full volume and crashing drums on school nights, partying, drugs, and so much music. So it came as a huge shock the day my holier-than-thou folks decided to tell me I was no longer allowed to listen to secular music—ever. *What the fuck do you mean? No AC/DC, no Madonna, no Cyndi Lauper? Surely this is a joke.* It wasn't. (I'm not complaining though—Crystal Lewis, DC Talk, and Carman fed my soul.)

Music had been my only escape. One Christmas, I was gifted a little yellow boom box with a tape recorder built in. I would sit outside in my driveway for hours recording music off the radio, and then between songs I would do my own DJ show. This is what replaced hanging out in that damn boat. I recorded hours and hours of tapes. My DJ name was Lacey Carter, and I was bringing you the hits! It was one of the few joys I had as a child—and now they were taking it from me. I didn't have a choice but to abide by their Bible-thumping rules, even if it hurt like hell.

But every night when it was time to go to sleep, I would put my little yellow boom box under my pillow and turn on the radio as low as I could without getting caught. It was my only sense of normalcy until I woke up one morning without any music playing. I lifted my pillow up and saw that sometime in the middle of the night, Mindy had come in and cut the black wire to my boom box. How could you do that to a child, knowing it provided their only sense of peace? I got ready for school in shock and cried my eyes out on the school bus.

I could now only watch G-rated movies, so at least that took care of the porn, and we'd left Andi behind in Houston anyway. No TV was allowed—ever. So that meant no more of the MTV that I'd practically been raising myself on. Add in dresses down to my ankles—that Mindy decided she wanted to sew herself. Just envision *Little House on the Prairie*, and I was Laura fucking Ingalls. Bill and Mindy took our newfound faith to the absolute extreme. Church was every Sunday morning, Sunday night, and Wednesday night, and there were Bible studies and Bible camps and youth groups too. If I wasn't babysitting Baby Sis or doing my list of never-ending chores, I couldn't do anything but eat, sleep, and church. My life was so restrictive, it felt like I couldn't breathe or think for myself. It was so forced and abrupt, and enough to turn anyone off religion.

I had whiplash from the shock of our new life. In the midst of this transition, I got a special job. I was the offering girl, and I'd carry the plate around collecting cash from the congregants. Whoever decided I was trustworthy enough to have even this title must have been fooled by my angelic smile and big, bright eyes. They didn't see that my horns were there to hold up my halo. It didn't matter if I went looking for it or not—trouble always found me.

Think of the cartoons where the angel is on one shoulder and the devil is on the other: That's my entire life. I was a natural-born hell-raiser. I've always been a rebel without a cause. So, as I carried that plate, loaded with singles and fives, I wondered, *Why on earth would I not swipe some for myself?* I was doing the Lord's work, wasn't I? I was only nine when this was happening, so did I even know any better? *Wink wink.*

To this day, I feel awful, and I've since apologized to that church publicly. But as a kid, my eyes popped out of my head when I saw all that cash. *They're trusting me with this plate full of money? No one would notice five dollars missing.* Candy bars were calling my name. Whatchamacallits were my addiction, and I was going to feed it any chance I could. I was like a crackhead for some chocolate. At home, Mindy governed everything I ate. I was never allowed to freely take anything from the fridge or cabinets. And to be able to snack between meals? Never. I was only allowed to eat what was served to me at dinner—which was a one-way ticket to an eating disorder. Sugar wasn't allowed in our house, so that was another secret I kept along with the string of others I'd learn to collect over the years.

No one ever caught me stealing from the offering plate—or maybe they did and just never said anything. But we moved on from that church after a short time and the 'rents were ready for a wannabe megachurch down by the Strip.

I actually started looking forward to the Bible camps because I could get away from my shackles and cage and just *be*—because even if Bill and Mindy were thumpin' their Bibles with fervor, they were anything but good and loving Christians at home. The abuse didn't stop—church just gave them new rules to enforce and new punishments to dole out. The hypocrisy disgusted me. But the worship leaders were different. They were the first adults to ever give me grace, and they would show me that not all adults are out to hurt you. They just tried to help me understand that I was a child of God.

XO

A FEW YEARS OF LOVING the Lord and hearing testimonies encouraged me to speak out about things that happened to me as a child. By the time I was twelve, I was feeling confident in myself and in my walk with God. I finally decided to confide in my parents about what had happened with our family friend's son. I didn't say anything about Andi—I've never said a word about that until I sat down to write this book.

This was the moment I was going to tell them where so much of my anger was coming from so hopefully they would be able to see me like my pastors and friends at church. You would think that being good Christian people, their hearts would have softened, but it was still a military base at home. Still, I was finally ready to tell my truth.

"You're lying, Alisa," Mindy said without any hesitation. It felt like being slapped in the face. She and Bill exchanged looks—and then they laughed at me. I was so stunned by their reaction I couldn't even process it. All I knew was that for the first in what little life I had lived, I truly felt alone—and most certainly unprotected. Fuck all the ass whoopings, fuck being grounded all the time, fuck them not even liking me because I was a reminder of the past. I was sitting there telling them a man touched me, and they were calling me a liar? *Fuck you.*

I realized I never wanted to be like them, and I vowed never to confide in or trust my parents again. It sparked a rage inside of me I had never felt before.

Years later, I was proven right when that same guy ended up in prison for serial rape—on top of what he did to his own flesh and blood. *Checkmate, bitches.*

With years between me and that horrible abuse, all I can say is: If a child ever comes to you, believe them. They've already been through enough trauma at that point. There's no need to add to their therapist bills later in life.

XO

I'D ALWAYS KNOWN THERE WAS a higher power, even in my earliest memories. I have six planets in the eighth house, and if you know anything about astrology, that means I'm obsessed with all things spiritual, occult, mystical, and dark. Lucky me. I've been seeing ghosts and spirits since I was a child. I guess that's why I can read someone in five minutes flat when they walk into my energy.

I remember the first time I saw a ghost—I now know it was a spirit who was playing with me. I was in my room throwing a fit because Bill was practicing with his band across the hall from my room, and I wanted to hang out but Mindy had said it was bedtime. *How dare she.* As I kicked and flailed my arms, I grabbed my pillow over my head and screamed in it. When I took the pillow off my face, my entire Strawberry Shortcake bedspread was suspended in midair in the shape of a ghost. The hair on my neck stood up, and I walked on air running to get out of my room—which of course landed me an ass whooping because Mindy didn't believe me.

She threw me right back into the haunted house, and I had no choice but to make friends with this spirit. By that time, my blanket was back on my bed, but I could just feel its presence in the room. After I collected myself, I found comfort in knowing a spirit was trying to make me laugh when I was so distraught. And my spiritual openness would go on to save me from plenty of near-death moments. Ever since then, I've never feared the world beyond—until I went through my suicidal depression in 2020. We'll get there—trust me when I say that was one of the scariest times of my life. I've always been curious about the supernatural. It was obvious to me then as it is now that we're not alone out here.

XO

I WASN'T ALLOWED TO EVEN think about boys. Sex before marriage was shunned and you were made to feel dirty if you ever had "bad" thoughts. It's crazy how Bill so freely engaged in sexual acts my entire childhood, but the minute Jesus stepped foot in our lives, everything we once knew was bad. Now, we were all pure thoughts, all the time. Talk about confusion. Can you see where my anger stems from?

I'd watch the adults kiss up to the main pastor or try to impress him with their faith and hefty tithes—and for some reason, the pastor was held up on the world's highest pedestal. He had the perfect family, with a beautiful wife and daughters. Gosh, they were beautiful—and they set one hell of an unrealistic standard for perfection. But seeing my parents sweeten up for church and go home to be the same profane people I'd always known got me questioning, and I started paying close attention. I'd overhear Bill and Mindy gossiping about other churchgoers, or my friends would confide in me about what happened behind their families' closed doors. Soon enough, I knew what all these people did at home, away from the pastor and from the eyes of the other congregants. I saw the hypocrisy—especially around the fear. My God, the fearmongering was constant. Step out of line, burn in hell. The point was to be scared shitless. Deep down I knew this wasn't how faith was supposed to be.

I'll never forget the day a traveling evangelist came to the church and all the families showed up to hear his message on why secular music was so bad for kids. He taught about "back-masking" and played records backward to reveal demonic chants. He especially went in on Madonna—Madge had been the soundtrack to my life. He must have felt the daggers coming from my eyes because he walked over to me and stuck a mic in my face.

Mindy looked over and beamed with pride at the attention from all the pastors and their families and the congregation. Her pride would be short-lived.

The evangelist asked me to name as many Madonna songs as I could. So I did. I named them all. I named so many he yanked the mic away.

"And there you have it, folks. That's how much of a hold Satan has on our youth. That this young lady could name that many Madonna songs off the top of her head." Mindy glared at me. And when we got in the car, she screamed at me the entire way home for humiliating her in front of the congregation.

To this day, I don't think God's as black-and-white as the church told me He was. Jesus was a Capricorn, after all, and we share a lot of those Capricorn traits because I'm right on the cusp. He's all about the gray. But in those Pentecostal church pews, there was good and evil, clean and dirty, God and Satan. And when you have a family like mine, where I witnessed sexual abuse, affairs, violence, pornography, lies—and then you're told that all that same shit sends you to hell—you get massive anxiety and religious trauma. It's why I call myself spiritual more than religious now. I cannot stand organized religion—and I truly feel Jesus can't either.

The church had me questioning every thought in my head. *Am I a hypocrite because I cuss? If I kiss a boy, am I going to rot in hell?* I kept on rebelling against any authority figure I could. It was how I was surviving in the world. But it weighed on me every day—a panic that I'd see some kind of divine retribution for the bad thoughts I had, or for being angry or scared.

I figured I'd go to hell for being a normal, angsty kid.

Man, does this shit stick with you. I still can't take the Lord's name in vain—it scares me too much. If my daughter or my husband says it, I tell them to stop right away. God has been nothing but my divine protector. But it's like a habit I can't break: the unknown of heaven or hell.

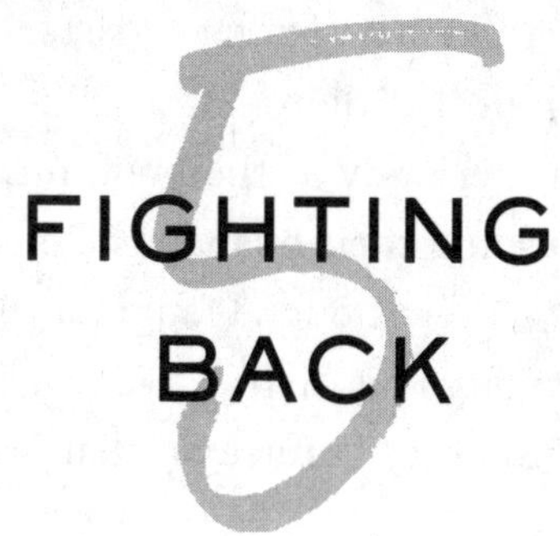

5 FIGHTING BACK

WE'D LEFT MY AUNT ANDI BEHIND IN HOUSTON, BUT MY parents couldn't wait to ship Baby Sis and me off for the summer. By junior high, Andi had roped her a millionaire named Henry and moved to Kentucky. She might have been crazy as shit, but she was still drop-dead gorgeous.

Henry was sweet, and he loved my aunt. She towered over him at six feet, and poor Henry was short, stocky, and couldn't have been more than five six. But all that mattered was he loved her. I'm sure the bank account helped. And he was nice to us—even if he didn't know what would happen when he left the house. I was too young to judge the situation, and I was too young to understand their dynamic or to realize how much older Henry was than Andi. It was normal to me that an older man would be with a much younger woman. But there was one thing I knew for certain: Henry thought my beautiful aunt walked on water.

They spent weekends at the country club, and Andi would turn on the Southern charm and pretend to be the perfect wife and aunt, just like her two-faced sister, Mindy. The acting gene must run in that damn family. She went looking for a reason to flaunt her body at the pool in front of the other country club wives and their husbands. So she signed me up for the diving team, even though I fought it tooth and nail. I'm not coordinated enough for diving, and I wasn't thrilled to be risking my life with every bounce on that board. But I didn't have a choice.

There wasn't a moment I didn't feel out of place around all that country club–style wealth. I've made a lot of money for myself, but even today, I still feel like an outsider around that kind of money. Old money. Hell, my husband and I *lived* in a country club, and I still didn't feel like I belonged.

Our summer with Andi just dripped with fake charm and fake happiness. It was almost like she was trying to prove to Henry she was mommy material when in reality she was Mommy Dearest. And the minute Henry wasn't around she turned on the physical and verbal abuse. Every minute with her was a nightmare. She was a ticking time bomb. I eventually even tried to tell Mindy and Bill how abusive she was, but of course no one ever listened and thought I was being dramatic or exaggerating. So Baby Sis and I had to sit there and take her tirades and act like we enjoyed it for the whole summer, especially on calls home, because Andi would sit right in front of us every time we were on the phone, listening to every word.

One night, I was fucking tired of being a human punching bag and I snapped. I heard something funny from the bathroom and found Andi holding Baby Sis's little head under the water.

"What are you doing?" I screamed. "Leave her alone!" I ran up and started pounding on her back.

I realized what I'd done and backed away, but Andi turned and looked me up and down. She grabbed Baby Sis out of the tub, carried her to the room next door, threw her down on the bed, and pressed a pillow over her face. I didn't even have time to think. I just jumped onto Andi's back and started screaming at her to get off my sister. I doubt my little fists were doing much, but I fought like hell and got her loose. You know when someone pushes your face so far down into the mattress you can't breathe? Andi slammed her hand down, holding my face until there wasn't any air. I was screaming and Baby Sis was too, while Andi beat the shit out of me. I didn't think I'd make it.

Finally, she stopped. Henry must have come home, but whatever it was, she snapped out of it. Right after, she tried to hug and console us and tell us she was sorry. Talk about a complete mindfuck.

The violence I was subjected to by the people who said they loved me and called themselves my family has left scars on my heart. Growing up, I could never understand why I was so angry and so violent, but writing these pages makes it crystal clear. There was no way I wouldn't have been. Children are sacred, and sometimes people don't deserve them.

XO

HEADING BACK HOME AT THE end of the summer was small comfort. Instead of Andi screaming at us, my parents screamed at each other, and Mindy screamed at me—always. It would go on for hours and hours, and it was always about money or my dad's cheating—I guess even the Lord couldn't help Bill keep it in his pants. No wonder I couldn't ever stay faithful either.

One night, the arguments reached a new level of TMI—clearly, we had zero boundaries in this damn family. Bill told Mindy she wasn't fucking him enough, and so she went on a tirade. Now, I don't really blame her, but at the time, all I could hear was this woman piling verbal abuse on my dad. I was so attached to him, even with all his problems, and to hear and see him insulted and abused emotionally hurt me. I would get so upset listening to this woman talking to my dad like that, but he wouldn't say anything. He'd just take it, and I couldn't fucking stand it. Women like Mindy would be his weakness until his last day. Maybe it's because of the little boy in him who was never loved that he wouldn't stand up for himself. Maybe if he couldn't be faithful, at least he could let them manipulate him and he'd take their verbal abuse. For him, it must have been what love was—or at least a fair trade. And even as it was eating me up inside, I couldn't say a word either. I just had to watch it all happen. It made me resent her even more.

The argument turned to money like it always did, and Mindy was being a cunt about my school clothes. She laid into him about how much I cost—and remember, Mindy made it clear I wasn't part of their family. Why should she have to pay for my clothes?

My dad and I went outside to the front yard to catch a breath from the war zone we called home, and I tried to defuse the situation. Maybe I could just make it all go away.

"I'm sorry you have to buy me school clothes, Dad," I said, staring at the ground. "I'll wear what I have." He didn't say *This isn't your fault* or *I love you. Don't listen to her.*

"You're under my roof until you're eighteen, Alisa," he said. "Until then, you're my responsibility."

"I'll be out of here before then," I said flatly. No way I would stick around for the screaming and abuse. I was still in junior high school, but I was already reaching my limit.

"Shut up, Alisa," he said. "You're here 'til you're eighteen."

Wanna put some money on that, Mr. Carter? 'Cause I'll never lose a bet.

6 HELL-RAISER

I'VE ALWAYS BEEN A WILD HYENA—WE'VE ESTABLISHED that by now.

By junior high, I was fighting constantly. Everywhere. Church, parties, bus stops. I was fighting in school too. I was never one to start shit—but I sure as hell would finish it.

One day early on, I got jumped at the bus stop by three girls—probably because I looked at one of them the wrong way. I got my ass handed to me. I'm talking steel-toed boots to the face, three on one. I went home tail tucked and crying. You would think your parents would coddle you and help lick your wounds, but nope. Instead, Bill took it upon himself to teach me how to fight.

"Life is hard, Alisa," he told me, "and just because you get your ass whooped doesn't mean you lie down and cry about it." As if I hadn't been getting my ass whooped for years already—by his wife. But okay. Go off, Pops.

We went out in the back yard, and he held his hands out in front of him.

"Hit me," he said, and I took a swing. He caught my hand and threw it back down.

"That's not how you throw a punch. You don't make a fist with your thumb like that. You do it like *this*." He taught me to square up and rotate my shoulder, and I was outside until dark punching my father's hands.

We practiced every day after school. He taught me to kick or pull hair if I couldn't get a good hit in. My favorite was yanking someone by the hair and slamming their face on my knee—it became my signature move. That and always throwing the first punch.

XO

BY THE TIME I LEARNED how to throw a punch, I was attending Fremont Junior High in Vegas, and all the anger I accumulated over the years was barreling out as I lashed out at everybody. I'd become the kid whose friends' parents wouldn't let come around. I was a *bad influence*, and I reveled in it.

My parents assumed the nonstop fighting and detentions were because of my school environment, so they put me in a private, religious junior high school associated with our church, Trinity. Maybe they were hoping I'd calm down or that private school would be less hardcore. But it didn't take long before I made friends with a fellow troublemaker—Nicole, who had jet-black hair and stick-on tattoos. Not to mention, her mom was pretty and let her do whatever she wanted. I was so jealous that she had a mom who was her best friend—but the jealousy didn't have any teeth. I just loved what she had and wanted it.

I loved that girl. We spent our days drinking and smoking between classes. And to add to it, I had Randi, my best friend from church too. We got in trouble for passing explicit notes back and forth talking shit about our teachers, but we did it all to make each other laugh. I just could never focus on school. It was near impossible for me to learn anything, and I'd sit there in class with my mind racing a thousand miles an hour. There had to be more to life than sitting in a cage for eight hours a day doing math. I just wanted to have fun in between worship and Bible study and school uniforms and being told we're going to hell. A little laughter at the teachers' expense was perfect—until we got caught. Busted. Off to the principal's office the three of us went. The intercepted letter was so explicit they called our parents and read the letter out loud to them. Yup. Grounded again.

My days were numbered at that school. Mindy refused to let me buy lunch or any junk food. Remember, she had me on a strict diet. And she sent me to school with chicken cacciatore for lunch, and like every kid, I just wanted to be like everyone else. It was humiliating pulling a huge Tupperware out of my backpack and not even being able to heat it up. So I did what made the most sense at the time. I walked into the girls' bathroom and flushed that chicken cacciatore and white rice down the toilet. I didn't think anyone would notice, and I'd just go buy lunch like everybody else.

Backing up the entire school's plumbing system was the straw that broke the camel's back for me at Trinity. I hadn't been trying to get in trouble—and how was I supposed to know that rice would clog up the whole fucking drainage system? Who knew rice swelled that much? I sure didn't. They handed me an expulsion that day. But hey, at least it wasn't for fighting. We were making strides.

Freshly expelled, my parents put me in another private school, Harbor Christian Academy. The school was no bigger than a thousand square feet with maybe six to eight kids per classroom. Every single lesson was on a VHS tape from 1982. It felt like a last resort for troubled kids. The good news is that it was right down the street from my house, so I could ditch and run home to hang out while Bill and Mindy were at work.

Not one to shy away from adventure, when someone handed me a can of spray snow after school one day, I tagged my name on a brick wall on campus—my entire government name. How the hell was I supposed to know it would look like spray paint or that it would stick? *Why did I write my fucking name?* Combine that with my attitude toward adults and constant ditching and, well, you guessed it, they showed me the door. Back to public school I went—and yet somehow in the midst of all this chaos, I managed to graduate eighth grade. High school was next.

I was used to being a bad influence and a big man on campus. Not there. At my high school, I was the low man on the totem pole. It all felt like some kind of humiliation ritual, and of course all the kids made fun of me. It was clear I didn't fit in. I didn't know any of their slang. I was too innocent. Me? Innocent with a clean mouth? It's honestly shocking—I was the worst kid at my private school and now the most innocent at my public school. Here's a little perspective: Maybe I hadn't been such a bad kid, after all. Maybe I was just a normal kid who craved some love and needed some help.

I got tired of the bullying. I wanted to be like everyone else. One night, I sat in my room practicing mouthing off with every cuss word I could think of. I recited all the dirty jokes I'd ever heard out of Bill's mouth. I was tired of being the innocent girl. I wanted to be the bad girl—like how I thought of myself—and like the villains in the movies I loved.

I joined every sports team I could in high school. Sports were an escape from home, and I loved the team mentality and working toward a goal together. But I also got to run off all the extra energy I always felt, sitting in my throat and choking me.

My parents never came to a single one of my games. Sometimes, when I would see the other kids' parents cheering them on, it would hurt my heart. But then, I would think how embarrassed I'd be if Mindy was there yelling at me, or Bill, critiquing my every play. Then I'd let it go. Plus, who had time to wallow in self-pity?

XO

I'LL NEVER FORGET THE FIRST time I saw Tasha. She was a cheerleader with long, curly blond hair—and even longer legs. All the boys in school drooled over her, and once you saw her, you didn't forget her. When I walked into my theater class that first day, I noticed her right away. Plus, we were both freshmen in a sea of seniors.

We were a little standoffish with each other at first, but we weren't mean. We always worked in the same groups and did scenes together, but we didn't really talk outside class. She had her own set of friends, and I had mine, having finally broken free of the bullying bullshit.

One day we were in class and the door to the theater flung open.

"Where the fuck is Tasha?" screamed one of the senior girls who was notorious for fighting. "I'm going to beat your fucking ass, Tasha! You fucked my boyfriend!"

I swung my head around to find Tasha onstage, obviously caught by surprise. The girl walked across the auditorium, closing in on Tasha, and I could see that Tasha didn't want to fight her. So before this senior could get to her, I stood the fuck up.

"Mandy, get the fuck out of here," I said. I knew Mandy, and we'd talked a few times in the hallway. When you're both known for fighting, you develop a mutual respect. I didn't know the details of Mandy's beef with Tasha, but I wasn't about to let it explode in our theater class.

Mandy stopped dead in her tracks.

"Stay the fuck out of this! It's between her and me."

I stayed super calm, no matter how pissed she was.

"Nah, it's not," I said. "Get the fuck on." By that time, the teacher had caught wind of what was happening and sent her straight to the dean's office.

"Thank you," Tasha said to me. I just smiled.

"No problem."

We were instant friends after that.

XO

I'VE ALWAYS PREFERRED HAVING FEMALE friends over male. I like to think it's because in a past life, I was a witch who belonged to a coven of powerful, spiritual women who scoffed at the men who fell to their feet and cast spells on any who wronged them. I've just always felt safer in numbers with women as my allies. And in high school, my crew was Tasha, my cousin Stacy, Michelle, and Lisa. We were all from the most dysfunctional families and somehow—like the wayward get-along gang—we found each other. They're still by my side today.

I got to know Tasha pretty quickly after that day in class. She came from a broken home too. Dad wasn't around and Mom popped in and out. When Tasha and I started hanging out, she was living with her aunt. She was one of the prettiest girls in our school, but it's almost like she didn't realize how beautiful she was. She also had a Blood boyfriend, like Barbie and gangster Ken.

Her family of misfits is honestly what drew me to her. They were as trailer trash as could be, and I loved it. They would barbecue and sing classic rock songs, and even though they fought like cats and dogs, they still stuck by one another's side and welcomed me into their raging vortex with open arms. They knew how fucked up my life at home was, and soon enough, my family was on Tasha's family's shit list.

Michelle has been one of my best friends since second grade. She couldn't be more polar opposite than me, but that girl has always had my heart—her mom, Sherri, does, too. Hers was one of the few houses I was allowed to go to and stay the night. Boy, did we abuse that privilege. I wanted to stay every night if I could, because her house was full of love and happiness. Her mom was the sweetest woman I'd ever met and knew what was going on at my house. She hated sending me home. She knew what was waiting for me.

Michelle and her mom stood by each other up until the day Mama Sherri passed away. The only way I could honor Ms. Sherri was to send her off in the best funeral Michelle could possibly put together for her. We dressed her up in the most leopard-print-clad way we could, and I could feel her soul smiling down on us as we sat by her casket. She was such a special woman, and she's the one who gave me memories of childhood love.

And then there was Stacy—a fucking lunatic. A lovable lunatic, but a lunatic all the same. She was adopted by two lesbians when she was a baby—the story's changed a few times, to be honest, but Phyllis and Kate raised Stacy with a little more money than the rest of us. I mean, they had a pool, for God's sake.

You never knew what kind of mood Stacy would be in, but when it came down to it, she was always there for you. Even if she didn't want to be—and trust me, you knew when she was there but wished she were somewhere else.

Phyllis and Kate kept an eye on us, because they knew that together we were trouble. But they overlooked a lot of my colorful behavior because of what I had going on at home. Now that I look back, it's clear that everyone else's parents hated my parents. At least I wasn't alone.

Lisa was the "mom" of the crew. She was responsible, had a great family life with parents who loved her, and a longtime boyfriend she'd been with for years. She lost her virginity to him and they stayed committed. If you ever needed anything, Lisa was the one who would show up on time. Her mom was the sweetest and always welcomed me in their house with open arms too. I could never officially live with them, but she would always let me crash when I needed to and never let me go without a meal if I was in her house. Lisa was the all-around good girl. How she got mixed up with us, I'll never know. But thank God she did.

I still love these women, our little wayward rat pack. We've all been through hell together, and I wouldn't trade them for the world. Nothing means more to me than having these friendships for my entire life. No matter how much space or distance or breaks in between, we've always picked up where we've left off. And that I'll cherish forever.

7 GIRL, INTERRUPTED

LIVING IN THE WAR ZONE I CALLED HOME MADE ME cold. Cold and mean. If someone ever popped off at me, I didn't say shit. I just swung. I just had so much anger. School, home, church. Didn't matter. I was trained to go.

I ran away for the first time in fourth grade. Somehow, I conned a classmate into taking off with me. We ran away to a desert across the street from school and stayed there until dark. She started crying and wanted to go home—but I wanted to stay. I also knew that sleeping in a desert fort wasn't something I could do, so I reluctantly bailed with her.

By fourteen, life at home was suffocating, and I just wanted out. I no longer wanted to be a human punching bag and couldn't keep listening to Bill and Mindy arguing every fucking day. So I started running away for real. It didn't matter where—I just ran.

I'd stay at one of my girls' houses—anything to get away from those maniacs. Home was no longer an option for me, even if it meant leaving Baby Sis behind.

I'll always be Baby Sis's big sister, but you'll notice she's not too present in this book, and it's for good reason: She's just not really a part of my life. I love her and I always will, but the fracture between Baby Sis and me was probably predestined from the minute she was born into that home. I don't think we'll ever be able to overcome it.

Eventually, my parents got smart and wanted to cover their asses, so they started calling the cops and filing runaway reports on me. It meant that if I had any encounters with the law when I was away from home, I would be brought right back to Bill and Mindy. It was miserable. I never understood why they wanted a child they hated so much to come back home so badly.

At home, the fear that I might jet meant that the last shred of privacy I had got taken away. They put a leather strap of literal sleigh bells on the front door so they could hear me coming and going, and eventually, nailed my windows shut. Then they took my bedroom door off the hinges, and I was made to sit on my bed with my hands in my lap, staring at white walls for hours on end. I was only allowed outside my room if it was to complete a chore. I was officially in prison.

When I was under their roof, every minute felt claustrophobic, like I was being strangled by invisible hands. With my door off the hinges, everyone could see into my room, it was like a fish tank, and I was the guppy everyone was staring at. I couldn't get a second of peace.

XO

I'D PRAY ALL THE TIME for an escape.

Why, God? Why is this my family? Why am I here?

As I rounded fourteen, the anger was just bubbling over. I had some height on me—and a lot of strength. I wasn't easily pushed around. I'd even fight dudes if I had to—whatever I needed to do to protect myself. No one else did.

Mindy would constantly poke and poke and poke. Until one day, I saw red. She picked the wrong one to fuck with. I don't remember what she was mad about that time—or if I'd even said anything to piss her off. But when she raised her hand to hit me, my voice got cold and low.

"You put your hands on me one more time, I'm going to fuck you up," I said.

She took that as a challenge—and lifted me up off my feet and put my head through a door. For all my hazy memories, I remember this crystal clear: Every amount of anger I'd pent up from years of her beating on me came tearing out of my soul. I pulled myself up, turned and faced her, and just started whaling on her with every ounce of muscle I had. I beat the shit out of her. I barely felt it when I connected over and over. She felt my wrath that night.

Of course, she played the victim card to my dad, widening the rift between Bill and me. But she definitely learned not to touch me ever again—and she didn't.

But Mindy had another plan. She wasn't going to give up control that easily.

XO

"TIME TO WAKE UP, HONEY," Bill said, shaking my shoulders. I blinked my eyes open and looked around at my uncle B.'s house in California. We'd shown up the day before after a long drive from Vegas. We were going to Disneyland—a rare family vacation. We never did anything together—especially the older I got. All work, no play.

Normally, I would have stayed in bed as late as I could, but not that day. I had a date with Disney. And something about the idea of our trip to the Happiest Place on Earth made me feel full of love—I was excited to spend the day with my dad and sister. Hell, maybe even my evil stepmom.

"Where's Mom and Baby Sis?" I asked.

"They'll meet up with us later," Dad said. He was being weird, but I didn't want to push it. We never got one-on-one time anymore. Mindy didn't allow it. So I wasn't about to question alone time with my pops.

The sun hadn't even come up yet, but I finished my breakfast and ran upstairs to get dressed. I barreled back down and yelled "Ready!" Dad didn't smile.

We got in the car and set off for Disneyland, hyper and excited.

An hour or so passed before the car slowed down and Bill turned into a parking lot. By then, the sun was up, and I could read the sign. It was some kind of hospital.

"Are we stopping here before we go to Disneyland?" I asked, confused.

"We aren't. You are," he said flatly. Dad led me inside, and it took about two seconds to figure out where we were. A mental hospital.

XO

A SHRINK MET US AT the door—she'd been expecting me.

"Do you know why you're here?" she asked. Her voice was kind, and she seemed nice.

"I'm rebellious and I don't listen to my parents," I said. "And I'm always running away." This wasn't my first rodeo with concerned mental health professionals. My parents had put me in front of counselor after counselor, trying to break my spirit and make me more docile. Instead of asking me questions or trying to get to know me even a little, they'd just berated me to try to scare me straight. But the psychologist looked surprised.

"Do you know why you do these things?" she asked. I smirked.

"I hate my home. My stepmom is mean to me, and my dad doesn't listen to anything I say." Before I could say more, Dad chimed in.

"Doctor, we need to figure out what's wrong with her. Maybe she has a chemical imbalance and she needs to be medicated. Whatever it takes."

She raised her eyebrow at him, had him sign the last paper, and directed him out the door.

"Keep an eye on her. She'll run away if she gets the chance." *No shit, Sherlock.*

I wouldn't cry in front of him, but with Bill gone, I was free to let go of the angry tears I'd been holding back. I was so stupid. I thought my dad was taking me to Disneyland, but instead, an orderly led me into a room to put on scrubs.

"Do you want to hurt yourself right now?" She looked at me so intensely, it was like she was looking *into* me.

"No," I said. "No suicidal thoughts either." I knew this game.

They led me into a brightly lit room without a TV—or much of anything. It was a twenty-four-hour suicide watch, they told me, where I'd be monitored the whole time. I sat down on the bed and tried to close my eyes, but the fluorescent lights dug into me. I cried my eyes out. *My life is over.* I turned over and found the only thing to look at in the whole room—a Bible on the nightstand. I guess it was just me and God again.

I stayed in that room, thumbing through the Bible, trying not to go stir-crazy. Outside my door, I could hear voices that sounded like girls my age. I peeked out my window and saw into a common area—there were kids! They looked like they ranged from around eight to teenagers.

A girl with long blond hair and the prettiest blue eyes walked up to the window and glared at me through the glass. I waved and smiled, but it didn't move her. I wondered if she could even see me. What was she looking at? The lights were on, but no one was home.

I draped myself across the bed and flipped off the camera they were using to spy on me. I was defeated. I had no idea what time it was. I made myself go to sleep. Tomorrow would be a new day.

XO

BANG BANG BANG!

"Carter, wake up!" Someone was pounding on the door. I rubbed my eyes and noticed that whoever was there had gone—and left the door ajar. This was my chance to run. I walked out into the common room where I'd seen the kids the night before. I slinked against the wall, watching them all eat breakfast and looking for an exit. I could tell right away that these kids had been through some shit and were medicated out of their minds.

I saw the blond girl with the pretty blue eyes from last night eat her breakfast. Another girl who looked like Janis Joplin sat next to her and spotted me.

"Come sit with us! You gotta eat!" she called. I wasn't hungry. I was looking for a way out. But I went over anyway.

"I'm Amber. This is Janey, Todd, Mike, and Sarah," the Janis Joplin clone said. To my left, a kid banged his head against the wall. Janey, the blond one, looked like she was still on the best acid trip of her life.

"I'm Alisa," I said. I couldn't stop looking at the kid who was banging his head against the wall. Amber noticed and shrugged.

"They haven't given him his lithium yet."

"And this one?" I asked, pointing at Janey.

"She's permafried," Amber said.

"Permawhat?"

"Permafried. You know when you take too much acid?"

"No," I said, "but I do now." Amber seemed normal. And unmedicated.

"Why are you here?" I wondered, and then realized I'd accidentally said it out loud.

"I'm a cutter!" she announced proudly as she rolled her sleeves up for me to see the scars she had engraved in her arms. I'd never even heard of cutting.

"What about you?"

"I'm rebellious, I don't listen to my parents, and I run away all the time." I was used to repeating it over and over.

"That's it? Nothing else?" she asked. It was like I wasn't even good enough to be in the loony bin. "You'll be outta here in no time."

On cue, the psychologist from the day before appeared and waved me over. I left my new friends behind. Maybe I'd be told I could go home.

"How are you feeling today, Alisa?" she asked, looking over her glasses.

"Honestly? I'm confused, mad, hurt, and ready to leave," I said. I snapped my arms over my chest in defiance. But she just smiled.

"I saw you talking with Amber. She's a frequent flyer."

"A what?"

"She's been here numerous times, sweet girl. Just very disturbed." I was getting tired of the chitchat. I wanted to move things along.

"Do I need to be on medication? Are you guys going to put me on medication?"

"I don't think your issues will be solved with medication. I think you are just what you say you are: an angry child whose parents don't hear her."

I almost fell over. I couldn't believe what I was hearing. The psychologist agreed with me? Am I on *Candid Camera*? This couldn't be real life.

"But we're going to keep you for another twenty-four hours or so, just to make sure," she said. Fuck.

For the next day, I went to group counseling and meals with my new crew. They were doped up out of their minds, but I was surprised to realize they were cool—that we'd faced some of the same stuff. Hypocritical parents. Addiction. Violation. I was one of them: an outcast. We thought differently, and we were misunderstood. But we didn't think we had to explain ourselves to everyone else.

By the fifth or so day, I was almost starting to like my surroundings. I'd always been curious about people, and I wanted to unravel them to understand how they worked. I soaked up counseling sessions, and being around those other kids was super therapeutic. I wasn't alone. I wasn't misunderstood. I was heard.

"Carter!" that same male nurse screamed. I jumped up and followed him to the psychologist's office, where she sat at her desk smiling.

"Alisa, there's nothing wrong with you. You're just a teenager who doesn't like her stepmother. It's very common. Honestly, I'm appalled that your dad even brought you here. And you get to go home today!" she said, waiting for an excited response. She dialed Bill's number, and he answered with his usual "Yello?"

Hearing his voice made me want to rage. I scrunched down in the chair and blew my bangs out of my face.

"Mr. Carter," the psychologist said. "After numerous counseling sessions and observation, I'm happy to inform you that Alisa will be discharged today. She won't require any medication, and we truly believe that with the right counseling, we can get you guys back to a healthy, happy family."

The psychologist and I sat in silence, waiting for Bill to answer. He took his damn time, and finally I could hear him over the other end of the line.

"I don't want to come get her today. I don't want her home. Are you sure she doesn't need medication? I would like to keep her there longer if possible." The psychologist's jaw twitched.

"Excuse me, Mr. Carter? Am I hearing this right? You want us to keep your daughter in a mental facility?"

"Why not? My insurance will cover it," Bill snapped. If shock treatment had been an option, I'm sure he would have gone for it.

"Mr. Carter. There's nothing wrong with your daughter. And if you don't pick her up today, we'll have to involve the authorities," she said.

"I'll be there tonight," my dad said. *Click.*

She and I sat in silence, trying to make sense of the call.

"It's all clear to me now," she said.

I shook my head in disgust. Sure, he'd fucked up by standing by time and time again while his wife beat me and treated me like a second-class citizen. Sure, he'd fucked up when he chose to follow God and religion in a way that suited his wife and her need for control. Sure, he cheated and watched porn and drank and did drugs and didn't believe me when I confessed to being molested. But in that moment—as he tried to have me locked away in a mental hospital with no end date—my dad broke my heart for the last time. After that, I stopped waiting for him to get it right.

LATER TEACH

WHEN BILL AND MINDY WOULD CALL THE COPS ON ME, it was to cover their own ass. They didn't really want me home, but they just didn't want to get in trouble themselves, so they looked the part of concerned parents.

Once, cops caught up to me in a routine traffic stop when one of my friends got pulled over. Turns out there was yet another runaway report out for me, so the cops called up Bill and Mindy.

"Don't bring her home," they said. "Let her go to WestCare."

For those of you who aren't from Vegas and don't know what WestCare is, let me enlighten you. WestCare is a nonprofit that provides support for addicts, HIV/AIDS patients, domestic violence victims—and runaways. It's not the best place for a confused and angry runway, but it at least put a roof over our heads.

So, the cops dropped me off at WestCare. The staff checked me in and showed me to a dimly lit room. I was told to pick a cot. I blinked in the near darkness—the room was filthy, like something out of a hostel horror movie. Kids lay out on cots all around me.

I headed to my cot, sat back, watched, and listened. My ears perked up when one of them mentioned leaving.

"Hey, did you just say we can jet if we want to?" I called over to one of the other kids.

"Yep! You can just walk out and they won't chase you or anything."

That's all I needed to hear. I hung around for maybe fifteen minutes before I headed straight for the door and tumbled out into the old downtown of Vegas. I didn't care where I was going. I just knew it wasn't WestCare, and it sure as fuck wasn't home.

XO

I BOUNCED AROUND HERE AND there, and landed for a few nights back at the "perfect" home of Bill and Mindy. I spent all day arguing with Mindy and Bill until we'd all finally had enough.

"Get in the car." We drove in silence until we got to Tasha's house.

Bill stopped abruptly, reached in his pocket, pulled out a crisp $20 bill, and handed it to me.

"Have a nice life," he said flatly. I was surprised, but I didn't question him. I got out of the car and walked up to my friend's house. I stayed with her until—yes, you guessed it. My parents called the cops. It was a sick game they played.

Some months later, I got picked up by the cops—yet again—and they called my house.

"Take her to juvenile hall. Let her stay the night there," good ol' Bill advised. So off we went to juvie. Unlike WestCare, I was locked in a cell. And couldn't escape.

"This is what your life is going to look like if you don't get yourself together," the cop told me, slamming the cell door closed. He really thought he was teaching me a life lesson.

I found the tiny window in the cell, and by standing on the bench connected to the wall on my tippy-toes, I could watch the world pass by. I did that all day, and when the sun finally went down, I stared at the sky and counted the stars. I felt no remorse for my actions, just more reasons for why I'd never go home.

The next morning, Bill and Mindy showed up to save the day. I don't think I even spoke two words when I saw them.

"Did you learn anything being locked in that cell?" Bill asked.

Hell no.

XO

I SOMEHOW, MAGICALLY, MADE IT to tenth grade. Ask me how and I couldn't tell you. I think I was just getting passed so the teachers didn't have to deal with me. I barely went to class—between the ditch parties I had to attend and running away from home, that didn't leave much time to show up.

But I was feeling studious one day, so, off to school I went, not realizing it would be the last time I ever set foot in a high school.

I was in the cafeteria, hanging with some friends at their table and minding my business—for real this time. I noticed a group of girls at the table across from us kept whispering and pointing at me.

I just shrugged it off, because honestly I'd had enough of everyone's shit. I figured maybe they were talking about someone else at my table. *Wrong.*

The next thing I know, two of them got up and started screaming at me. Then one of them stuck her finger in my face. *Here we go.* I swung first and I didn't stop. It was like something took over me, and I couldn't stop punching this girl.

I went flying through the air and landed so hard on the tile floor it knocked the wind out of me. When I finally came to my senses, all I could see was my four-hundred-pound principal sitting on me to hold me down.

"Alisa! Stop!" he shrieked, panting.

"Why are you sitting on me, Mr. G.?" I asked, perplexed. As if I wasn't just beating the dog shit out of some girl I didn't even know.

"You wouldn't stop. You just wouldn't stop," he said, standing me up. He kept his hand on my shoulder and walked me in the direction of his office. "You're just too violent, and we can't have that here. I'm going to have to expel you."

"Wait, wait, wait—expel me? Like as in expulsion? Like I can't come back? Ever?" I gasped.

"It's been two years of nonstop violence, problems with authority, and honestly, you don't seem like you even want to be here."

I sat there in silence and stared at the floor for what seemed like twenty minutes. I knew there was no reason to even try to keep defending myself. For what? It felt like a losing battle. And honestly, he was right.

"Tell Stacy to take you home. Clean out your locker and go."

Damn, he didn't even call my parents. He let my underage bestie drive me home.

All I could think about on the way home was that Bill was going to whoop my ass. Bill rarely put his hands on me unless he was really mad—or if Mindy egged him on. But the ass whoopings were so severe that I still remember the majority of them. Getting thrown up against walls and manhandled like a rag doll as a young girl will stick in your mind. His specialty, though, was whippings with metal-studded leather belts.

Or there was the piece of wood he cut himself that he loved

to call "the board of education." When my dad first presented me with this board, I drew its name in Old English letters, trying to make it look official and make him laugh. We laugh at our pain in this house, don't we?

Another school, another upheaval. I had to get the fuck out of that house for good this time. I knew there was so much more to life than this.

I knew I'd be safe with my coven of misfits. My best friend, Tasha, and her mom would take me in for a few nights, or my cousin Stacy and her two moms. Our friend Tonya's grandpa had invested in Walmart, so she had her own whole house and she was just barely eighteen. There would be plenty of places to crash. I wasn't scared. I knew how to protect myself and I wouldn't let anybody put their hands on me. Plus, anywhere was better than here.

I went to my room and started making plans. Back then we didn't have cell phones, but I snuck out to the living room when they all went to sleep and made a quick phone call.

"Meet me at midnight around the corner," I told Lisa. She was the only one in our crew with a car besides Stacy. "I'm leaving for good."

No one checked on me all night, which gave me plenty of time to unscrew the screws Bill had put in my window frame. My parents had thought I wasn't smart enough to figure out how to get the window open, but it was child's play. I packed up all my clothes and put them in two big garbage bags. How the hell they didn't hear all the rustling around that night is beyond me. Maybe they did and just didn't care.

I slid the window open slowly and lowered the bags into the shrub outside my window and waited for midnight. I was the anti-Cinderella—I came alive when the clock struck twelve.

Midnight struck and I slowly lowered myself out my window,

trying not to wake my sister, whose window was right next to mine. I grabbed my two garbage bags and hauled ass to the dirt road we lived on.

Lisa was there, waiting around the corner in her car. I threw everything I owned into her trunk and we drove away. I was finally free, and I was never going home. I smashed that rearview mirror and never looked back.

9 THERE'S A FIRST TIME FOR EVERYTHING

LISA COULDN'T HAVE ME AT HER HOUSE THAT NIGHT, so we paged one of my other friends, Kim, on her beeper and she called us back on a pay phone. It was the middle of the night in Las Vegas. I picked a crazy time to run away.

"I need a place to stay," I told her. "I'm leaving home for good." Kim didn't bat an eyelash.

"You can stay the night at mine," she said, but when I got to her house, Kim's mean-as-fuck mom kicked my ass out. That tiny Asian lady didn't play. Kim clearly felt bad, so she left with me.

"Let's walk the Strip," she said. "We'll figure out a place for you to crash later."

Kim and I spent all night under those bright-as-fuck flashing lights. There were people smiling and laughing everywhere, but I squinted my eyes at them. *Are these people really happy? What does happiness even mean?* It was all hitting me: I was fourteen. I'd left home. I didn't belong anywhere, and I didn't have anywhere to go.

My protective instincts kicked in, and my brain started spinning, trying to figure out my next step. I needed to find a way to make money and take care of myself. Giving up was not an option.

I looked at Kim and felt gratitude for her washing over me. Kim was a senior, but we always had a bond. We kept that bond until the day she passed away. She was too good for the world.

By the time the sun started coming up over Vegas, Kim figured her mom was asleep and she took me home.

"When you wake up, you gotta go."

XO

I CRASHED ON DIFFERENT COUCHES for the next few days before landing at Tasha's for what would be the best time of my life. By then, Tasha's mom, Theresa, had straightened up enough to be in Tasha's life more consistently, and Tasha, her baby brother, and Theresa lived in a tiny little tinfoil trailer we called the Roach Motel. But the roaches didn't bother me, because that trailer was full to the brim with love and laughter. There were Christmas lights up all year long, and the kids who lived in the park became our extended family.

Theresa's dudes, though. She had a habit of dating men who put their hands on her, and one time, she came home with a black eye. And all I ever knew was to stand up for the ones we loved. So, Tasha, me, and all the kids in the trailer park jumped this grown man and beat the shit out of him the next time he came around.

Theresa called up some more biker friends for backup, and the trailer filled up with dudes on bikes ready to kill people. We knew we were safe with Theresa and that nobody could fuck with us. It was the first time in my whole life I'd ever felt protected. She was and still is a true badass.

XO

JORDAN WAS SIX FOOT TWO, half Asian, and fucking gorgeous. He played football and had the most innocent, sweet smile I'd ever seen—not to mention that his Richard Gere eyes used to make me melt, along with the freckles sprinkled across his nose and cheeks. Poor kid never even knew what he was getting himself into with me.

We met as freshmen and instantly had a thing for each other. For some reason, it was always the privileged rich boys who ended up wanting to be with me. Maybe it was some other-side-of-the-tracks thing. Maybe it's because I gave off damsel-in-distress vibes—or maybe, just maybe, they thought I wouldn't run from them. But that boy fell for me and then we fell hard for each other.

It was your regular old high school ditch party at someone's house where we decided it was time to give ourselves to each other. We were both virgins, though my childhood and life at home had more than prepared me for all things sexual. But when it came down to it—we were both nervous wrecks.

I took his boxers down and saw his penis for the first time. Now I know for a fact it was on the smaller side, because I'd seen plenty of porn. But I wasn't disappointed—it made me less afraid. I figured if he was smaller, it wouldn't hurt so bad.

I laid myself down on the bed and pulled my panties off so he could get on top of me. Unfortunately, he was so small that being on top meant it would barely go in. He was so unsure of his movements that he wouldn't go deep enough and was just laying it in the very entrance of my vagina. I was starting to get frustrated. *Pop my cherry, my guy.* But sweet Jordan couldn't figure it out.

"Let's take a break and get a change of scenery," I said. We both threw our clothes back on and I went into the bathroom to give myself a pep talk. I looked in the mirror, took a deep breath, and knew what I had to do. I walked out of the bathroom, into the hallway, and grabbed his hand. I led him outside.

In the backyard, I told him to lay down on a lawn chair.

"I'm going to ride you," I said. This is my *first time ever having sex.* How would I have known how to ride somebody? Like always, I'd figure it out. He looked at me in disbelief.

"Are you crazy?" Why does everyone say that to me?

"Yes, I am," I giggled as I threw him down onto a perfectly positioned lawn chair. You can't tell me the universe didn't provide.

I started kissing him and took off my top so he would get rock hard again. *Bingo.* I slid his pants down to his knees and took one leg out of mine. I wanted to be able to cover ourselves just in case we were caught in the act.

I slowly straddled him and grabbed his hard dick with my hand and slid it inside me and then bore down. *Pop!* I winced in pain, but as I kept moving, the pain faded away and was replaced with the best feeling I'd ever felt. I only had that feeling for a minute flat before he busted inside of me and it was all over. I'd popped my own cherry the first time I had sex.

Tell me that's not the story of my entire fucking life.

That night, I realized how much control I had—control over him, control over myself, and control of what I wanted. It was like a lightbulb went off in my head: Pussy is power. If I learned how to control every situation with sex, I could get whatever I wanted in life. What a lesson to learn.

XO

JORDAN AND I COULDN'T WAIT to fuck each other again, and by the third time we knew what we were doing. But as with everything in life, because I'm ruled by Daddy Saturn, all my fun comes with lessons. Brutal ones.

Midway through that third time, he came inside of me again. I felt a quick pain like a needle going through my uterus. I grabbed my stomach.

"I just got pregnant," I said.

"You're crazy," he said. "There's no way you'd be able to tell."

"I'm definitely fucking pregnant." He rolled his eyes and rolled off me.

A few weeks later, I was a raging bitch—gaining weight and feeling nauseous constantly. At another ditch party—even if they'd expelled me, they couldn't keep me away from the parties—I told Jordan I was scared and wanted to take a pregnancy test, so he left with some friends to go buy some tests and bring them back to me.

With kids partying on the other side of the door, we sat on the edge of the tub and waited for the pee stick to marinate. And when the three minutes were up: *Positive.*

The room got super hot and tiny, and my brain started spiraling. *Oh my god. Fuck. I can't have this baby.*

"We can't have a baby," he said, but I barely heard him. My brain was going a mile a minute. *Fuck. Fuck. What do I do? Should I have this baby?*

"Alisa. I cannot have this baby. My parents will kill me," he said. He was right. We were just sixteen. There was no way we could be parents.

"Fine," I said. "If you can pay, I'll get an abortion." Both of us stared wide-eyed at each other.

"Deal."

That week, Jordan stole three hundred dollars from his parents and handed me the cash.

XO

I WAS A RUNAWAY LIVING on the streets. I couldn't even take care of myself. How would I ever raise a kid? Sitting in the clinic waiting room with Stacy and other pregnant teens was mortifying for me—they all knew what I'd done and what I was about to do. I didn't even ask Jordan to come with me. This was my problem.

The nurse opened the door, called my name, and we went into the back operating room.

It was cold. And the staff was so unwelcoming. I'm not sure what I expected.

They handed me a gown and laid me on a stainless-steel operating table under bright lights. It was a tiny room with an ultrasound machine. There weren't any pictures on the wall—nothing at all to look at. Just my feet in stirrups.

The nurse came over and rubbed gel on my exposed tummy and placed the ultrasound device over my uterus. She moved it around on each side going back and forth until she paused and hovered for a minute. No words, just clanking on the keyboard and snapping what sounded like a picture of the little baby she could see on the screen.

She printed out the photo and handed me an ultrasound picture of my baby. *What in the actual fuck, lady?* I looked at her blankly. Was she hoping I'd change my mind? Was this a keepsake? Tears welled up, but I fought them back.

She started an IV in my arm and told me that soon I'd feel relaxed.

To this day, I don't know why she showed me that picture, but I didn't have time to ask questions before the drugs started kicking in. The room went fuzzy, and the doctor walked in.

It was like something out of *American Horror Story.* A dingy, dark operating room with a doctor who wouldn't even speak to me and that I could barely even see because the drugs made my eyes so blurry. He shoved what felt like a vacuum nozzle inside of me. The pain was intense. All I could do was scream on the inside.

"No," I mumbled. Something had shifted, and the second he started, I knew I'd made a mistake. "I want the baby. Stop." The doctor didn't listen. He continued the procedure and it felt like being split open and having my insides ripped out. "You didn't give me enough medicine," I wailed. "It hurts. Please stop."

He didn't care about anything I had to say. I was sobbing and inconsolable, and it felt like my body wasn't mine. In the recovery room, I bawled my eyes out for a couple of hours alone. I just wanted someone to hug me.

I didn't know then that the doctor had messed something up during the procedure. My insides would never be the same again.

XO

STACY DROVE ME BACK HOME while I waited for the anesthesia to wear off. I called Jordan to come over that night, and we lay on the couch watching TV. I put my head on his chest and tried to breathe through the pain. I felt so vulnerable.

It seems crazy now, but we had sex that very night. That's how disconnected from pain and abuse I was then—and from my own body and what it had been through. And looking back at that sixteen-year-old who made the choice she thought was right at the time, she probably just wanted to feel loved and cared for. Maybe it's not so crazy, right?

A couple of weeks went by, and Jordan's dad found out he'd stolen the money.

"I need that money back," he said.

I didn't want Jordan to get in trouble, so I somehow got the money together and paid up. Nothing's free in this life.

XO

TASHA WAS DATING A RICH kid named Dan who lived in Summerlin, the ritzy, immaculate development on the edge of Vegas. He'd throw lavish parties where people would be huffing gold paint in the corners of every room. His mom was a single mom with a sugar daddy who provided a life of comfort and luxury for both of them.

I always thought rich kids were the lucky ones but I learned quickly that more money meant more problems. I was definitely a troubled kid and I loved to party, but huffing just wasn't for me. By then, I'd tried glass, but not in the quantities Dan was bringing out at his parties. One night, I ended up in a bathroom with Dan, Tasha, one of Dan's friends, and a tray with more glass in a mound than I'd ever seen.

Maybe I was dumb or showing off, or maybe I truly didn't understand how bad methamphetamines were, but I laid out twelve lines. Six in one nostril, six in the other. I can't say exactly what I was thinking as I snorted, but I know that back then, taking risks with my body was just part of the deal. That girl just didn't think of herself as something worth protecting.

Within a minute, my nose started pouring blood. It looked like an artery had ruptured. Tasha started screaming, and the room got darker and darker and—

"I don't feel good. I need to lay down." I knew they wouldn't call the cops—if you called the cops, someone was going to jail. I started shoving toilet paper up my nose to get the bleeding to subside, but it wouldn't. My skin was crawling.

I somehow made it to an empty bedroom and lay on a bed,

spinning. I started puking and praying. *God, just let me get through this.*

One hour turned into three fucking days of not moving, not eating. People would come and check on me, but I could barely even answer when they asked if I was okay. It was my first time overdosing, and I didn't have the energy to do more than groan in response.

What the fuck did I do to myself? How am I still here?

It would take years for it to finally sink in: that I was worth more than rotting from the inside out. That ultimately I could take control of my own life and my happiness, that I could forgive myself for how I'd treated myself the same way everyone else had treated me, and that I could choose to care for myself and heal. But even if it would be another decade and a half before I could truly help myself, at least that morning I was awake—or awake enough—to get my ass up. Some part of me was starting to see trickles of the truth: Life waits for no one. And I had so much more life to live.

NOT AGAIN

WITHOUT MY PARENTS IN MY LIFE, I WENT ON A RAMpage. I bounced around houses and did whatever the hell I wanted. You always hear that girls get attached to the men they lose their virginity to, but not me. After my first time and the pregnancy and abortion with Jordan, I grew restless—and that only fueled the wild streak inside me.

There was a party every night of the week, and back then, Vegas just had a sparkle. The city felt bright and alive—or maybe we were just so young that we hadn't lived enough to realize how dark the city really was.

I was still working odd jobs to put money in my pocket. I started at Fatburger, which was short-lived when I quickly realized that I hated being around all the grease. So I got a summertime gig at Wet' n' Wild as a lifeguard for a few summers. I never missed a day on that job—this water baby found so much joy in a bathing suit and pool all day.

But my real hustle was stealing expensive clothes from Dillard's, with Stacy as my partner in crime. Stacy was Pinky from

Pinky and the Brain—she didn't stand more than four foot nine with dark brown hair and big, beautiful, sky-blue eyes, but would make you want to crawl in a hole if you ever crossed her. And anytime there was a scam going on, Stacy was front and center.

Remember the big Starter jackets that were all the rage back in the day? We would buy XL jackets, take a box cutter, slit the lining ever-so-perfectly, pull the stuffing out, and leave the jacket empty. Usually, our targets were whatever name brand jeans were trendy. We would grab every pair we could and act like we were going to the dressing room to try them all on. Inside the dressing room, we would stuff those Starter jackets with as many pairs as would fit. This was way before alarm tags—I like to think we actually had something to do with that particular innovation.

We were like pirates returning from sea when we got back to Stacy's house with our loot, sorting our booty and reveling in our haul. We were some of the best-dressed criminals in Vegas, because we always kept some of the stash for ourselves.

After sifting through everything, we'd drive over to the deep Eastside, to a place called the Attic, and they would buy all the items we stole with price tags intact. They must have known what we were doing, but it was their hustle too. We'd steal a two-hundred-dollar pair of jeans, and they'd give us fifty dollars for each pair and turn around and sell them for a hundred dollars.

Honestly, I'm thankful for those dudes at the Attic. They kept me afloat in one of the hardest times of my life. Because of that fifty dollars a pop, I was able to survive.

Stacy and I kept that hustle up for year—until one day, we were finally caught and arrested. Our faces were even in the local newspaper, because law enforcement thought we were such crafty thieves. I guess they wanted to show copycats they were onto us. To this day, I'm proud of that one.

XO

JEFF WAS OLDER—MAYBE TWENTY-THREE OR twenty-four, and I was still sixteen. He would pull up to the high school in his lowrider and pick up underage girls right after they got out of chemistry class. But I was young and didn't see how creepy he was. He just seemed hot and popular and him being older seemed cool, not dangerous.

One day, he pulled his lowrider up next to me. It was obvious what he wanted, and I was definitely into him. But I'd only just had that abortion, and I needed to take things slow.

"I like you," I told him, "but I'm not ready to have sex. I want to hang out." He nodded like he understood.

The third or so time we hung out, Jeff took me to a party at his friends' house: brothers who were big shots at school. Someone handed me a plastic cup of the Goldschläger everyone around me was knocking back.

I'd never tried it before, and I took a sniff of the glittery drink—*Wowee, that's strong. Fuck it.* It sparkled, so I was in.

It was fucking disgusting. But I wasn't going to look like a pussy, so I kept drinking. Before I knew it, Tasha and I had damn near finished the whole fucking bottle between the two of us, drinking until we could no longer taste that sickly sweetness.

But Jeff wasn't partying like everyone else—he wasn't even really drinking. He was just sitting back and watching me as I got absolutely shit-faced. It was like he was waiting.

I was blacked out, but I do remember going into the bathroom to try to make myself throw up. If I could just puke, I'd get my head straight. As I leaned over the toilet with my head slung low in shame, the door opened. Jeff, all hazy in my blurry vision, came in. I crouched lower in front of the toilet so I didn't look so pitiful, but I must have pulled myself up, because I remember flashes of us making out, and then it's just all black.

I woke up with my face pressed against the cold bathroom floor. From another room, I heard that same party music still playing, and when I looked down, I realized my pants were off. I pulled myself up, still unsteady, and it hit me.

Oh my God. He raped me. I couldn't make sense of it. I couldn't believe it.

I stumbled out of the bathroom and went upstairs, just trying to find a place to lie down. I found a room with no one in it and I passed out in one of the brothers' beds. Fade to black, again.

XO

IT WAS MORNING WHEN I woke up, with one of the fuckin' brothers on top of me, trying to stick his dick in me. *No, no, no.* Waking up with your pants taken off twice in twenty-four hours is enough to send any woman into a rage.

"What are you doing? I don't want to have sex with you," I yelled. I managed to get him off me and get up before anything could happen—thank you, God—and ran into the next room, where I found Tasha passed out.

"Tasha. Get up," I yelled, shaking her shoulder. She opened her eyes, took one look at me, and we got the fuck out.

XO

NORMALLY, WHEN BAD THINGS HAPPENED to me at that age, I'd figure it was my fault. Even if I knew that Mindy and Bill weren't particularly Christian in their parenting and had put me through hell, eventually I started to think that I must have deserved it. I'd done something wrong or acted crazy or been too rebellious, and so, naturally, something bad would come my way as some kind of cosmic punishment. But for the first time in my life, I felt violated in every single way. It didn't matter how much I'd had to drink, throwing back those Goldschlagers in the brothers' living room. Jeff had no fucking right, and I was mad as hell.

I had a beeper that Jeff kept blowing up, but I just wasn't interested in speaking to him. He called every friend I had as well, looking for me. But what was I even going to say? My mind was spiraling through rage and anxiety, and at one point, I even felt bad for *him*—maybe he missed me, or maybe he felt guilty. For the next fifteen years, I'd watch myself and the women around me try to love away the anger or violence of their men, to feel their pain deep inside us and try to take it on. But that weekend, my empathy was just a flash, and it quickly dissipated and returned to anger.

A few days after the party, I was hanging at Lisa's and the phone rang. She answered, put her hand over the phone, and turned toward me.

"It's Jeff. Do you want to talk to him?" Hell, yes, I did. I had sat with this anger long enough. Maybe he would apologize. I grabbed the phone out of her hand.

"What's up?" I said.

"Where have you been? Why haven't you haven't called me back?"

"Because of what you did the other night."

"What are you talking about? I didn't do anything." Oh, *really.* Rage was building up inside of me, and hearing his voice made me even angrier.

"Jeff. I know what you did. It's fucked up, dude. You're a piece of shit," I said. "You had sex with me when I told you I didn't want it. You fucking r-r-r-raped me." I felt so helpless that it was even hard for me to get the word out.

I slammed the phone down. I was not very good with boundaries. I'm still not. But I felt so wronged in such a disgusting way that nothing would move me to speak to that man ever again.

Funny how life always circles back. I heard about him over the years. He married some girl from my high school class, treated her like shit, had an affair. *Fucking loser.*

XO

EVEN THOUGH I'D BEEN EXPELLED, I still went to the football games. Part of me missed being in school—deep down, I just wanted to be a regular kid. One night after a game, a red Eagle Talon pulled up in front of a party at a friend's house. I'd never seen a car so nice in my life. *What was it doing in this neighborhood*? The door opened and out came Tony, a rich kid from the other side of town in Green Valley.

His mom and stepdad were loaded—and Tony had a job as a dental assistant, but I wasn't easily impressed. I was always the pickier one of my crew with the men I selected, even from a young age. So when Tony somehow finessed me into going on a date, my whole crew was shocked.

Tony and I fell fast, and for a moment in time, he was my world. As with all young relationships, we were wild. And he had money and a car, so that meant the world was our oyster. Tasha's mom even loved him and accepted him into our tight-knit family. Tony was here to stay. Or, at least, stay awhile.

XO

I'D GOTTEN PREGNANT WITH JORDAN one of the first few times I had sex, and with Tony, I slept with him right away. Man, I moved fast. Sex had become my way of expressing my love—but now I can see how it filled the huge hole in my heart for feeling so unloved as a child.

I wasn't a virgin, but Tony was a whole lot of firsts. My first blowjob, my first guy who had his own place, my first time doing harder drugs.

"Let's move in together," he said, looking at me all wide-eyed. "That way, you can get a job, and I can help you. You won't have to be on the streets anymore."

I thought it was cute that Tony wanted to save me. I said yes.

XO

WITH THAT WALMART MONEY FROM her grandpa, Tonya found herself with a million dollars at eighteen. She'd used it to buy a cute little house on the Eastside and a nice car on rims. And Tony had the idea that we should rent a room from her together.

As he promised, Tony paid Tonya one month's rent for a small room in her house that only had a mattress on the floor. But we didn't care. We were just happy to have our own place—kind of.

It was all sex and drugs on that mattress, and one night, we were so fucked up that I got a bright idea.

"Let's see how many times you can cum," I said. Tony was never one to turn down a dare. We fucked all night—and he ended up cumming twelve or thirteen times in a row. We set a damn record that night. But around session nine or ten, I got a familiar feeling and grabbed my stomach.

"What's wrong?" he asked, panting.

"You're not going to believe this, but I think I just got pregnant," I said. I expected him to react like Jordan, but he wasn't fazed.

"Good," he said. He didn't bat an eyelash. We went back to it.

XO

A FEW WEEKS LATER I was at my new, postexpulsion school, showing my face on campus for a class or two, when the cramps started. I figured it was my period, but it hurt so bad I could barely stand up. After a few hours, I couldn't see straight, so I went to the school nurse.

"It sounds like appendicitis," she said. "I need to call your mom."

"Please don't call her," I begged. "I'm not living at home." The school knew I was a constant runaway, and for whatever reason, they let me be—which in retrospect is a weird way to take care of a kid. But in this case, the nurse didn't have a choice.

Big shock—Mindy raced in pretending to be a concerned mom who loved her stepdaughter more than anything. She was always good at that, able to put on her sweet Southern drawl and fake a big love bomb.

I hated the fakeness in her. It made my skin crawl. But to my surprise, I was relieved when I saw her. Even if it was fake, I was scared, and I really needed a mom right then. She hugged me with a worried look on her face.

I was in too much pain to do much of anything besides let myself get loaded into her car and try to keep breathing as she brought me to a clinic across from Sam's Town, the massive casino way off the Strip. Inside, I peed in a cup and waited in the exam room, shivering in the paper gown they made me wear. I tried to ignore Mindy asking where I was living and what I had been up to.

A doctor came in with my chart and cleared his throat.

"You're pregnant, Alisa." *Oh my God. Not again.* Just like the first time, I'd called it. I looked over at Mindy. *Fuck. Here we go.*

"You're having an ectopic pregnancy. It means the embryo's growing outside of your Fallopian tube. Your baby won't survive and neither will you if it bursts. We need to get you into surgery right away."

From that moment, it gets blurry—just another traumatic episode I blocked out. I do remember Mindy rushing me to the hospital and that I was scared shitless. They took me back right away, sedated me, and did the surgery. Nobody told me what was going to happen to my body. No one told me shit before it all went black. Again.

XO

I WOKE UP A FEW hours later in a hospital bed to the sound of my heart monitor beeping steadily. My dad and Mindy came into focus sitting at the foot of my bed. My throat was dry, but I managed to say, "This doesn't mean I'm coming home."

"Please, Alisa," Bill said. "This isn't working out for you." I wouldn't respond, but they kept asking—until Tony showed up. He was pale and worried about me and heartbroken that we'd lost the baby. I must have called him before we left the clinic, so he'd only known I was pregnant for a few hours. But a few hours is plenty of time to get excited about a baby on the way.

I ended up going home with Bill and Mindy because the hospital wouldn't release me to anyone else but them. I was a wounded warrior and just needed to heal. But it didn't last. I stayed a few days to let my body get back in the groove of life and then I was gone. That house wasn't my home anymore.

I didn't know that it would be the last time I'd see my dad until I was about twenty-two. Bill ended up leaving Vegas and moving back to Texas a few months later. They gave me an ultimatum through my friends to come with them—that they would wait for me on moving day. But I never showed up, and once they left, I was really free. And really on my own.

While I was healing at my parents' place, Tonya tried to hook up with Tony, he told me, so he left. His mom and stepdad hated me, but he convinced me to sneak into his house one night after they had gone to sleep so I could sleep next to him in his bed. We must have been giggling too loud, because his mom came knocking on his bedroom door. We panicked and he shoved me under his bed. He opened the door pretending like nothing happened, but she wasn't going for it. She walked straight over and looked under the bed.

"Get her the fuck out of here, Anthony!" she screamed. And then we were off to his dad's trailer.

His dad lived in the hood of Henderson. He was an addict and had a rough life but a good soul—and that man loved me from the jump. But a junkie lives like a junkie, and there were trash and needles everywhere. That trailer probably hadn't been cleaned in years. I'd stay there for a whilc, trying to figure out my next move.

XO

TONY WAS PROTECTIVE AS HELL over me—especially after what he'd seen me go through. The nights I didn't want to stay at his dad's we stayed in seedy motels, living off his dental assistant salary and the money he made dealing on the side. He'd become a drug dealer for no reason. He didn't need the money. Deep down inside, I think Tony yearned to be from where I was from and where all my boys were from. He was fascinated with our culture and wanted to live like he wasn't a rich kid—I can't understand why.

I was a teen runaway, crashing in shithouse motels with my boyfriend or in his junkie dad's trailer—even if he was the sweetest man alive for letting me stay—or on my friends' couches. I'd been pregnant twice. My mind raced. *This is my fucking life. I'm never going to get out of this shithole situation.* I was spiraling and couldn't get ahold of my emotions.

I was disgusted with myself. And then everything that I'd endured hit me all at once. Waking up in the bathroom with my pants off. The abortion doctor who didn't use enough anesthetic. Mindy. Mindy's piece-of-shit sister. The molestation. That sick fuck man who whipped his dick out in front of me as a child. It was all closing in on me. Tony and I were fighting over the phone, and I hit a wall. I slammed headfirst into it. This was it.

"Fuck you," I said. "I'm going to end it all. I don't want to be here." I hung up before he could respond.

Across the street from wherever I was crashing that night was a stretch of desert, and I walked out there, bawling my eyes out. I sat down and really, really wept with my whole body. Tears the size of raindrops fell in my lap. *Why the fuck was I born? What purpose do I have to be on this earth?* It was pitch black in my mind. There was no light through the cracks.

I saw a broken bottle a few feet away, and my body moved without thinking. I was on autopilot.

I took a shard and started hammering away at my wrist as deep as I could. The pain was unlike anything I'd ever felt before—amazing, clear relief. With every slash, more blood poured out and I kept gashing away, hoping and praying I'd hit an artery and bleed out.

I've got nothing but empathy for cutters who think the pain's the only way out. Back then, I didn't know any other way, and it was the calmest I'd felt in ages. As bad as it hurt, the peace I found with that release was almost euphoric.

Out of nowhere, Tony appeared.

"Baby. What are you doing?" He reached down and shook me, tearing the glass out of my hand.

"I don't want to fucking be alive anymore," I wailed, tears streaming down my face.

"I love you," he said, flipping my wrist over to assess the damage. "You're so much better than this. Please don't ever do this again." He grabbed my face to kiss my forehead and pulled me in to cry on his chest.

We both sobbed as we held each other in the middle of that desert. He gently took my hand and we went home and cleaned and wrapped my wrist.

Decades later, I found out Tony took his own life. He never moved on from the heartbreak of losing our baby and us breaking up. But he saved my life that night. I sure as hell wish I could've saved him.

11

THE BULLET AND THE DARKNESS

I WAS LIVING ON AND OFF WITH STACY BY THE TIME I HIT my late teenage years. She was very moody and unstable, so I was always walking on eggshells around her. But I loved her for who she was and not who I wanted her to be.

There were plenty of times when Stacy's moms, Phyllis and Kate, would catch us climbing in or out of bedroom windows—and we were always grounded. Her relationship with her mothers was a rocky one, but all I saw from the outside was a spoiled and rebellious kid. Years later, I'd learn where her anger stemmed from, but it's not my story to tell.

Phyllis was the butch of the relationship and a lot of the times she would lay the smack down on us. She never raised a hand to me, but poor Stacy definitely had her share of ass whoopings. One night, Phyllis was waiting and ready for us as we snuck back inside. The minute we locked the door behind us, the light flipped on to reveal Phyllis in the living room ready for attack. I honestly was tired of seeing Stacy get smacked around, so when Phyllis made a beeline for Stacy with her hand raised, I stood in front of her, willing to take the hit. Before Phyllis's hand landed, she stopped midair. Without missing a beat, her angry fist turned into an angry pointed finger, and she screamed at us to get up the stairs.

"Hey, thanks for doing that," Stacy said, her big eyes peering in through a crack in my bedroom door.

I smiled and put my finger to my mouth. *Shhhh.* I didn't want us to get in trouble again.

Stacy and I always had a strong bond, even though she could be the biggest asshole. There would be mornings I'd wake up and she would have taken the blow-dryer and curling iron with her just so I couldn't use it. Other times, if I dared to go into her closet to borrow a shirt, she would lose her mind. But I'll never forget the night Stacy tried to take her own life. It's when I realized just how badly she was hurting inside.

Stacy and the moms had been going at it again. She had come upstairs in tears and disappeared into her moms' bedroom for the majority of the night. I would periodically go in to check on her and just see if she was okay because she had the TV on so loud, but every time I peeked in, she was smothered up in covers and appeared to be sleeping.

It was getting late so I went to my room to try to fall asleep—until I heard Kate screaming.

"She's not breathing!! Call 911!"

I ran across the hall and found Kate lifting Stacy's lifeless body off the bed. Her arms were limp, her skin was gray, and she wasn't responding to Kate's shrieks.

By the time the ambulance got there, Stacy was slightly coherent. I remember her puking nonstop, but because I was so scared, my memory has blocked out the majority of that night. By then, my brain was well accustomed to papering over the worst of my pain, and in some ways I'm thankful to my body for letting me survive. I don't know that I would have made it through those years if I'd been lucid. But eventually, I'd have to face the pain head on. I'd have to excavate and process it all—years down the line—to finally heal.

We found out later that she'd downed an entire bottle of Valium. After that night, I knew Stacy wasn't okay—in her mind or in her heart. I told myself no matter what we have to go through as friends—even when she wasn't always lovable—I'd love her through it. And I did.

XO

WEEKS LATER, AFTER STACY HAD started therapy and seemed to be doing better, the moms decided to go out of town for the weekend. Thinking we had hit the lottery, we instantly planned a huge fucking house party. When I say huge, I mean massive. Stacy and I were known for throwing pretty amazing kickbacks at her place, and this would be no different. We invited everyone we knew. We even printed flyers and handed them out around town. All high schools were welcome.

Come the night of the party, we had to start turning people away. Over two hundred people showed up for ya girls. Kids we knew from school, boys who ran with different crews, anyone who was looking for a good time or trouble walked through Stacy's door. And one of them was a handsome Italian boy named Mark.

Maybe I shouldn't say "boy," because Mark was in his twenties, and he was just about the most beautiful man I'd ever seen, with full lips and jet-black hair. Now listen, I've never claimed to be a saint, but men were always my weakness. I love love. Actually, strike that. I love lust. So any chance to have a short fling filled with twitterpation? Sign me up.

But because I'm such a Pisces Venus lover girl, I also love to ignore all the red flags that come flapping toward me. My favorite color is red—wave those flags, boys! We young, impressionable teens thought an older dude liking us meant we were special. Wrong. Obviously, what happened with Jeff wasn't enough to steer me clear. My seventeen-year-old self jumped at the opportunity to be with this *man*. This hot Italian Stallion thinks I'm the kitty's titties? I'm in.

We flirted all night, and he told me about his big Italian family. He had two brothers and a sister who all looked like him—full of Italian pride. He even wore a spiraling Italian horn on a chain around his neck for good luck.

I'd had the abortion with Jordan and the ectopic pregnancy with Tony. My body was still in survival mode then—I hadn't given it any time to recalibrate or even rest. When it came to all things traumatic or painful, I'd always push forward, figuring I'd deal with the fallout later. I hadn't even begun to try to figure out how I really felt inside after all I'd been through. Bill always said, "Rolling stones gather no moss," and that's exactly what I was doing.

I had a bad habit of overlapping relationships, and breaking hearts was all I knew. But by the time I met ol' Mark, I was a free agent. I was ready to pounce.

He became my new toy. He wasn't in any of the crews I knew. He was older. And the fact that he was a d-boy and a gangster had my little heart beating.

XO

MARK RAN GAME FOR SURE. He had a slick mouth and knew exactly what to say to manipulate any situation. He was a hustler—that's what they do.

He told me a whole story about how he'd just broken up with his crazy ex-girlfriend and was single. Ladies, word to the wise: If any man refers to his ex as crazy, it's either *him* who 's crazy or he *made* her crazy.

For the first few months, he would pick me up in his white Ford Explorer with tinted windows. We would go on little dates and fuck and he'd bring me back home. So cute, right? Wrong.

One day, I was at Stacy's house and a number popped up on my pager. I called it back thinking it was Mark. It was a girl on the other end.

"Hello?"

"Hi," I said, confused. She didn't sound like any of my girls.

"How long have you been talking to Mark?" she asked. I could hear the sincerity in her voice. She was hurting. I could barely speak—I was stunned. This had never happened to me before.

"Probably about three or four months," I said. "Who is this?"

"This is his girlfriend. Jess."

I felt like I'd been punched in my stomach. Jess and I talked for a couple of hours, comparing notes, and turns out, I liked her. We agreed to meet up and confront Mark together—and ask him who he really wanted to be with.

Mark had cheated on his girlfriend with *me*. I was the other woman. I'd never done that before, and I had no idea what I was getting myself into. She offered to pick me up the next day, and wouldn't you know, she showed up in the little white Ford Explorer with tinted windows. That man had been driving me around in *her* car. I opened the passenger-side door, and in the driver's seat was a gorgeous blond-haired, blue-eyed girl with freckles all across her cheeks. I couldn't even believe he was cheating on *her* with *me*.

We had an awkward hug, but we were both checking each other out. I don't think either of us had any idea where this situation was going to land. As we rolled down his street, Jess slowed down and started panicking. They had been together for a few years, and the reality was setting in. She parked and tried to slow her breathing.

I hugged her and said, "I'll never talk to him again. You can drop me back off right now and I'll lose his number."

Her big blue eyes had tears in them.

"No," she whispered, "because then I wouldn't know which one of us he really wanted to be with."

I was gutted. I was mad. Why the fuck had he put us both in this situation?

We pulled up in front of his house and my stomach filled with butterflies. Handsome as Mark was, he had a temper on him too. And he had no idea he was going to find both of us in the car.

When he got to the passenger door, I rolled the window down and we both smiled at him.

"Funny seeing you here!" we both shrieked. Mark looked like he'd seen a ghost.

"What the fuck is wrong with you bitches?" he asked. Automatic gaslighting.

"What's wrong with us? What's wrong with you? You've been cheating on me for months!" she yelled. They started going at it, screaming at the top of their lungs over me. I leaned my seat back a tad just to get out of the line of fire.

"I'm done with this shit!" Jess yelled through snot and tears. "Pick who you want to be with *now*!"

I glanced at her and glanced back at him. I waited for him to pick her.

"I want to be with Alisa," he said.

My head snapped to the right to look at him fast enough to give me whiplash.

"Wait. Dude, I will seriously go home and you'll never hear

from me again," I said. "Don't say that just because you're mad. You've been together way too long to let me come between you." I was *fine* moving on—and seeing Jess hurt made me hurt too.

"We've been done for a long time, Jess. You know that," he said. He opened up my door and pulled me out, shutting the door behind me.

"Go home, Jess."

I was beyond perplexed, and I didn't feel good about it. It had been me and her against him five minutes ago. *What about—*

He walked me up to his house, pressed me against the wall, and started having his way with me. I gave in to it. *Never mind. I'll ask questions later.*

XO

DO YOU THINK KARMA WAS going to let me have a loving, happy, healthy relationship with this man? *Always remember, you lose them how you get them, sugar.*

Mark was jealous and possessive as hell, and he wanted me around him all the time. That meant my seventeen-year-old ass was stuck in this house of loud Italian big-time drug dealers.

Chronic and guns were Mark and his brothers' game. If you needed a pound of weed, they were your guys. They acted like the mafiosos they'd seen on TV, pretending they ran Las Vegas like the Godfather.

We all lived together in a rambling house, where the voice volume level was always at 10.

I got close to the mom and sister, but it didn't take long to see why Mark was the way he was with women. His mother enabled the fuck out of his impulses, and she was always in our relationship and seemed kind of obsessed with her son, like *cut the damn umbilical cord, woman.* Her obsession seemed limited to Mark;

she always said it was because he had almost died during childbirth. But as the years went by, it seemed like a weird excuse for her to just paper over all the shitty things he did.

Trying to keep up with our mob-family image, I cooked, cleaned, fucked him when he wanted—and worked nights at a restaurant on the Strip across from a massive club called Utopia. He would come by or call to check in on me all the time. He hated when men would leave me big tips or their phone numbers on receipts. He didn't like that I was around men in general. As if my long hours and graveyard shift weren't enough—I had to deal with him tracking my moves. He decided he wanted me to be a "square girlfriend" who worked an office job. So I quit.

I was so submissive then—it was survival—and so I was obliged to make my man happy. I interviewed for a nine-to-five, regular-ass job at a pest control company. I showed up in a cute white T-shirt and blue jean overalls. Who shows up to an interview in overalls? But the owner, Karl, hired my eighteen-year-old ass on the fucking spot. And to this day, he will tell you the overalls are what got me hired.

I loved Karl. He was a family man, businessman, and sweet spirit. We developed a friendship—at work and outside of work. I had no idea back then what was right or wrong. I just knew he was my buddy. How could I predict he'd end up becoming my first sugar daddy?

Back then, I had no idea what a sugar daddy was—and we definitely didn't use that term to describe our relationship. But Karl would overhear Mark and me arguing and see me struggling to find some independence. He bought me my first car and my first cell phone. He helped me with my first apartment. He gave me a salary big enough to support myself and save up a little too. He watched me grow up, and he provided for me. He's still a friend, and I'll always have a soft spot for him.

He was my first taste of having a sugar daddy—even if I didn't have the sexual part down back then. But I sure as hell liked the feeling of a man like that spending money on me.

I guess you could say he created a monster.

XO

WE HAD HELLA GUNS IN the house at Mark's—assault rifles, semiautomatics, and guns I've never even heard of. Under beds, in closets, in attics—name it. They bred German Shepherds, and Mark had his beloved all-white man's best friend. She never left his side. I had Dana Dane, named after the rims.

Mark and I lived in a guesthouse in the backyard, and we could see the front yard from our window. I woke up around five in the morning one day because our dogs were barking like crazy outside. Mark was at the window, squinting out into the dawn. The sun was barely peeking through the night sky.

"Something's not right," he said.

The next thing we knew, cops were running through the yard in gas masks and shields.

"Freeze!" the cops yelled, loud enough that we could hear them out back. Lights came on in the house, and we saw cops laying everybody down. I barely had time to be petrified before a few stormed out to the guesthouse, took us outside, and sat us down on the porch with our hands behind our backs while they searched the property.

All around us were police in SWAT vests pointing guns at our faces, yelling at us to keep our hands behind us. When you're raised in the streets, you're taught not to like cops, and every second of this situation confirmed it. When people tear your house apart—throwing and tossing everything you own—it feels fucking awful. After what seemed like hours, the cops arrested Mark's youngest brother, and eventually let us go back inside.

The house was torn the fuck up, and the family went into overdrive looking for a lawyer, calling other family members, and making a plan to get his brother back home. In a crisis, they banded together, but the bond would be short-lived. They'd be back at each other's throats in no time.

XO

MARK WAS IN A CAR club, and on Saturday nights, you could see beautiful lowriders cruising the streets, and empty grocery-store parking lots turn into what we lovingly would call "a hop." You'd bring your car—which you spent tens of thousands of dollars on—to hit hydraulics and try to hop other cars' heights. It was good ol' fashioned fun, and it gave all the boys something constructive to do with their d-boy money and time.

One night, we went out to a rival car club's party at the Q Club. We were out in the parking lot at the end of the night, when—

Pop pop pop pop.

Mark grabbed me and threw me behind a car's massive tire.

"Get down and stay down," he yelled, putting his body over mine. He hung on to me tight as bullets flew past us. They were getting closer until *whoooosh.* A bullet whizzed right past my fucking ear. I froze like a deer in headlights.

"What was that?" I yelled.

"A bullet," Mark said, squeezing me tighter. "Get down lower."

If I'd moved half an inch, I would have taken it to the side of the head. See what I mean? God's always had a hand on me.

I don't know what started it all, but Mark and his brothers

were always talking shit to someone or starting shit. All I know is once the bullets stopped, we got the fuck out of there.

XO

THE FIGHTING WAS GETTING OUT of control. Sometimes I'd leave, but I always came back. And that familiar feeling started, the one where everything is so fucking miserable and overwhelming that I just wanted it to be over, but there was no way out.

So, alone in the bathroom, I downed thirteen Tylenol PMs, thinking it would be enough to end it all. Mark found me sleeping and groggy in bed, and when I'd told him what I'd done, he laughed in my face. And then he made me go to work so he could go out and do God knows what. I don't know how I made it through that shift, trying not to fall asleep. I fought hard to keep my eyelids open, downing Mountain Dew, hoping it would reignite some life in me.

It wasn't the worst time of my life, but I don't know why I didn't tell that dude to go fuck himself. But we were so twisted—and he would make me the responsible one so he could fuck off and do whatever he wanted while I was at work.

Shit was spiraling in my life again. I just didn't know how bad it was about to get.

12

NEVER BREAK A PROMISE

I WAS NINETEEN. MARK WAS BANGING SOME HOSEHOUND stripper named Hope. She was scraggly as shit, but Hope had something I wanted: She was making money dancing. I'd always wanted to be a Vegas showgirl. I wanted that glitz and glam. As a little girl, I'd swung from the post of my Strawberry Shortcake canopy bed. One time, I swung so hard I snapped my imaginary stripper pole in half. You can imagine how that went over with Bill and Mindy.

In my teens, I realized I had power over men, and I loved it. But the fact that men would have to *pay* me to touch me at the club was even more tantalizing.

I knew many girls who danced, but Mark absolutely wouldn't let me go to the clubs to work. Instead, I had to make a dirt salary with a fucking square job where I'd keep my clothes on so Mark would never feel like he had to share. He even made me leave Karl's company because he knew I was getting too independent and financially secure. By the time I found out about Hope, I was working odd jobs at restaurants for minimum wage and barely making tips.

And when I found out he was sleeping with that stripper behind my back, something inside me snapped after years of being told what to do. I was done being the obedient house mouse. I said, *Fuck that. I'm going to fucking strip, too.*

All the girls I knew worked at Cheetahs, and if you were hot shit, that's where you would go. I already had an outfit prepared, so I threw on my teeny-tiny bikini with a schoolgirl skirt and clear heels and sashayed my way out onto the floor.

I was nervous as fuck, but my girl Veronica was with me, and she was a seasoned vet. The OGs who had been dancing for a while called us newbies "green"—and let me tell you, the men could always spot fresh meat. They were drawn to innocence like moths to a flame.

My first customer signaled me over, and I anxiously walked toward him, trying not to teeter in my sky-high heels.

"I want you to kick me in the balls. I'll pay you seven hundred dollars," he said—no hesitation. I jerked my head back, totally appalled. Veronica was watching, and she raised her eyebrows at me, like *What the fuck you waiting for?*

"Absolutely not," I said. *Kick him in the balls? How? Wouldn't that hurt him?* I'd never heard of such a thing. Now that I think about it, my innocence was kind of endearing. Talk about green.

But Veronica the Vet didn't hesitate and swooped in like a vulture on prey.

"If you're not, I'm going to take him in the back and do it," she said.

"I can't do that!" I said, shaking my head.

"You better get used to weird shit, Lis. All these motherfuckers have fetishes. You just have to decide which ones you're okay with." She fixed her face with a smile and walked up to the guy. She took him by the hand and they walked back to VIP together.

Great. So now I have to kick dudes in the balls? My heart was racing. I was getting more nervous by the minute, and I could feel my stomach was churning. *What kind of shit happens here? What have I done?* Before I could turn back around and catch my breath, a bachelor party signaled me over and asked me to dance.

It was a group of about ten men. It's out in the open. Surely they're not *all* ball kickers.

I wasn't about to bitch out again.

Shaking, I stood in front of one of the bachelors. All eyes on me, I could feel their stares as they undressed me with their eyes. The butterflies in my stomach were overwhelming. The pressure to perform was building up.

I turned around to plop my ass into the bachelor's lap and start grinding. My stomach bubbled and—

A fluff slipped out. I just couldn't hold it in anymore. Luckily, it was silent. *Phew.* My relief morphed into panic within seconds. I was grinding my ass off as we wafted in the smell of a rancid fart. It had a *kick* to it. I couldn't believe it had come from me. *I'm going to be known as the fart dance girl for the rest of my stripper career.*

"Bro, you ripped ass!" one of them yelled. I whipped around to try to defend myself, but to my surprise, the bros were pointing at each other. Nobody thought that smell could come from li'l ol' me.

I finished dancing for them as the smell dissipated and ran to the dressing room mortified. *Fuck this shit. I'm never dancing again.* I didn't think I belonged there, and a moral battle was raging internally. Everything I was ever taught in church said this was evil. So what was I doing?

I put my clothes on, took the single shred of dignity I had left, and ran the hell out of that place. I was fucking disgusted. With myself. With stripping. With men.

Maybe I just wasn't one of the "cool girls." I figured I was destined to be a square after all.

XO

SURPRISE, SURPRISE, ONE NIGHT WE were fighting because some random girl was calling his phone, so I went out with my girl Erin. I knew Erin from Mark's car club—she was one of the other members' girlfriends. And that night, I took X for the first time.

If you're ever going to take X, you sure as shit should not do so while *The Devil's Advocate* is playing on the damn TV. Don't do it in some stranger's house—especially a stranger whose mom collects haunted horror dolls. When that X hit, those fucking creepy-ass dolls came to life as people going up in flames while Satan laughed. Too bad I didn't take my own advice.

Instead, I watched in horror and spiraled into a scene straight out of hell. I started puking my brains out—for the life of me I couldn't stop throwing up. I didn't even want to stop puking—I wanted this drug out of me. I hated how it made me feel and the severe anxiety it instantly gave me. I puked myself silly, until the muscles in my throat were so relaxed I couldn't get any more out, even if I stuck my whole hand down my throat.

I was fucked up beyond belief. I felt completely outside my body with zero control—and I was overheating like crazy. Was I going to die? *What was in this pill?*

My brain worked long enough for one clear thought: *I need to get to my car. I've got some Panda Express in there. If I can just get some food in my stomach, it will make me feel better.*

I got my ass over to the car and found my take-out box of

fried rice. I downed it—just shoveled food into my mouth. Dry rice with nothing to drink is a fucking health hazard, by the way. How I survived that, I'll never know.

After getting the food into my stomach, I was still terrified. There was only one thing that had ever gotten me through hell before: Prayer. *God will see I took an illicit drug and I'm freaking out and have mercy on me, right?*

It was worth a shot. I got down on my hands and knees in the middle of the street and talked to God.

"Lord, please let me fucking live through this. Just get me through this and I promise you I'll never touch another drug again."

My friends thought I had lost my mind, but I didn't care. At least if something happened to me, Big Homie upstairs would let me through the Pearly Gates. *Amen.*

I pulled myself together and told Erin we needed to go somewhere. I needed to be anywhere but that house with the creepy fucking dolls. Erin had taken the X too, and we were fucked up when I got behind the wheel of the 1997 red Honda Civic that Karl had bought me. We only made it by the grace of God. I should *not* have been driving—I took a turn and all the streetlights and road blended together like a watercolor painting. We somehow got to Erin's apartment. The last person I wanted to see was Mark—he would have lost his mind seeing me in that state.

The sun started coming up and we couldn't sleep, so we laid in the room staring at the ceiling. This was the worst drug I'd ever taken. Erin and I rotted in bed for two days, sick off our asses. When the drugs finally started to wear off, we both had black circles under our eyes. Her boyfriend came in periodically to check on us, and even he couldn't deny that we looked like death warmed over.

"What the fuck did you take? You look like you're on fucking heroin," he said.

Later, we found out that the X we'd bought *was* laced with heroin, and that's why we were so sick. But I'd survived. God had my back again, and I pulled through.

XO

AFTER THAT, I WOULDN'T EVEN take an aspirin for years. I still drank, but I wouldn't pop a pill if you paid me. After the X, I started having full-scale panic attacks. It's like that pill had unlocked Pandora's box in my brain. I genuinely thought I was losing my mind. The anxiety would get so bad that I'd drive myself to the hospital and just sit there until the panic would subside. I was such a frequent flyer that I learned the doctors' and nurses' first names. The only place I felt safe was in the hospital, but when doctors would prescribe me medication, I refused to take it.

Later, down the road, I'd cave and start taking the Xanax a doctor prescribed me. But at the time, I just knew something was building inside of me that was eventually going to explode.

XO

I WAS GETTING READY FOR work when I felt a dull pain on my side. At first, I thought it was period cramps, but it got so bad I had to call out of work. I prayed it would stop. It didn't. I braced myself on the bathroom sink and looked at myself in the mirror. *There's no fucking way. Please. No fucking way.*

But I knew I was pregnant again, and I knew what was happening.

I dialed Mark.

"I'm really hurting," I told him.

"What do you want me to do about it? You're always going to

the fucking hospital," he said. "So why don't you go to the fucking hospital?" I hung up and went and found the only person I could think of to help me: Mark's mom.

"I think I'm having an ectopic pregnancy," I told her. She shook her head.

"There's no way you're pregnant," she said. *Wait. What?* I was baffled but in way too much pain to argue. I also didn't have time to go down that road with her. I just knew I needed to get myself to the hospital.

As soon as I walked through the double doors I greeted the familiar nurse.

"I think I'm having an ectopic pregnancy. It's my second." Her eyes widened and she took me straight back to a room. They immediately did a pee test and an ultrasound.

Yahtzee! *Fuck. Another one.*

I called up Mark's mom looking for some sort of comfort and told her the news, using every ounce of energy to keep my voice calm.

"I *am* pregnant, and I'm having an ectopic pregnancy." She responded just as evenly—it was almost scary.

"If you're pregnant, it's not my son's. There's no way he got you pregnant. His sperm isn't strong enough." *What the fuck? Who says this shit?*

"Listen to me. They're about to take me to the operating room. Can you just let Mark know that I'm about to have surgery?" *Click.* I hung up the phone in disgust.

I was alone. I was scared as fuck and I was losing another baby. One of the nurses was standing by and saw everything. She came over and started rubbing my arm and told me everything would be okay. Thank God for women who bring comfort to other women.

They wheeled me into surgery, and when I woke up hours

later, Mark still wasn't there. No one was. I couldn't drive, and they wouldn't release me alone. I had to call around, groggy and nauseated from the anesthesia, until I could find someone to find my boyfriend and tell him to come get me.

Hours later, Mark finally crashed into the hospital room, pissed as hell I had inconvenienced him by having a medical emergency. He hurried me out, not saying a word as we walked to the car. I crumpled myself into my seat, still groggy. *I just lost our baby,* I kept repeating in my head. *Why is he treating me like this?* It's almost as if I were trying to take mental notes so that this time I wouldn't forget.

At home, I headed toward the guesthouse where I lived, but his family redirected me upstairs into some dark, spare room away from the family. Like they were throwing me in a hole. Like I was in quarantine. I lay down and bawled my eyes out. I'd been trying for so long to keep a damn smile on my face and keep everybody happy by cooking, cleaning, and being perfect, no matter what I'd been through. My spirit was finally crushed. Up there in that dank little room away from everyone, I finally, truly broke down, and to this day, it gets me emotional to think of my teenage self up there all alone, just begging for the universe to cut her a break.

Mark never came up to check on me—even one fucking time. I lay in that bed for days, not eating, not talking to anyone, not watching TV, not existing. I didn't care about anything besides watching the sun rise and set every day.

There was one bright moment: I'll never forget when Mark's friend, Mike, poked his head in. His was the first face I'd seen in days.

"You okay in there?"

"Not really, Mike," I said.

"Do you need anything?" I couldn't think of anything in the

world I needed more than what he'd already given me, which was just an ounce of care.

After Mike left, I got to thinking. *You know what? I am never, ever going to let a motherfucker make me feel like this again.* Alone, scared, and angry, I decided right then and there that my life was going to change. I promised myself, and I never break a promise.

MOVIN' ON UP

OLD HABITS DIE HARD, AND IT TOOK A WHILE TO GET rid of Mark. I had to start devising a plan to separate—and he had no idea it was coming.

When I woke up from that postsurgery haze in the dark hole his family had stuck me in, I got my ass up and started looking for my own place. I wasn't ever going to let anyone make me feel as low as I did lying in that room—and I fucking meant it.

I had just turned twenty and was working an escrow job doing title work, so I had enough money coming in for my own rent. I found a house of my own, but it wasn't far—just a block away from Mark's mom's house. I'd never had my own place. I had always lived with other people and their families—or in my parents' house in a room without a door.

But Mark decided he wasn't giving up on me. Funny how men want you when you don't want them. Stop chasing a man and he'll start chasing you.

Unfortunately he followed me to the new place—and the man ended up moving in with me. I know. But I was so run down—I had no energy to fight. Everything was catching up with me: the years of abuse, the fallout from the heroin-laced Ecstasy trip, the medical trauma, the trying to make everyone around me happy. But did I deal with any of my trauma then? Hell, no.

Mark and I continued to fuck and fight—shocking—for the next year, but by the time I was twenty-one, I'd had enough. I was burnt. Exhausted. Disconnected. We were practically living separate lives anyway.

Tasha and I had fallen out for a few years, but after I got my own place, we reconnected. She'd had a beautiful son named Aalijah, and she was doing the mom and dancer life all at once. One day, Tasha came with me to pick up one of my paychecks. She took one look at the total and freaked out.

"Bitch, that's how much you made in two weeks? You could make that in one night at the club."

I thought about my failed attempt at dancing from a couple years back—how I'd been so nervous I farted on a whole-ass bachelor party. But I was working my tooter off trying to save up enough money to finally shake Mark off for good and move across town. I wanted to get away from the Eastside of Vegas, away from all these fucking memories.

And I was done slumming it. I wanted a fancy life, the one with glimmering lights like the showgirls in Vegas. I wanted to wrap myself in beauty and glamour to insulate myself from the ugliness of my childhood and teen years.

I needed to make a shitload of money. *Fuck it.*

Tasha had a year of dancing under her belt and was already established at the Olympic Gardens, or OG's, as we so lovingly called it. I still have a picture of us out in the parking lot with our hair and makeup done like the *Playboy* models we aspired to be. I had on massive fake eyelashes, the kind where if the wind blew, my eyes looked like butterfly wings flapping off my eyeballs.

Tasha was there to teach me how to ask for dances and get paid. I trusted her completely and knew she had my best interests in mind. And after an hour or so, I was ready to spread my wings and fly. I started moving through the club on my own, figuring out what I liked and what I didn't.

I gave the stage a try, but it was definitely not my thing. I'm always so mesmerized by the women who know how to do pole work. It's so beautiful and so elegant—which I am not. And it didn't make much financial sense either. Why would I go onstage and make a few dollars when I could be in the VIP room and make a hundred? *If it don't make dollars, it don't make sense, baby.*

I walked into that club so damn innocent with no idea how to act. I walked out with $2,000 in cash in my pocket. I was two grand closer to being able to get away from Mark once and for all.

XO

I SWEAR, WHEN I'M GENUINELY over someone, it's like the universe just sends someone right into my path to make sure I never go back. I'd seen Bobby around Mark's car club. He was hard to miss—a blond-haired, blue-eyed cutie. He was an absolutely fucking adorable little baby boy, and the complete opposite of Mark.

I was dancing one night and looked up and saw sweet Bobby in the club lights with his best friend. They were so fun and free-spirited. They were everything I needed. He spent the night drinking with me until we were shit-faced—and when I told him *Let's take this party outside to your truck*, he didn't hesitate. I've always loved being a seductress—it's a kink to be an earthbound siren of sorts, I'd say. I also love newness: new cars, new houses, new relationships. It's a habit I would later have to learn to break.

We fucked in the club parking lot, and I figured he'd be my

dirty little secret until I could end the relationship for good with Mark. It felt *so* good to finally be a shady bitch behind Mark's back after everything he had put me though. At that point, he'd slept with half of Vegas behind mine.

But I've never been good with secrets. Maybe fucking Bobby gave me the courage to really separate myself from that disaster of a relationship. I knew I couldn't live there anymore—I was just down the block from Mark's mom, and his brothers, and, obviously, fuckin' Mark was in the place that was supposed to be all mine.

Tasha and I had hatched a plan. We really wanted to get to Green Valley, so we applied for places. We got approved for a McMansion. This was it! This was my time to shine! I was beaming ear to ear when we got the call—I was finally independent and going after what I wanted. But nothing would feel better than getting to watch Mark's world crumble when I told him I was finally leaving him. Forever.

"I'm getting a place with Tasha. Keep the fucking house," I said. "I'm done. I'm leaving you and I'm not coming back. And by the way, I've been fucking Bobby from your car club the past six months."

I was free. I packed up my shit again and moved across town. I remember driving up to our new house knowing Mark was finally in my rearview mirror. I cried tears of happiness the whole way home. I finally felt like I was turning my life around.

I started really unpacking my new place in Green Valley—the nice side of town, far from the Eastside trash I'd come from. We were moving on up. We were doing something with our lives—and you couldn't tell me shit. I was living in a part of town I'd only dreamed about growing up. I had my best friend and her son in this huge house. I was free. Life for the first time was—dare I say—happy.

14
GREEN VALLEY

OUR MINI MANSION IN GREEN VALLEY WAS THE ULTImate bachelorette pad. It was a huge, two-story number, with *five* bedrooms, in a gated community. We even had a sprawling backyard with a trampoline.

There were two master bedrooms, so I took the one downstairs and Tasha took the one upstairs to be closer to her son. Coming from the couches I'd crashed on through my teenage years, it might as well have been Wayne Newton's estate. I was so fucking proud of us. We'd made it.

Our girl gang would visit every day like something out of *The Golden Girls*—we were our own little family. It was our compound—and men couldn't enter without an invitation.

Aalijah had one hell of time growing up in that house of girls who would fawn over him and take care of him. We loved to barbecue out in the backyard, jump on the trampoline, and lie out in the sun. There was so much love going around, and it was always laughing and dancing and rock 'n' roll blaring in a never-ending blondetourage. It was truly one of the happiest times in my life.

XO

IT WASN'T PARTYING THAT GOT me hooked on what would become my chemical love affair. It was my damn wisdom teeth.

I made it to twenty-one before I had to have my wisdom teeth pulled. I always called my front indented tooth my "Jewel" tooth—like the singer with one pushed-back tooth. I had the same exact tooth, and I hated smiling. I left home before my parents could have put braces on me. Not like they would have in the first place.

Now I was ready to fix my own teeth, and my wisdoms were up first. One guess who went with me to the appointment? Fucking Mark. Why did I always have these exes hanging around? I never could seem to shake them. But it turned out that Mark and I were better friends than we were lovers. I still have an extremely bad habit of befriending my exes—there's something in the *We survived that together, congratulations. You can be my friend for life.* The doctor opted out of putting me under or giving me much of anything in the way of a numbing agent—to this day, I don't know why that was allowed, or if he was just too shady to follow basic rules. He just yanked and ripped my teeth clear out of my jaw. Poor Mark had to watch the barbaric surgery front and center. He almost passed out a couple of times. It left me with two black eyes and a face so swollen you couldn't recognize me. It was horrific, and I was absolutely miserable.

Back home, I was trying to muscle through the pain like I've done with everything in life. Blood trickled out of my mouth every so often onto my cheek, which was swollen as round and big as the damn moon. Tasha and I were floating in the pool, and I was desperate for anything to make the pain go away.

"Why don't you just take one of your pain pills?" she asked. My head throbbed, and the raw, vacant gums screamed in razor-sharp pain.

"I don't want to take a pain pill," I snapped.

"Bitch, you won't be in pain if you take the damn pill," she snapped back. She got out and grabbed me a Percocet, and I reluctantly swallowed.

Thirty minutes passed and the minute that pill kicked in, it was like *sweet heaven, 7-Eleven.* I was euphoric, just wading through the water, letting it wash over me. That perc had me in a chokehold instantly. I didn't have a care in the world. Anxiety, where? Pain? Gone. I was floating down the river of love.

Tasha had her own stash on hand, and the two of us laughed our asses off together in the pool that day. Tasha was used to pills, but I sure as shit wasn't. It was nothing to her, but I was on another planet. It was the most amazing thing that had ever happened to me. Little did I know that opening up the drug gates again was a gate to hell. Because once my fear had subsided around percs, I started in on other pills too. First it was Lortabs. Then more Percocets. Then Norcos. And once I felt steady with those, I moved on to Xanax, the ones the emergency room doctor tried to give me so many times. And those little pills changed my life.

I'd never known peace like I did on Xanax—not even for a minute of my twenty-one years. It felt like all the muscles that had been twisted up so tight for decades could finally relax. It was peace of mind for the first time in my whole life.

XO

TO TELL YOU THE TRUTH, dancing was hard for me when I was getting started. All the religious trauma came rearing its ugly head. So I made a deal in the beginning: I worked my square real estate job during the day while I danced at night. I figured that if stripping wasn't my main job, I was only part-time sinning, and I could live with that.

I told myself that I was dancing so I could work my way up in life. I'd work nine to five and then dance from ten till two. The burden on my body was intense, and honestly, just downright exhausting. But I made myself juggle. I couldn't be a full-time sinner.

I was making good money during the day—but I wasn't making the kind of money that made this hustle worth it. I could make five or ten grand a night dancing. And those numbers stacked up pretty heavy against my moral guilt. I could pay my bills and take care of myself without sacrificing my body—because what had this guilt gotten me? A busted body and soul and not enough in the bank to do anything about it. Remember, if it don't make dollars, it don't make sense, baby. So I up and quit my square job.

If I was going to be a full-time sinner, at least I would be getting paid.

Dancing back then in the early 2000s wasn't like it is today. It was much more taboo, and it was so glamorous. The girls were beautiful. They'd be in elaborate gowns with stunning hair and makeup. And all the girls worked together. We didn't compete or get catty. It was one big family. The bouncers were our big brothers or uncles, and they protected us. The house moms loved us, and they always had meals for us to eat during breaks. We took a lot of pride in our looks: Our nails were done, hair was perfect, makeup on point.

I'd die without my girl Hailee who does my makeup nowadays, but then, we sure as hell didn't have professional makeup artists getting us ready to dance. As glamorous as it was back then, we learned to smoke out our eyes as black as night and gloss our lips so glittery they sparkled under the club lights. We were our own glam teams, and it meant we brought another kind of creativity and artistry to the work. The way we looked wasn't just sexy, it was *art*.

When I'd get too low on nights at the club, we'd all snort rails off each other's naked asses or dirty bathroom sinks—or even worse: the back of the toilets.

It was all money flowing and *Playboy*'s heyday and celebrities rolling up for VIP dances. It was rock 'n' roll, and it was sexy. I don't think there will ever be a time like that in the clubs again. You fucking bet there were plenty of seedy parts of the business, but it also had a kind of innocence that could only exist before cell phones or cameras or clout chasing for social media. It was iconic, and I miss those days. They were singular and wild, the kind of magic you just can't re-create.

XO

PLAYBOY WAS ALWAYS IN THE background, and a lot of my friends were in the magazine. It was what we all wanted, and it was another step up into the glamorous, sparkling life. *Playboy* scouts came into the clubs all the time, looking for girls with the perfect look. By the time I was twenty-three, I'd already headed out to Santa Monica for a test shoot. I still have that series of Polaroids. I look so young, tiny, fresh-faced, and excited. I still have the letter they sent me saying I wasn't a good fit too.

Back in Vegas, *Playboy* held casting calls all the time. I decided to try again, and I walked into the conference room in some hotel. All around me were the most beautiful girls I'd ever seen. Everybody wanted to be in fucking *Playboy.*

I waited until they called my name, and then stood in front of a few scouts. One of the guys—who was nothing to write home to mom about himself—looked me up and down.

"You're cute for a chubby chick," he said.

"What the hell does that mean?" I didn't weigh more than 120 pounds.

"Honey, if you want to be in this magazine, you have to lose fifteen pounds."

If that man wanted me to lose fifteen pounds, I would've looked like Skeletor—and who the fuck was that pleasantly plump scrub telling to lose weight? But the shitty comment sent me into a spiral. At the time, I was sure he was right. My self-esteem jackknifed, and—obviously—I didn't get a spot in the magazine.

But that doesn't mean I stopped trying. Today, I'm so damn embarrassed, but I booked a reality show with PlayboyTV. It was like most reality shows back then: Four or five of us moved into a mansion to see if we could find love. And to be honest, it was fucking dope. The producers loved me, and we had a blast. But at the end of the taping, a producer called me outside.

"Alisa, I really need to sell this show." I didn't understand much about the business then, that we were shooting a pilot that had to be picked up by the network.

"Okay," I said. "So?"

"So I need you to hook up with Matt," he said. Matt was one of the dudes who lived in the house with me, and I was *not* interested.

"I'm not doing that," I said.

"Name your price."

This dude is going to pay me to act like I'm fucking some guy?

"Five grand," I said.

"Perfect," he said. He didn't stutter.

"You're serious?"

"Yeah."

So I went back into the house and started flirting. Even Matt knew I wasn't into him. I tried to convince him, but we ended up faking it for the show. We went under the covers naked and pretended to have sex by making the noises—but Matt got so fucking excited, he came in my eye. The load of semen shot across the bed into my fucking eye. And they have me on camera saying that. Goddamn.

They sold the pilot, and I got my $5,000. It wasn't like I'd turned a trick. But it planted a seed. One day, if I wanted to, I could make some serious money. And as I learned very young, pussy is power.

TRICK OR TREAT

MY TWENTIES HAPPENED DURING THE GOLDEN AGE of porn—porn was absolutely popping. The OGs Jenna Jameson, Jesse Jane, and Belladonna were at their prime, and business was booming. Rock stars dated *Playboy* models and porn stars, and the paparazzi were obsessed with toxic love stories and couldn't get enough. It was Pamela Anderson and Tommy Lee's world, and we were just living in it.

Porn wasn't the shit you can get today on a website with a million pop-ups trying to sell you dick enlargement pills. It was an elite industry, and those girls were glamorous and beautiful. It was hardcore as shit, but it was still soft enough to be passionate and sexy.

Everybody in Vegas wanted to be a stripper or a porn star. It was just what girls there did—and it was the path to the high life. Sex, drugs, and rock 'n' roll the dice.

I guess you could say I was the luckiest-little-stripper-in-the-world, because porn scouts started hounding me every single day—including a major, major scout who contracted with Vivid.

Vivid was the cream of the crop, the top dog in the porn industry at that time, and if I was going to do porn, I was going to go big.

Mikey Fuckin' B. walked into my life at just the right moment—or so he thought. He was an old white dude who wanted to try his pasty hands at being my manager. I stumbled upon his lap one hazy night at the club, and he sold me dreams. His first plan was to turn me into some kind of sexpot Vegas lounge act, but when the porn scouts started circling, he switched gears.

Plan B was for me to become the iconic Jenna Jameson's understudy—or so he said. Jenna was the queen—nobody did it like she did. But Mikey claimed that he had industry knowledge that she was planning to retire soon, and I'd be the one to slide my ass onto her lube-covered throne. Who the hell knows if he was talking out of his ass or if he'd really heard something around town. I went to a meeting with Mikey and some scouts, and right away I could feel something was off. These were weird fucking people, and the whole scene was seedy as fuck. People in the porn industry who aren't doing the performing give me the creeps—the directors and the producers who get to keep their clothes on and make money off performers always looked so damn dead-eyed to me. Just soulless.

And let's be real: Stripping and porn are close cousins, but they're two different things. And once you step over the wall into porn, there's no coming back.

These creeps were coming on strong. They placed a contract in front of me, and I could almost hear them panting like dogs.

"We're going to change your name," one said.

"Change my name? Why?"

"Yeah. We're gonna call you Crystal Method," the other one said. I shifted in the vinyl seat. That feeling of something being off got even stronger. Isn't that a drug?

Today, I'm wary of contracts—I've always felt uncomfortable

tying myself financially to anyone. Maybe in another life, someone had made me sign a contract and then kept me under their thumb, because my body physically revolts against such authority. I sure as hell didn't trust the contract these men put in front of me. I didn't want *anyone* to own me—least of all these creepy dudes.

"I'm not signing shit," I said, and Mikey's pale face turned fire-truck red.

"If you want to fucking work, you need to sign this," he said in a sharp tone. We'd been working together for months at that point, and nothing had come to fruition. First it had been record execs who ghosted, then it was showgirl auditions that never happened, and now he wanted me to sign a contract without legal advice? And wasn't my manager supposed to fight *for* me? Why the fuck was he on their side?

I haven't gotten anywhere in this life without trusting my intuition, and my intuition was screaming at me to get out of that room. There were so many times when all I had was trust in God and trust in myself—and without them, I wouldn't have survived. I wouldn't have survived the two kidnapping attempts when I was just a kid. I wouldn't have survived being a homeless teen runaway. My instincts were everything. They were all I could count on.

"You can go fuck yourself," I said right back.

I didn't need a manager. I could handle my own affairs.

XO

SUNNY WOULD COME INTO OLYMPIC Gardens all the time. He owned a huge car chop shop not too far from the club, and he'd stop by for a dance or a VIP. He'd bring his boys—and they loved to drop money on us. He'd always say, *Nice to see you, you sexy motherfucker*, to Tasha or our girl Katie or me.

That man loved blondes—and so he loved Tasha and me. But he *really* took a liking to Katie. That girl was absolutely gorgeous. She looked just like Pamela Anderson. She was also your stereotypical blonde—the ones they talk about in movies. The lights were on, but no one was home. It was impossible not to love her.

One night, it was getting late, and Sunny and his boys had already spent thousands on us. But he had something else in mind.

"You ladies should come back to the shop with me," he said. His banged-up wedding ring flashed. If he was going to cheat on his wife, his place of fucking business was as good a place as any. The girls and I took a beat to talk it over. I wasn't convinced, but Tasha and Katie were ready.

"Come on," Tasha said. "Let's just go."

"Well, how much money are they going to give us?" We agreed on our number, and I took it back to Sunny.

"We want two thousand dollars to go back with you," I said. "Each."

"Done."

"Really?" I asked. He didn't blink. It was that fucking easy?

"Yeah," he said. "Each of you want two thousand dollars? I'll give you two thousand dollars. Get your clothes on."

We headed to the back to tip our house mom out and get dressed—our house mom kept the dancers running, helped us with our day-to-day like bringing us dinner or keeping the dressing room clean. Those women have seen it all. Love or hate your house mom—they could make a dancer's life hell—but at the end of the night, we'd give her a portion of our tips for her service.

Sunny took us to his shop, and—surprise, surprise—the shop had an upstairs with a set of bedrooms. I guess this was a regular thing for him.

"We're not doing anything until he gives us the money," I whispered to Tasha and Katie.

I'd learned the ropes of the game a long time ago—when I was just seventeen—and all these years later, I have nothing but respect for girls still in it. Back when I was still living between my various girls' places, I met a dude named Anthony, who was dating my other bestie, Michelle. He drove a Cadillac on rims, and he had freckles, long hair, and long nails.

Pimps in Vegas are flashy as fuck, and Anthony was always trying to get me to choose up with him—basically agree that he'd protect me if I'd make him money. I had zero interest in choosing up with any pimp, but I wanted to learn the business. I wanted to understand the ins and outs of the underworld. I wanted to know what made the people inside the industry tick.

So I'd tag along with Anthony and Michelle to the clubs, even though I was underage, and get him liquored up so I could ask him all my questions. He explained all the levels of the game to me, everything I knew back then.

It all fascinated me, except for the part about handing over your money. I couldn't imagine making all the money those girls were making and giving it over to a man—a man who usually treated them like shit and had other girls too, all stacked against one another in some kind of twisted hierarchy. I'd heard horrific fucking stories of pimps beating on their girls. One pimp even put a fucking hot curling iron in his girl's vagina because she didn't come back with enough money. None of that appealed to me.

If there's a jump between stripping and porn, there's sure as hell a jump between stripping and hooking. But there was something different about this job—I was in control in a way I wouldn't have been in porn. It was *easy*, and that feeling of running the show was electric.

I was about to have my first customer, and I remember what

Anthony had taught me: You never turn a trick without getting your money up front.

We took the cash—and we'd keep it all, by the way—and it was on.

I tried not to wince when he took his shirt off, since he was covered with wiry, gray hair. He was furrier than a Persian rug. Katie and Tasha weren't first-timers like me, and they had no fear. But I was scared, so they went first, while I secretly hoped he'd cum before it was my turn. In between each of us, we switched out the condom, washed his dick off, and put a new one on. From that day on, whenever a group of us shared a trick, we always played it safe.

When it was my turn, I straddled him and double-checked that his condom was on. *This dude is so fucking gross*, I kept thinking the whole time.

And then I started focusing on the money. I was just an actress getting paid to do a scene. I started riding him while Tasha and Katie made out—we were giving him his own little personal porn scene. *When is this going to end?*

It was over faster than I could remotely have anticipated. I must have ridden him for no more than two minutes. He finished, and me and the girls took our money and left. Driving home, I decided it wasn't really so bad. I didn't feel guilty or even that gross. Two minutes of that fucker inside of me, and I got paid and left.

What I really, really liked was that the motherfucker had to pay to touch me. He couldn't do a damn thing to me unless he paid me first. If I said no and didn't take his money, he didn't get me.

And I thought that was the most beautiful fucking thing I'd ever heard.

XO

AFTER THAT, I DIDN'T MIND turning tricks. I could dissociate my way through them and watch my cash stack grow. I knew I was supposed to feel shame about doing sex work, but it was becoming obvious that sex work was a tool. I could use it to gain some control over my body—which helped heal my childhood trauma—and I could get revenge on men who didn't see it coming.

After that first night, Sunny became a regular. And it was easy to make money from other men, too, because honestly, sometimes I just robbed them silly.

Super-rich guys would come into the club, looking for the full VIP experience. They'd get hammered, the girls and I would bat our eyelashes, and they'd fall in love. It was so predictable—that's when they'd ask us to come back to their room.

By this point, they'd already dropped a few grand on me, and so I could name my price. I'd say *another three grand* or even more, and these guys always came ready to play. *No problem*, they'd say. Sometimes, they'd pay me right there in the club and just slap a stack of bills into my hand.

And when they paid me right there, I just took their money and went on with my night. In fact, I've been fired from just about every club in Vegas for robbing people. It's what I was known for—I didn't care what people said. I didn't care about my reputation. I was in the driver's seat for once, and I couldn't get enough.

The smart customers wouldn't pay me until I went up to the room with them—but I always stuck to my guns and got my money first. *All right, honey, I hate talking business, so let's just get it out of the way so we can focus on the fun*, I'd say, and it worked like a charm every time. The ones I didn't rob kept coming back for more, so my list of regulars started to grow. My clientele were high rollers and VIPs—locals who owned major businesses in town or celebrities, like actors or pro athletes.

I wasn't thinking about part-time or full-time sinning anymore. I was fully supporting myself now. In fact, it was probably the first time I was being kind to myself, or so I thought. I was in control. I didn't mind what I was selling. I just cared that the price was right and that the clients were buying.

HEY, MA

I'VE ALWAYS BEEN A COMPUTER NERD. I GET IT FROM Bill. I love to figure apps out and study algorithms. It's all very Rain Man. And when the dial-up modem came on the scene when I was twenty-two, I danced my ass off one night to buy myself my own brand-new computer. I proudly turned my guest room into an office—I'd arrived. Even if it was just a white room with a desk, a computer, and a lamp.

After a shift at the club, I'd come home sloshed and hop on AOL chat rooms with my friends—or sometimes alone to read the crazy shit strangers would post. I'd have the watered-down vodka and cran I'd drive home from the club with in one hand, and I'd type away on the keyboard with the other. Getting behind the wheel intoxicated was probably one of the worst decisions I've ever made in my life. Take it from me: It doesn't make you look cool. It makes you look stupid and sloppy. Not only are you risking your life, you're risking other people's as well. Don't drink and drive, kids. Nothing good will ever come from it.

It was like any other night browsing the World Wide Web when an instant message popped up on my screen.

SASSA KAYE: *hey, i'm your mom*

I snickered and rolled my eyes. It was obviously someone who had me mixed up with someone else or was playing games.

fuck off, I responded. I x'd out of her chat window. I'd never even seen the name Sassa Kaye. Besides, my mom's name was Vanessa. But she popped up back up onscreen.

SASSA KAYE: *no, this is really me. Is this miss alisa?*

I froze. *If someone is playing, this is such a cruel joke.* I'd only ever spoken to my mom once in my entire life.

I was eight when the phone rang. I answered, and the woman on the other end said, "Hi baby. It's your mom." I was scared about what Mindy would do, so I slammed the receiver down as fast as I could. When I told Bill and Mindy who'd called, they changed our number and went on like it had never happened. No one ever spoke to me about it again.

So sixteen years later, sitting in the spare bedroom I called my office, I stared at the screen illuminated in front of me. *Bling bling bling!* She kept sending messages, probably trying to prove who she was as quickly as possible before I could block her. Pictures started popping up in the chat: baby pictures of—*is that me?*, my dad and Vanessa, me and another girl I'd one day find out was my older sister.

hi mom

It was all I could say. I'd been dreaming of talking to my mom since I was a little girl. This definitely wasn't how I'd envisioned it.

She sent me a phone number, and I jumped at the chance to hear her voice.

The second she picked up, she started bawling—it was a trait that would eventually drive me crazy. But I just listened and let her cry. I was so happy to finally hear her voice.

XO

I'D HEARD SO MANY HORROR stories from Mindy that by the time I turned eighteen, finding Vanessa wasn't on the top of my list. And Vanessa had left *me*. If she wanted a relationship, she needed to come find me.

I wasn't even allowed to see a picture of my mom when I was growing up, so I spent most of my life not knowing what she looked like. Somehow, I remembered her jet-black hair and piercing blue eyes from those first three months of my life—I remembered enough to know that the woman who tried to kidnap me in the bathroom at Bill and Mindy's wedding resembled her. Even if I was just a tiny baby, something about Vanessa had imprinted into my memory from the start. She was written into my neural pathways, even if it would be months or years before anything else stuck.

But a month or so before Vanessa found me online, Bill and Mindy came to visit. When I dropped them at the airport, Bill walked Mindy onto the plane and came running out back to where I was waiting. He wrapped his arms around me, acting like he was going back for one last hug.

"Hurry. Take this. Hide it," he whispered, slipping me a bag. I grabbed it and put it under my shirt. I could feel Mindy glaring from the plane.

They took off for Texas, and I raced back to my car. I flung the door open and yanked it out from under my shirt where I'd been keeping it safe.

It was a pile of pictures. I shuffled through photos of my dad posing with a beautiful woman with piercing blue eyes and a smile just like mine. They were holding a baby. I kept flipping through, my eyes wide. They were pictures my dad had saved of the three of us. That was my mom.

I broke down, alone in that parking lot, and sobbed like a baby. I studied my mom's face, and she felt so familiar, even after all those years. For a moment, I had a flash of anger at Bill for blindsiding me, but then I pictured Mindy losing her mind. It was better this way.

So just a few weeks later, I had my mystery mom on the phone. Maybe I'd belong in her world, and I could finally have a real family. And she came with an older sister—it was a dream.

We talked for hours, and neither of us wanted to hang up.

XO

I LEARNED VERY QUICKLY THAT the one thing that won't leave you—and would never tell you it doesn't love you—was money. My hustling was unmatched. I started escorting and dancing every single night to stack money and make sure I always had cash in my hands at all times. I was never again going to be the broke little girl walking the Strip with nowhere to go.

For me, trauma has always shown up as a need to do more, more, *more*. So I decided to also get another square job—something stable. I was married to the game and loved it, but at the same time, I craved some sort of normalcy. I signed up for real estate school.

I flew down the 215 to that first day of class, my stereo bumping Brotha Lynch. I was feeling proud of myself—sure, I made thousands of dollars every night dancing for skeevy dudes, but it didn't make me feel accomplished. It was just a hustle—it was survival. This would be something *real.* I pulled up to the school on two tires, figuring I'd make a grand entrance like always. I needed everyone to know I had arrived.

There was no one in the parking lot.

But head held high, I marched up to the classroom. I scanned the room for an empty desk, and my eyes locked with a beautiful brunette sitting at the back of the room. She had long hair, tan skin, green eyes, and freckles kissed all over her face and body. She was gorgeous. I instantly knew we'd be friends.

The only open seat was across the room from her, and for the next few days, I threw myself into absorbing every word the teacher could possibly tell me. I wanted to soak up all the knowledge and be the best real estate agent that I could ever be, because remember, I'm *very* competitive—but mostly with myself. The hottie in the classroom and I hadn't spoken to each other yet, but I could tell we were feeling each other out.

In one of the lessons, the teacher asked if we would be willing to sell a house to a couple with a young child—if a pedophile lived next door. A *convicted* pedophile at that. The sale would be a huge payout for us as agents. Everyone in the class nodded yes—they wanted that big chunk of money. I was totally appalled. I couldn't believe what I was hearing.

"Absolutely the fuck not," I said. Loudly. The classroom went dead silent, all eyes on me. "You'd be willing to risk this child being molested—or even worse—just for a sale? That's bad juju for one thing—and just morally incorrect."

The teacher glared at me.

"Aw, look. We have a hero in the room." The class laughed, and I felt my chest turn red with anger, and before I knew it, I was arguing with the entire classroom. The teacher smiled at the chaos, and the fighting was so intense, I even questioned if I was in the wrong. Sooner or later, the teacher and I were exchanging verbal character assassinations. He went low, but I went to hell. You could never outinsult me.

"She's not wrong," said the sassiest drawl from the corner of the room. "What's wrong with y'all? Risking a child's innocence for a payday. Y'all are fuckin' disgusting."

I whipped my head around to see who had my back. It was the beautiful brunette. Now that I had someone on my side, the teacher kicked us both out of class for the remainder of the day. We both giggled profusely as we walked out of the classroom.

"Thanks for that. Sorry I got us kicked out," I said.

"It pissed me off watching them gang up on you," she said with that beautiful smile. "I'm Grace, by the way."

"I'm Alisa." I smiled back.

"You a stripper, too?"

"How did you know?"

"I can just tell," she said. "We all stick together."

She was right. And then . . . we were inseparable. Over the next few weeks, Grace opened up to me slowly. She'd been a call girl in Texas and fell in love with one of her tricks. They called themselves boyfriend and girlfriend and lived together in a fancy townhouse on the west side of Vegas. I didn't believe in dating tricks, but it didn't bother me that she did. Different strokes, right?

We both ended up dropping out of that real estate class—things went from bad to worse with the teacher. It didn't take long before we joined forces and became a dynamic duo in and out of the clubs.

Grace was like my instant soulmate—and even if she was a single year younger than me, she became my little sister. I just felt so protective of her. And we fought like sisters too. I've never argued with a woman the way I did with her—but by the next day, we'd be completely fine. We were just riding the wave of her Gemini bipolar energy—and half the time, we were also coming down off copious amounts of drugs. Throughout our almost decade-long friendship, she would teach me how to be free. How to have fun. Before Grace, all I did was work—I didn't know how to enjoy the moments I was given because I was always so wrapped up in responsibilities. But her wonder-filled eyes would always win me over, and instead of going home and going to sleep, we'd wind up being out until nine the next morning. She would beg me, *Lis, puhhhleeeeaseee can we go out?* and poke her bottom lip out. I'd always cave. I wanted to be the fun party girl too. I brought Grace into my little coven of females. All my girls became hers.

XO

IF I THOUGHT I PARTIED before, damn was I wrong. Partying with Grace was on a whole other level. It was all GHB, cocaine, and X, and we even dabbled in meth together. We would go to all sorts of parties, and half the time we didn't even know the people. It didn't matter. Grace was fucking wild.

She was notorious for getting lit and stripping off everything but her heels. Her long legs always gave her this runway model presence and she owned it. It didn't matter who, where, or what, she was gonna strut. We ended up at a party one night with all these gangsters and dealers—so everyone was strapped. Guns on tables, guns in waistbands. She was strutting around, buck naked, and somehow Grace grabbed someone's gun. A loaded gun at that.

Everyone froze, and our eyes got as big as cartoon characters'. Throwing her head back laughing and lying back on a counter, Grace spread her legs and put the tip of the loaded gun on her pussy hole. We were all shaking—if she accidentally pulled the trigger, it would be a horror movie. But in typical Grace fashion, she gently rubbed it on her clit, giggled, and then crossed her legs and set the gun down.

You could hear a collective sigh in the room. The party kept going, and we never spoke about Grace and the gun again.

XO

WE WOULD ROB TRICKS BLIND right in front of their faces. We would party so hard with them until they passed out, or we would feed them Xanax so they would pass out and we wouldn't have to touch them. And our clientele was elite: We partied with lawyers, politicians, and doctors—we even had regulars in the operating rooms in Vegas hospitals.

"I love playing God with the patients in the OR," one of the surgeons told me, coked out and smiling ear to ear.

I was always good at snagging sugar daddies and keeping them around, so they would hand over credit cards. Even though we had our own houses, we'd pick a casino and I'd rent us a room on Sugar to party for weeks at a time.

We often flew to LA to get away from the Vegas scene, and once we ended up staying at the Beverly Hilton for three weeks on a drug bender. I barely even remember leaving the room for food—and you have to figure that anyone who got a look at us knew we were up to no good.

We eventually overstayed our welcome, and the fine establishment asked us to leave. Coked up and grinding our teeth, we hopped on a flight back to Vegas, sneaking Newports in the airport bathrooms. When I'm doing cocaine, the only thing I want to inhale is menthol smoke.

I would get extremely high and then need to bring myself

down, so I'd take Xanax to balance out the cocaine. And when we didn't have Xanax, we would drink bottles of mouthwash. We'd be too fucked up to go buy real alcohol, so the mouthwash hit the spot. I am not proud of this fact.

Eventually, the drugs stopped hitting like they used to. But we weren't about to give up on getting high. Lucky us, one of our tricks taught us to do cocaine enemas. You'd lay out a line like you were going to snort it and put it into a syringe without a needle. You'd add water and shake it up and then *up the wazoo.* It was the best high I'd ever felt.

The booty blasts only lasted us a short time before they became child's play. We were so deep in a haze that we didn't realize we were full-blown addicts. We thought we were just looking for a higher high.

Even if I dabbled in meth here and there, I looked at it as a poor man's drug, and I mostly stuck to what I called my "designer" drugs. But in reality, they're all the same—and we tell ourselves all kinds of lies about the risks we'll take with our lives when they're nice and pretty.

Grace had been on a meth kick for some time, and she told me it was a way better high than coke. *Fuck it.* Grace handed me the glass pipe and I breathed in.

"Hold it for as long as you can," she said. "But not too long. Your lungs could crystallize." I blew out the biggest cloud of smoke I'd ever seen come from my body. And then it hit me. I'd snorted glass and meth plenty of times, but this wasn't the familiar, amped feeling—it was *relaxing?* I smoked crystal meth and it relaxed me? I was hooked.

Grace and I would hole up in hotel rooms and smoke meth for days on end. We would gamble, we would have my sugar daddies come and split the money they gave us, or we would go fishing down in the lobby and pull tricks. The money bought more meth.

We were so far gone that we didn't even notice how rough we were looking to the outside world. We were both dealing with legal troubles—I had a DUI and some other charges hanging over my head—and we shared a lawyer. When we went to drop off payment one day, he looked us up and down.

"Girls. You know you both look terrible, right?" We were stunned. In our minds, we looked the best we ever had.

"Excuse me?"

"You guys are strung out. It's obvious. You look like you're on meth."

"How can you say that? We would never!" We denied it to the fullest. How dare he say we look like crackheads?

"Listen. My opinion doesn't matter. But you're both beautiful women. Don't ruin yourselves over drugs."

We both nodded and walked out, staring at each other. *Was it that obvious?* You would think his warning might have swayed us. Not in the slightest.

XO

WE RAGED ON, UNTIL ONE drug-induced manic episode finally caught up with me. I'd decided I wanted tattoos on my arms, and I found myself in some random dude's garage where he was banging out backyard tattoos for free. We both hit the glass dick together and bonded over our love for Dear Old Methany.

I wanted two big stars on each wrist. So he started drilling away on the first one. *Done!* It only took five minutes—total cinch. He moved on to the next one, and for some reason, the pain felt good. I wanted more.

"Go deeper," I said, tweaked out of my mind.

"You sure?" He looked at me, nervous, and I nodded.

For hours, this man dug into my flesh with a tattoo needle

all because I said it felt good. It went so deep that he hit my wristbone, and I started bleeding so much he finally had to stop.

"You're pretty twisted, girl," he said. I took it as a compliment. I wrapped my wrist and headed home.

By that night, my wrist began swelling. The pain became overwhelming. I was on enough drugs that my body didn't have a chance in hell of healing itself normally, and the fact that I'd had ink drilled into my bloodstream didn't help. I got sick and feverish, so I took a shower and lay down. I couldn't get out of bed for two days, and I ignored my phone. I was too sick to speak. Grace knew something was wrong, so she showed up to my house and somehow—thankfully—she got in.

"Bitch, why the fuck aren't you answering the phone?" She pulled the curtains open to let some light in, and I slowly raised my wrist. My entire arm was infected. My wrist was the size of my biceps, and my fingers were swollen like balloons. The whole room smelled like death.

"Alisa! What the fuck!" she screamed. "We have to get you to a hospital right now." I shook my head.

"I don't have insurance."

"Oh hell naw. We're going to see Dr. What's-his-face. The one who likes to play God. He'll help you."

"Fuck no. That dude scares me. I'm not going. It'll go away."

Grace yanked the covers off me and told me to get up. She was never serious, so to see her all business got me moving. Reluctantly I threw on sweats and she got on the phone and tracked the good doctor down.

"He's working at a hospital in Parhump," she said. Parhump is a little town an hour outside of Vegas, full of chicken ranches. Apparently, he worked there once a month, helping out the working girls from the local brothels. Must have been my lucky day.

"That's so far," I whined.

"Shut up. I'm driving. Let's go."

I slept the whole drive, but when we got there, Grace pulled me through a back door. The doctor was waiting for us—I was getting the VIP treatment. To my horror, he took one look at my arm and panicked.

"Oh my God. You're going to lose your hand."

Well, that's about the last damn thing you want to hear from a doctor. I burst into sobs. I knew just how bad it was.

"Get her on IV meds now, two bags. STAT," he snapped at the nurse. Someone whisked me away and I had an IV in my arm within minutes. The minute they started pumping those antibiotics into my veins, my entire arm—from fingers to shoulder—was itching violently. It was brutal, and I had to sit still for what felt like hours being pumped full of them.

Grace tried to make me laugh—anything to distract me.

"If you lose your hand, let's make you a blinged-out hook."

"A hook?" I asked.

"Yeah, bitch. We'll call 'em hook-ers," she said. It worked. I burst out laughing. For a minute, the pain faded.

After a few hours, Doctor God swaggered back in.

"If you'd waited ten minutes longer, I'd be amputating your hand," he said, before launching into a lecture about my addiction to meth. He'd seen all the drugs in my bloodwork.

"If you don't get clean, you're going to kill yourself. Your body just doesn't have any defenses left. You've depleted everything you need to survive."

He sent me home with antibiotics and the fear of God. I was done with meth. I would never touch it again.

17 LOVE AND MONEY

I MIGHT HAVE BEEN DONE WITH METH, BUT I WASN'T DONE with drugs. I'd nearly wound up with a hook for a hand from meth, so I took my ass back to Xanax.

I'm almost certain it was around my twenty-sixth birthday that my friends left me alone to die, but I'm bad with dates, and when you were partying like I was, it's hard to remember. We didn't know much about Xanax in those days, and docs were handing scripts out like candy. I didn't know people were forgetting huge chunks of their lives and overdosing—or what it would do to me. All I knew is I fucking loved it.

You probably wouldn't expect it, but I'm shy and full of social anxiety. Back then, I needed Xanax and alcohol and drugs to bring me out of my shell. Just one little pill made me feel a peace I'd never known. It washed over me like a glowing blanket of fairy dust. It made me the life of the party that my friends, family, clients, sugar daddies, or anyone who crossed my path wanted me to be. I even obtained the ever-so-eloquent nickname Xanna Nicole, because I became the ultimate seductress on those things, a sexy vixen with no fear. The goal was to get fucked up enough not to remember the night before or feel a trace of anxiety. It was perfect, and I couldn't believe I was brave enough to do some of the things I heard about the night before. I relished the aftermath stories.

By then, I'd started selling pills and blow at the clubs—no sweat, easy money. I'd been dating a dealer named Mateo, and he kept plenty of coke around my house, all bagged up and ready to go. If one of my customers at the club wanted to buy and I didn't have anything on me, I'd just call Mateo between trips to VIP. An eight ball would cost me eighty dollars, and I'd turn it around for three hundred. Big homie tax.

I bet I had a million dollars pass through my hands before I turned twenty-two, but I never had anything to show for it. And by twenty-six, I was squandering cash like I didn't have to sell my body. The truth is: I wasn't Mateo's main girl. I was the side bitch—unknowingly at first, the sweet delusion of a twenty-something-year-old. *Lucky me.*

In the daylight, I was going to beauty school and trying to make something of my life so I could leave sex work. *Thanks, Pops, for the religious trauma and unwavering moral compass.* I moved around constantly, most of the time to get away from whatever dude I was living with who had trashed the place in one of our knockdown, drag-out fights. Like I'd done my whole life, I was clawing my way toward survival. After being told by so many people I'd never amount to anything, I was determined to be something, to be someone. I just didn't know who.

XO

WE WERE OUT AT A club like we always were, and I got an idea.

"I'm gonna see how many bars I can take!" I yelled, and everyone cheered me on. I counted each yellow "ice cream" bar, as we'd lovingly called them, that I swallowed, and my crew kept getting rowdier and rowdier. *One, two, three, four . . .*

I was feeling good. Why stop? *Five, six, seven . . . More.*

That night, I took fifteen yellow bars of Xanax. I must have had a death wish, or I was just *that* fucking stupid. When you're young, you can convince yourself you're invincible. You don't have any idea about your own mortality. Nothing can touch you.

Mateo put me in the back of his Hummer—and he was pissed. *How dare I be so unladylike? A boss's girl should never act like that in public, let alone around any of his compadres.* He was always cool, calm, collected, and he never raised his voice at me. Instead, he'd give me the silent treatment and disappear for days—sometimes weeks—if I made him mad enough. I don't know which was worse: not hearing from him or just wishing he'd yell at me.

"You're fucking disgusting," he said. Even though most of what happened is hazy in my memory, his tone is still clear as day. "You can't live like this."

I'd gotten too fucked up for a man who made his living off people like me. Don't get me wrong—Mateo definitely got high off his own supply too, but I was his woman on the side. Sloppy bitches were never cute. It didn't occur to me that maybe I needed some help instead of punishment.

To teach me a lesson about embarrassing him, he dumped me at my house, so fucked up I couldn't walk. I was so far gone I could feel my soul trying to leave my body. There wasn't anything left for me down here on Earth. I headed to my bathroom to look in the mirror at myself and what I saw was straight out of a horror movie. Lipstick smeared, mascara running down my face—very 1990s Courtney Love gone possessed. I'd also earned the nickname "the Green-Eyed Monster," because when I would be lit, so were my eyes. I had no pupils, and my irises were neon green. *Where was I?* I flicked the light off so I didn't have to look at myself anymore, and I managed to drag myself to my bed.

Mateo sent my friend to check on me. She found me choking on my own yellow vomit. At first, she thought I was playing, but then she realized I wasn't even conscious. She turned me onto my side and left. Walked out.

I've had my moments of being a bad friend, of letting people down even when I loved them and wanted to be better. But leaving someone unconscious and covered in benzo puke? I just can't imagine it. Months later, she told me, "I didn't want to be involved in it," when I asked her why the fuck she abandoned me. Looking at her, I could see how frail she'd become. My heart was breaking for me, but for her, too. I've seen the game ruin so many women. She was no exception. She was battling demons of her own, and meth eventually got ahold of her. At least she turned me on my side, right?

I came to later that night, projectile vomiting. I clawed myself to the bathroom, but the whole scene was warped, and time didn't make any sense. It was like seeing a series of camera flashes. Quick shot of my hallway. Quick shot of the bathroom door. *I just gotta get through this.* Quick shot of the bathtub. Then, pitch black, and I just kept trying to keep myself together enough to breathe.

God, please let me get through this. I'll never do another drug again. They were empty promises, but I was scared out of my mind, and something deep down inside me wanted to live. The only thing that's brought me comfort in these moments is talking to Him. It was the only thing that brought me peace, even if I knew I was lying to Him when I said I'd quit the drugs. But each time He always pulled me through.

The quick camera shots went dark. I woke up two or three days later. The bathroom walls had yellow handprints all over from me swimming in my own vomit. It looked like a psych ward where they'd keep you in a straitjacket, shooting you up with sedatives until you stopped wailing. It looked like somebody was trying to escape.

After waking up in that puke-stained bathroom, I knew something had to change. I couldn't quit Xanax cold turkey, but I figured I'd be more conscious of how many I took. I'd break pills into little pieces and let them dissolve under my tongue before I had to be social or if I just felt that anxiety taking hold of me. I'm not going to lie—to this day, I still crave that taste. Nothing beats how relaxed Xanax makes you. I will always yearn for that feeling.

Even though Mateo had his own money and didn't need me for anything, I still liked being in charge of my relationships, especially back then. I would get with a dude, fuck them, let them move into my place for a while, and then I was done with them. I liked being the breadwinner—my thinking was this: *If I'm supporting you, you can't control me.* And while those men weren't good to me, I wasn't good to those men either. If they told me no, I told them to get the fuck out of my life. I would cheat. I would hurt their hearts. I would push them so far that they'd cheat on me so I could use it to give myself free rein to be a piece of shit right back. And so when Eric gave me that look, I dropped Mateo without a second thought.

Eric followed the same pattern as the dudes who came before him. We fucked, and then he was mine. He was great in the beginning—tall, dark, and handsome. And he loved me, even though I was a nightmare dressed like a daydream. (Shout-out to T. Swift.) His parents hated me, and I don't blame them. I would *not* want my son to bring home a girl like me.

I consider myself a voyeur of sorts. I *love* watching people have sex. And at these clubs you could walk room to room and watch people going at it. Sometimes just a couple, sometimes throuples, and sometimes gang bangs—and always consensual.

I loved turning the men I was with onto this scene. The look on their faces when we would walk into this Sodom and Gomorrah was sometimes enough to get me off. So, one night, Eric and I went to the Red Rooster, and I swear to God we were drugged by the meatballs at the buffet. I know, I know—who the fuck eats from a buffet at a sex club? Me. The next thing I knew, we woke up at Eric's parents' house with all the lights on, the door wide open, and our buck-naked bodies covered in Del Taco. Why the fuck were we at his parents' house? No clue. I had my own place. *That's* how out of our minds we were. I was bad news for that dude, and today, my heart goes out to his parents for having to deal with both of us.

After that evening of mayhem, Eric moved in. He wanted to be with me 24-7. I thought he was the one. Between dancing and hooking, the money was flowing in. No one could tell us no, and we did what we wanted when we wanted.

Most men love the *idea* of being with a woman like me. But they can't handle it once it's their reality. Slowly but surely, Eric started getting *jealous*. He tried to get between me and my money, and that spells control. Once someone tries to control me, I buck like a wild horse.

I came home one night and caught Eric watching porn featuring ladies who—let's just say, had parts I didn't have. Now I'd never yuck anyone's yum. I get it. But how the hell was I supposed to compete? And he was so secretive about it. I'd go to the grocery store and he'd hop on the computer to whack off while I was buying a loaf of bread with money I'd made selling my body.

We were coming apart at the seams. I didn't trust him, and he sure as fuck didn't trust me. Pretty much immediately after the chicks with dicks saga, he got caught cheating or doing some other shady shit, and not one to *not* speak up about being pissed off, I cocked back and I hammerfisted the fuck out of his face one day in his truck. His nose started pouring blood.

"You broke my fucking nose," he said.

Eric and I fell into a dysfunctional pattern we'd repeat over and over for the next couple of years. Love, fuck, fight. Love, fuck, fight. Fucking exhausting.

One night, he thought I was out cheating, but I was really just sitting in my rented PT Cruiser in a parking lot, drunk off my ass and trying not to go home. But he kept calling, so I drove myself shit-faced into a metal construction sign, and then another, until I was dragging sparks behind me. They were flying everywhere, and suddenly, I *needed* a Del Taco cheeseburger. I mean, a girl's gotta eat.

So I drove that car—spewing smoke and flames on a flat tire—right through a Del Taco drive-through. You should have seen the drive-through attendant's face. *Like, is this chick for real?*

All the while, Eric was screaming at me to come home. I didn't want to fight, so I parked my car down the street to sleep it off, and that motherfucker called the cops and had me arrested for a DUI. Apparently in Vegas if you're intoxicated and behind the wheel of a vehicle with the keys in the ignition, it's an automatic DUI. But if the keys aren't anywhere in the car, nothing. Can you guess where my *extremely intelligent* ass kept the keys?

This motherfucker knew I was already in trouble with the law *and* had a court case for battery hanging over my head and he did *this*? Game on, dickhead. This launched an all-out war between us, and our battles were who could call the cops on the other one first.

He would threaten to call the cops and sometimes would if we were fighting—especially if we were drunk. And then I would be on my phone calling them myself because of course it became about who could get their story across first. I'd say he hit me, anything to get him away from me. I'd tell them to get him out of my house because he refused to leave. I manipulated the system. I always cried, and he was the one who ended up in trouble. It was a pretty sick game we played with each other and the judicial system. What the fuck did we think would come from all this?

After years of back-and-forth, Eric ended up with a domestic violence charge. When it came time for his sentencing and we knew for sure there was no way out of it, we had a great idea. What if we got married? Surely, then, the judge would drop the charges. Because marriage solves everything, right?

We got married at the courthouse despite everyone telling us not to. He wore blue jeans and a T-shirt with his signature beer in hand, and I wore a tight black sundress with my tousled blond hair in an updo. We were poster children for toxic love. We thought our brilliant move would sway the judge. It actually just pissed him off.

"You're married!?" the judge snapped. "You've called the cops one too many times. Both of you have played games with the court system and that's even more reason to keep you apart."

Keep us apart? But we were *so* in love, and I couldn't bear to think of him behind bars. The day before he had to turn himself in, he had one final fan-fucking-tastic idea.

"Let's get out of here. Let's go to Canada. They can't get us if we're there."

And just like that, we sold everything in our house, packed up a truck, and decided to go on the run.

XO

BEING LOCKED IN A VEHICLE for days was probably the worst thing Eric and I ever did to ourselves. We couldn't stand each other, but we couldn't be apart either. We made it to Washington before our toxicity exploded. And—you guessed it—Eric got arrested. Again.

And who do you think bailed him out? Again?

We got back on the road and made it to the border, ready to escape into the Canadian dream life we had created in our minds.

Anyone who says all Canadians are calm, polite people hasn't met a Canadian border patrol agent. Those motherfuckers are *scary*. They yanked us out of the car and started running our shit. We waited for what felt like hours, watching cars waved through—and surprisingly quite a few turned away. Finally, the somber agent came to loom over me.

"Do you know you have a harassment charge?" he asked. "A harassment charge? For *what*?" I was baffled. I knew I had battery and robbery charges. *Thug life*. But I didn't fucking harass people.

"Does the name Grace jog your memory?"

Son of a bitch, you had to be kidding me. I had threatened to beat up my best friend, Grace. As with any relationship with a Gemini, it was heads or tails. We fought like sisters. But she had taken shit too far.

Now where are we going to go? We can't go back to Vegas. Fuck, we're going to have to go back to my family. Texas. Maybe this will be a fresh start. Maybe we can become a family and be together and make lemonade from lemons. Maybe.

So we drove to Texas to be with my dad and sister. I tapped out all my sugar daddies to come up with the cash to rent us a house in a quaint, upscale neighborhood right outside of Austin. We were going to blend in and become an all-American young couple instead of fugitives on the run. I was worn out. But there we were.

Tapping out all my resources had pissed off every sugar daddy I had—they couldn't understand the abrupt move from Vegas to Texas. Now I had to make some money and support us, and I started dancing while I watched our relationship fall apart. I think we both silently swore to see it through to the bitter end.

I was trying to help Eric with all the legal trouble that I had helped get him into, but we never really managed to squash it. Even though we stayed together, I desperately wanted to move on. I soon met a guy while I was out dancing, Kdub.

He was the dope boy for Austin. Flashy clothes, cars, chains. He was a super-cute blond with a smile that would melt you. I met him in the club one night when I tried to rob him. I had danced for him and he said he wanted to take me home. Not realizing he was a regular, I quoted him a price and had him pay up front. He didn't even blink at the money and handed it right over. Then I went to the back, got dressed, and drove to White Castle to celebrate a long night at work.

I waited a few days to go back to the club, because I figured if the guy I ripped off was visiting, he probably would have left town by then. But when I got out on the floor, guess who was in VIP. *Fuck fuck fuck fuck.*

"Yoooo," he said, getting close to my face.

I giggled and flipped my hair. Maybe I could distract him enough that he wouldn't get too mad.

"You owe me," he said, leaning closer.

I can't lie, something about how he didn't cause a scene and was so alpha about what I'd done made me wet. I giggled nervously inside—never giving an inch. Back in the dressing room, I asked a few of the girls about him.

"Oh girl, Kdub is that dude—if you want or need anything, he's got you."

"Are you interested in Kdub?" they teased.

Evidently, he was well known in the area. He had money, was a d-boy, and all the girls wanted him. *Here we fucking go again.* I knew my type. I knew myself. Men were my absolute weakness. Especially these kind of men.

I fixed my hair in the mirror, stared at myself for a second, and walked right back out into VIP.

I wrapped my legs around him and whispered, "I'm sorry. I don't normally do stuff like that. I got nervous." I bit my lip and looked into his eyes. "What can I do to make it up to you?"

He saw right through it. Game recognizes game. But he did take the bait. We ended up getting wasted in the club together, telling each other about our lives. By the time the lights went up that night, I was in the backseat of his Escalade. He draped me across the center console and just stared at my naked body before he slid into me.

Why does he know exactly what he's doing? I thought to myself. This man flipped me every which way he could in that truck. And so started an exciting but short escape from reality.

Eric knew I was messing with that dude right away. I'm not a good liar. If I'm going to cheat, I'm going to tell you about it. Maybe directly, maybe indirectly. But you'll feel my absence even if we're sitting in the same room. Back then, something about watching that man's heart break in front of me brought me so much joy. Maybe it's because my father was my first heartbreak. Maybe it's because of all the shit these men had put me through so far.

I used to like to triangulate men and make them fight for my attention. It was like the affection I never had as a kid—*fight for me, motherfucker, if you really want me.* In some sick way, they were all paying for my dad's mistakes.

I was truly tired of Eric's shit. He wouldn't get a job—all he wanted to do was chase me around, act jealous, and drink beer in the shower. He even went as far as to come and stalk me at the strip club. Do you know how hard it is to make money when your husband is in the corner hawking your every move?

He pissed me off so badly that one night, I left the club with Kdub out the back door and left Eric in there by himself. He caused such a scene that my managers had to kick him out and eighty-six him from the club permanently.

It wasn't long until we both wore out our welcome in Texas. Cops were getting involved again. Old habits die hard, y'all. Except this time, I was smart enough to know the clock was ticking.

So we packed up and went back to Vegas. I rented us another house on another sugar daddy's dime, and the cycle kept spinning. We didn't even like each other, and by this time he had hooked up with one friend of mine and started talking to another one. I would beg and plead for him to leave, and when he did, I'd beg and plead for him to come back. We made a cesspool, and we called it a life.

Kdub visited Vegas frequently, because like most d-boys, he liked to gamble. I met up with him one night at the Luxor. I was with my girl Tamra—partially because I enjoyed her company and partially because I needed an alibi. We told Eric we were going to meet a client. But this wasn't work. It was purely pleasure.

We partied like we always did, and back in Kdub's room, I couldn't even form a proper sentence. Trying to be sexy, I suggested we take a bubble bath together. But Kdub wasn't having it. He could see how fucked up I was.

I wasn't fifteen bars deep, but I was lit as fuck. He told Tamra to take me home, because I was so sloshed and sloppy.

"Let me drive," she insisted.

"Just get us home safe," I said, reluctantly tossing her the keys to my Cadillac Escalade EXT. And there I was, just like I told you, singing along, feeling the cool night air on my skin until I got goose bumps. Riding on magic.

About halfway home, Tamra went to make a left turn. *WHACK.* The F-250 hit us at seventy miles per hour. You know the story: My Escalade flipped, and I didn't have a seat belt on. I flew through the car like a rag doll. Then finally, *crack.* My face to the windshield. My legs whipped behind me. *The crunch.* Tamra's body suspended by her seat belt.

"Tamra. You okay?"

"Yeah, I'm okay." *Thank God.* Smelling gas, kicking out the window as the car filled with smoke, calling Eric for help while he called me a *lying bitch*, running like hell from the police, *I don't talk to police!*, running away from everything in my life and being too fucked up to get very far. Strapped to a gurney. Dark.

XO

BEEP. BEEP. BEEP. THE SWEET sound of my heart monitor woke me up. I was in a neck brace with tubes hanging all over me and oxygen being blown up my snoot. Grace was there, and Eric too. *How did this motherfucker know where I was?* The first thing he said to me was "Give me your fucking phone." I had my phone clutched to my chest. *Had I been holding it the whole time?*

Even doped up, I knew not to give it to him. He'd find texts between Kdub and me, and I knew exactly what would happen: an explosion of catastrophic proportions. I was vulnerable, on my back, in pain, and connected to machines. Grace and I managed to kick Eric out before he could grab my phone, just before the doctor came in.

"Do you know what happened to you?" Doc asked.

"I was in a car accident. Is everyone else okay?" I asked, scared AF.

"Yes," the doctor said. Then he shook his head looking down at his chart. "I don't know how you were running from the cops. You split your C1 vertebrae in half like a wishbone. You should be paralyzed for the rest of your life from your neck down."

Fuck. Paralyzed? I wiggled my toes. I could feel my legs. I could make a fist.

"But I can feel my feet," I said.

"You're going to need surgery," he said.

Man, this was heavy. I was twenty-nine years old. I'd already been through so much shit in my life. But now I might be paralyzed? Where's my Xanax?

All I could hear was Bill. My dad always told me: Once they start cutting on you, you're never the same. Now, I've had surgeries since then. But I knew in my heart that *this* surgery wasn't for me.

"Honey," a nurse said. "I know you want to be tough, but if you even take your shirt off the wrong way, you could die."

It was the most pain I'd ever felt in my life. The shock was fading, and pure agony was now screaming through me. I couldn't believe what was happening. But something told me what I needed to do.

I told the doctors I'd take my chances. I said, *God's got me*, and I signed an AMA form.

My cousin Stacy snuck some Taco Bell into my hospital room the next day even though the doctor told me I wasn't allowed to eat. By then, I'd had enough of being strapped to a bed. I was alive. Bruised and beaten up, but alive. The nurse was taking too long for my liking to come and discharge me, so I finished eating, ripped my own IV s out, and walked my ass out of that hospital. *Very* carefully.

I wasn't supposed to survive. And while I still can't turn my neck all the way to the right, I'm still here. That split C1 vertebrae was just another thing that was supposed to stop me and didn't. That seems to be a running theme in my life. I walk right up to death's door and say *nope*. Not a lot of people get this many chances, and I'm grateful for every opportunity I've ever been given to be better and do better.

Maybe it wasn't as bad as the doctor had thought. Maybe my body just got it right this once and healed itself beyond what should have been possible. Maybe it was a divine miracle. Either way, God and the universe have never given up on me.

XO

I'VE ALWAYS SAID THAT IN order to get over one boy, get under another. So, always practicing what I preach, there was someone in the background of all that toxic noise of my first marriage to Eric and the adventures in the Escalade. Toward the end of our marriage, a dude named Paulie was lingering innocently—almost—in my MySpace messages.

The thing with Kdub had come and gone. I was completely checked out of my relationship with Eric. I just couldn't take it anymore. So, one night I messaged Paulie and told him to meet Eric and me at a rooftop bar. I had to see if he was as cute in person as he was online. What better way to scope out my next sancho than with my current sancho?

This tattooed, blue-eyed, blond-haired, beautiful cutie walked in and my heart just about stopped. Even more appealing was that something about him needed saving. He was a boy-damsel in distress, and I could be a knight in glittery heels.

Paulie was a womanizer with a hell of a backstory. He'd been a child model and a child actor in Hollywood, and he came from this massive, mobster-type Italian family. He was a walking red flag, and red was my favorite color.

I was holding hands with Eric, but I couldn't take my eyes off Paulie. When he walked by us, I whispered, "I want to make out with you" in his ear, my hand still wrapped around Eric's.

XO

I FINALLY KICKED ERIC TO the curb after the car accident incident—the dude wouldn't even come get me from a crime scene. *Let's meet up,* Paulie's message said. I was fucking ready. I pulled up in my crop top, miniskirt, sky-high stilettos, and the Shelby Roush Stage 3 a sugar daddy bought me. By then, I knew exactly what I wanted. We partied all night doing God knows what, but I sure as hell know how the night ended. Paulie walked me out to my car like such a sweet, sophisticated gentleman. And I draped my body across the hood of my car and looked up at him through my butterfly-wing lashes.

"Fuck me," I said. His eyes widened, and it took him a minute to get his act together. But he managed to kiss me, right there on the hood of my Mustang. It was sexy as hell, making out on that car. I wrapped my legs around him, and his hands were everywhere.

"Wanna race?" I whispered in his ear.

"Hell yeah, I'll race you," he said, smirking.

"Follow me home." I slid into the driver's seat and he got behind the wheel of his Charger. We sped through Vegas and I kept pushing on that gas pedal— 80, then 100, then 120 down the freeway. He kept trying to outpace me, and he must have been thinking there was no way in hell I'd keep pushing the speed. Wrong. I pressed down on my stiletto and put the pedal to the metal.

We made it back to my house in one piece—thank you, ancestors—but Paulie's eyes were just about bugged out of his head.

"You're fucking insane. You know that, right?" he said, but he couldn't keep his grin off his face.

"Oh, I know," I said, turning the key.

By the morning, he was mine.

XO

PAULIE KNEW I WAS IN the lifestyle from the get-go—there was no hiding that I had clients and sugar daddies paying my bills. And he showed up anyway and stuck around. I gave him the keys to my palace—and from that first night, we were inseparable.

I don't know how many men's rap careers I've tried to get off the ground, and Paulie wasn't any different. He really could have been something with the right mix of help, support, and motivation. I was ready to do all three. I wanted to make him a better person—because honestly, Paulie was the first man I really, truly loved. We laughed, cried, and argued, but we were best friends through it all.

True love or not, we were still toxic. We drank ourselves silly. He was on pills. I was on pills, chasing the sweet calm of my Xanax and trying to outrun the panic when they wore off. And we didn't fight a ton, but when we did, it was *bad*. He'd get in his feelings and wouldn't come out of them for days—and then things would blow up. And I was so cold. It was my way or the highway. No meeting in the middle for me.

To this day, Paulie will tell you that whatever he wanted in this life, I would have made it happen. I was always pushing him to be better and to get out of his comfort zone—because the only way that man's dreams were going to come true was if he fucking grew up. I would have done anything to make him realize his worth. But in a way, maybe that's my downfall, because I'd never really realized mine. So that's my gift to people: try to show them what no one ever did for me. The way I saw it then, I *did* anything to try not to have another failed relationship. I truly just wanted a teammate to build with. I was tired of partying. The late nights. The drugs, even if I wasn't yet clean. Even if I was so far from being healed enough to shake off the coldness, the need to control everything.

At one point, Paulie got it together enough to get trained and certified to be a bail enforcement agent. It's a dangerous job, and he'd have to get suited up in a bulletproof vest before he went out on calls. But I knew if I wanted him to stick with it, I'd have to encourage him and engage with the job as much as I could to keep him going. So we came up with the idea to use me as bait when he was after someone who did something particularly horrible, especially to women or little girls.

Once, Paulie was trying to track down a dude who'd jumped bail on some pretty heinous rape charges, and so I made a fake Instagram account and messaged him. Hook, line, and sinker—he wanted to meet up for a date.

I showed up at the bar we'd agreed on—no bulletproof vest or gun for me, just my usual high heels and miniskirt. But before he could get near me, Paulie and his partner jumped out of his truck screaming like psychopaths for the loser to get on the ground. They arrested him, and I went inside and got myself a drink.

XO

IN MOST WAYS, PAULIE AND I had a quiet life together when we were at home despite the occasional drunken fights. One time, we yelled at each other so loud the cops came and dragged his ass out, but Paulie never once put his hands on me. I picked him up the next day and bailed his ass out.

For the first couple of years, we lived in a house in Henderson and then moved around the area. And one day, a check for $25,000 showed up out of the blue. I hadn't expected settlement money for that car accident where I broke my neck, but there it was—not nearly enough, if you ask me, given that all these years later I still can't turn my head to the right. But we went to the bank and rolled out of there with $25,000 in stacks of $100 bills.

"I love you," he said.

"I love you too."

"Let's fucking get married."

My mind raced. Here we go again. But maybe this time would be better—and I wouldn't be marrying someone to keep him out of jail. I truly did love him. It was the best relationship I'd ever had, and I loved his family too.

Paulie and I flew out to Hawaii and got married at the town clerk's office. I wore a long, white wedding dress and a veil—since I hadn't done so my first time—and Paulie was in a black suit, a pink bowtie, and metal-studded belt. After signing the paperwork, we took a limo from the county clerk's office to the beach and took pictures standing out on the rocks as the waves crashed around us. It was beautiful. We were young, free, and happy.

XO

WE DID EVERYTHING AT THE highest possible intensity. We got fucked up all night, every night. The thing about drugs and drinking is that it's never enough, and over time, your consumption just grows and grows. It's impossible to sustain a real relationship when all you do is party. I'd started webcamming, and this was the beginning of what would be my eventual online following. I'd even use Paulie as my stunt dick to make videos. We got really good at taking money from old dudes—while I have a lot of love and respect for plenty of my sugar daddies, some were

Baby Bunnie

With Bill

Vanessa

Me and Vanessa

With Vovo

With Bill and Vovo

With Vanessa and Vovo

Around one year old

With a teddy bear

With Vanessa and Bill

Around two years old

Young Alisa smiling for the camera

Vovo styling my hair

Around three years old

Around five years old

At eight years old with Vovo

My fifth grade
yearbook picture

The high school
freshman athlete

Tasha, Lisa, and me, tenth grade

Tasha and me and my twenty-first birthday

At twenty-two

At twenty-two

Zanied out at twenty-two years old

At twenty-two

Drinking and driving at twenty-two

At twenty-seven

At cosmetology school

Me and Tasha

Me and Bill

Tasha, Mama T, and me

In my late twenties

just creeps. Paulie would take my phone and call up one of my lesser sugar daddies and put on some fake-ass voice.

"This is Dale Callahan from Pep Boys. Your girl's rims are out and it'll cost nineteen hundred dollars to replace them." And they'd send me over the money right away. *Thanks, Sugar.*

I figured out a new way to rob tricks too. I'd set up a date, take the money up front like I always did, and then *bam!* Paulie would show up screaming or pounding on the door, yelling that he was my boyfriend and was mad as hell that I was out cheating. He'd pull me out of the bar or hotel room and we'd drive home together, counting our money and laughing our asses off.

There was a hell of a lot of truth to that last hustle though. Paulie knew I didn't have any intention of stopping seeing clients. But he was starting to get jealous that other men had their hands on me, even if it was just a job. He was jealous of my sugar daddies buying me things, even if I never touched many of them.

I wasn't about to hang up my high heels for any man. Paulie wasn't much for ambition or a successful career after working as a kid, and he wasn't providing for us. He could barely take care of himself, so being an escort or a call girl or sugar baby or cam girl or whatever the hell you want to call it was paying our bills. I had no other choice.

And I was always straight with the dudes I was with that I was going to provide for myself no matter what. *I will always choose money over you,* I told them. I was never, ever going to be under some man's thumb. Not my father's. Not a shitty boyfriend's. Not a husband's. Sex work was keeping chains off me, and I am absolutely hell-bent on being free.

XO

I KEPT BUGGING PAULIE TO work. He decided to become a tattoo artist, so I forced him to get up and get hired at a shop. He got hired at the best fucking tattoo shop on the Strip. For a while, things calmed down, and he was making good money. It finally felt like we were a real team. This was marriage, right? You ride the waves with someone for the rest of your life even though it won't always be rainbows and butterflies.

When Paulie's parents got evicted, they moved into our house. I couldn't see any other way—I sure as hell wasn't going to let them sleep on the streets. This was a mob family that had been raided by the FBI and indicted on RICO charges, money laundering, and racketeering. They were facing ninety years between them—and they were coming apart. I knew it might destroy my marriage, but they were family, and I couldn't turn them away. The reality is that we were all functioning addicts, and we were all starting to spiral deeper into the pain. Even if we kept trying to make ourselves better, we just couldn't dial in. We were treading water on our best days.

Paulie and I made it five years before we started to unravel completely. Our fights were getting worse. I'd kick him out and he'd end up in jail and I'd go get him and then . . . we'd do it all over again.

Before Paulie, I'd caught Eric with porn that *definitely* didn't resemble me. Now, I don't give a shit if dudes watch porn, but those women had extra parts that I don't have, and it felt so hurtful because I knew I could never compete. It felt so sneaky and secretive—like he was hiding what he really wanted. When I caught Paulie watching porn with brunette college-teen-slut types, my polar opposite—it brought up that same hurt. I had gotten boob jobs and lip fillers. I'd bleached my hair just to be these dudes' fantasy girl. And now it felt like even that wasn't enough. It would be years before I'd realize that I *was* enough, and that my beauty, my brains, my *self* was for *me* and me first. That I didn't need to squeeze myself into smaller and smaller boxes until a man would give me the respect I deserved. The resentment became so intense—it was like Jenga, where you stack and stack and stack until something breaks.

I'm no angel. I'm a verbal sniper, and back then, I would push men to cheat. It was almost like I *wanted* to see if they'd do it just so I'd have an excuse to either do it back or to leave them for good. Hurting people and pushing them away was one of my specialties—and in all of my relationships, I share the fault.

Finally, I kicked Paulie out of the house in a blind fury during an argument and didn't speak to him for days after. He ended up cheating on me with some crackhead, and even though he came to me and admitted it, it was all I needed. Jenga!

XO

THE MARRIAGE WENT UP IN flames. There's something from that time, though, that will be with me for the rest of my life—that reminds me of how I tried my hardest and how I fight for love. What I carry with me most came from his mom—she was a beautiful woman with blond hair and blue eyes, just like her son. Around the time the family was getting indicted, she started calling herself "Kittie." I never knew why—but maybe it was a way to be someone else for a little bit. One day, we were in the kitchen, acting like a happy little family, and she waved me over.

"Come over here, honey," she said. "I absolutely love you. You're my little bunny."

And just like that, I became Bunnie.

I added the Xo later.

KARMA

THE NEXT DUDE'S PROBABLY GOING TO BEAT YOUR fucking ass," Paulie yelled at me.

I was single again and had zero interest in a new relationship. I was, however, on the prowl for a good time. I wonder if Paulie knew he completely jinxed me with those last words, because he was absolutely right.

I'm not a victim. I'm a survivor—in this relationship and in life. And when this relationship came around, I was not a good person. I know that now. Hell, I knew it then. But this man would humble me more than anyone deserves. It was extreme and some of it was beyond what I could endure, but if life hadn't humbled me the way this man was about to, I wouldn't be the woman I am today. And for that, I'm eternally grateful to the universe for teaching me, stripping me of everything I knew or thought I knew, and pointing me in the right direction.

His name was Karma—a fitting name for the retribution that was coming to me after years of crushing hearts, doling out physical violence, and being just downright mean-spirited.

Everybody was scared of Karma. He was a gangster boss, and everyone knew that if you didn't pay up, you knew what was coming for you. His violent streak wasn't a secret, and maybe it even added to his allure. He was a rapper in a group that was getting a lot of attention at the time, and he had girls throwing themselves at him. His ripped body was tatted up—including machine-gun bullets inked across his chest—and I was attracted to his darkness. He was confident and cocky enough to be tall, dark, and handsome even though he was short. It felt like nobody would fuck with you if you were with him, and I loved that. People were scared of him for good reason.

He seemed powerful to me, like he had his life together, he was in total control. *That* was exactly what I was looking for. He would snarl his lip when he walked through a crowd, with his fists clenched, ready to fight at the drop of a dime. He was the opposite of lover boy Paulie. Paulie had a good heart. Karma had no soul.

But Karma talked a good game. He could talk your fucking panties off. Literally.

XO

I'D MET KARMA A FEW times in passing as far back as when Eric and I were still together. We'd bought pills from him, of course, but I barely noticed Karma then. I definitely wasn't thinking about him like that.

But by the time I'd kicked Paulie out, all-powerful Karma was looking like exactly what I needed—a one-night stand of excitement and fun. Then again, every time I tried to one-night-stand somebody, it always turned into a full-fledged, yearslong romance. Couldn't a girl just have some fun?

I hit him up on Facebook and invited him to meet the girls

and me out at a bar. It took some convincing, and he seemed hesitant as we messaged back and forth. No wonder—dealers can't trust anyone, even women. That only made me want him more. When he finally agreed and rolled in, I was hooked from the first look. His no-fucks attitude, his swag in every step, and his style—my little black heart beat red. I'm a sucker for an alpha male. He sat down with us, and I instantly straddled him.

"It's about damn time," I whispered.

"I thought you were setting me up," he said, looking around at my girls.

"Why the fuck would I set you up?" I asked. "That's crazy." I wanted him there for me.

"I don't know. You're just so beautiful. I couldn't imagine what you would want with somebody like me."

Oh my god. Instantly wet.

The pull we had toward each other was magnetic, and everyone in that bar could feel it. My girls already knew what was about to go down, so they were all whispering and snickering to each other. We wasted no time—he was probably in my presence for no more than twenty minutes before I took his hand and led him into the bathroom—my body just moved automatically. He threw me up against the wall like he knew exactly what I wanted and shoved his fingers inside me. The next thing I knew, a tsunami was pouring out of me—a full flood, *grab a bucket and a mop*. Then he bent me over and fucked me in the bathroom stall. The entire floor was soaking wet. He pulled out, turned me around and kissed me as hard as he could, and whispered "Let's go outside." Totally dickmatized, I wasted no time throwing my clothes back on and running outside with him. We finished out in his car and collapsed in shock and silence. *What the fuck just happened?* It was so electric that neither one of us could put it into words. I got my ass up and sent him on his way—I'd gotten what I wanted. But ten minutes later, we were blowing up each other's phones.

bro, you're so fucking hot

you're my dream girl. what the fuck just happened? that was the most amazing thing that's ever happened to me

He knew exactly what to say—and it was the start of him being obsessed with me with a hands around your throat kind of passion. It was like nothing I'd ever experienced before. I wanted more of it.

XO

AFTER THAT NIGHT, WE WERE together every day. I think we were both looking for an intoxicating high for our shattered dopamine receptors. I was his drug and he was my fix.

The first three months were basically perfect. We'd go out every night, and he really brought me out of my shell. Nobody believes me, but I'm actually a homebody by nature. But all it took was for him to tease me a little . . . *What are you, fucking eighty-four?* and I'd put on my heels, do my makeup, and slap on a cute outfit for a night on the town. He was fun, and for the most part we mirrored each other. Two perfectly reflected psychos.

One night, we were so trashed that when we came home, I poured baby oil all over us and we just slid over and under each other and fucked for hours. I always say that dick is my love language and I've had chemistry with tons of dudes, but I'd never had such an intense sexual connection with anyone as I did with Karma. It was like we were animals clawing at each other. We got high off each other's pheromones. He made me feel like I was the only girl in the world, totally protected for the first time in my life. If a dude texted me, he'd text back. *Lose her number dork.* If a man approached me, all he had to do was walk into view and they'd cower. I loved it. No one could get to me unless they went through him.

I was so caught up in this totally addictive haze that I didn't question anything. There were so many red flags staring me right in the face, but honestly, I closed my eyes. There were rumors that he was a pimp, but I didn't believe them. He knew what I did for a living and would give me money just so I didn't have to work at night and could stay with him. And where I'm from, the game doesn't work like that. A pimp would never pay a girl—especially not to go to work. And when I asked him, he always denied it. His exes reached out to me and said he tried to break them—to become their pimp—or take their money. But being the complete narcissist I was, I truly felt like I was the one to change him. He wouldn't be like that with me.

Whenever we went out to strip clubs, I did notice that Karma had an unusual number of women around. Instead of asking questions, I befriended them all and we always had a great time. Who doesn't want tons of gorgeous women adorning their table?

There was one girl who was constantly in the mix, Cindy, and I couldn't quite see where she fit in. She didn't look like Karma's regular girls or anything like me. She was homely and quiet, and he told me they'd been best friends since tenth grade. Now, I'd only just shown up decades later, so who was I to ask questions? To be honest, she was no threat. She was always sweet to me and literally catered to Karma's every need. So she made my life easier. I wasn't trying to be anyone's wifey. I thought Cindy was my friend.

I'd stay at his house nightly, and she always slept in the other room. I knew she could hear us fucking, but she never seemed bothered by it and would even cook us breakfast in the morning. I honestly was baffled. *Where the fuck do I find a bestie like this?*

When we hit the three-month mark, his facade came crashing down. He had painted a picture of being a boss, moving weight, and having his shit together for months. And from what I saw, he wasn't lying—until all the pieces started coming together.

XO

IT WAS THE GIRLFRIEND OF Karma's friend who told me the truth.

"Bunnie, you know that Cindy isn't just Karma's friend, right?"

"What are you talking about?" I asked. "They're best friends."

"No, that's his girlfriend. That's his main bitch, they've been together for twenty years, girl."

Those words hit me like a slap in the face. *How the fuck could I have not seen it? There's no way!*

"Yeah girl. She funds his entire life. Her daddy is some big-shot doctor out here, and they con him out of money all the time."

What the fuck?

Now I was seeing red. How could he do that to *her*? And *me*? I absolutely hate being the last to know when it comes to shit like this. I drove straight to his house and ran up the stairs. He greeted me with a smile. I laid it out for him, but he didn't seem bothered.

"Who told you that?" I told him, and he picked up the phone and called his friend.

"Check your bitch," he said, and hung up. He didn't even put up a fight. He just admitted it: Behind closed doors, they were together—they'd been together since they were sixteen.

"Are you fucking kidding me?" I was in utter disbelief, but he didn't blink.

"She's been in my life for a long time, and I'm not ever going to be without her. She's my trick. You know, like the ones you have," he said, gaslighting me. "So if you want to be with me, you have to accept both of us. But we don't even have sex—I'm just using her for money, baby. Help me out and let me keep her around."

How the fuck was I supposed to argue with that? He ran complete game on me. But, as I saw it, Karma was no different from me. I still had my sugar daddies funding my life, so I looked at Cindy as a mousy sugar mama—and let's not forget that the lust I had for this man far outweighed any rational thinking. Because any normal woman would have hightailed it out of there immediately. But not I, Popeye! Fuck it—why not? Normal relationships never worked out for me, so maybe this lifestyle would.

If only I knew how much leading with my vagina instead of my mind was going to cost me.

XO

ONE NIGHT, WE MET UP with a bunch of his friends in a parking lot. We were shooting the shit and drinking and trying to figure out what to do with the night.

"Let's go to a strip club," one of his dudes yelled.

"Fuck yeah. Let's do it," I said joyfully.

I looked over at Karma for approval without realizing I had done something that could be considered disrespectful. He was glaring.

"Don't you ever fucking get excited when one of my friends mentions going to a strip club," he growled at me.

I didn't know what he was so upset about. Going to the clubs was a super-normal thing, especially in Vegas. And he'd just disrespected *me* in front of everyone by getting mad for no reason. I popped off and he wasn't having it. So we started fighting, yelling at each other, and we kept on yelling at each other all the way back to his house.

It was the first real argument we had ever had. And I was going to stand my ground. No one can tell me who I can and can't talk to.

He went on and on. *Don't act like that. Don't say shit like that. You don't even look my friends in the eyes, bitch. Keep your head down when they're around.*

I lost it. I went straight for the jugular with my insults.

"You know what? Me and fucking Cindy deserve better than you," I screamed in his face.

I didn't even see the punch coming, but I felt the impact straight to my ribs. I dropped to my knees. I had never felt pain like that. I was on the ground, trying with everything in me to breathe, but I couldn't get any air. I couldn't move. My ears were ringing, and I just kept trying to figure out what the fuck had happened.

Any sane human would have said *fuck this dude* and gotten the hell out. But the sucker for pain that I am, I crawled into bed with him like a wounded puppy. I lay next to him and cried myself to sleep. It hurt so fucking bad, but part of me felt like it was my fault. I'd been verbally attacking him, after all. I shouldn't have said what I said. It was my job to make *him* feel better.

In the morning, we woke up and had the best sex, even if I couldn't move much. He did everything to take away the pain. He apologized and said he'd never do it again.

Lies, lies, lies.

XO

AFTER THAT NIGHT, HE WAS on his best behavior for a few weeks—at least when it came to putting his hands on me—but there were other things I started noticing that I wasn't sure how to handle. His jealousy was outrageous—and his moods were all over the place.

I'd never seen his kind of jealousy before. And even though it would piss me off, I secretly liked it. It felt like he really loved me and wanted me all to himself. There were also times it got to be too much and I just needed air to breathe—like a long line of men before him, his love was so intense it would be suffocating—but man, the sex was phenomenal. It's what kept me coming back for more. I relished the fact that he couldn't live without me—he told me every damn night that he'd die if he lost me. No one had ever loved me so hard.

We had become kind of the "it" couple around town. He paraded me around like some show pony. I hid behind him and felt invincible when he was next to me. I was his beauty, he was my beast, and I had no problem siccing him on people who threatened me. There were plenty of nights when we had to run out of bars because he knocked someone out. We didn't care what damage we caused—we fed each other's dark sides. The monsters came out to play and then we'd tuck them into bed for the night—only to let them back out of the cage again the next day. It was a vicious cycle of fuckery—my specialty. If you had asked us we would have called it fun. At least it was familiar.

I was making a ton of money still working and doing calls, and he would go with me. In the beginning, we had fun and felt like a team. Had I finally found someone who accepted my lifestyle fully? We would gamble at the casinos or bars until seven or eight a.m. every day, blowing the money I'd made that night for the sake of "having fun" together. Snorting eight balls off each other's bodies and banging in every public restroom we could find. We didn't realize we were chasing the high from when we first met. Each time, we would have to outdo ourselves just to raise the bar. Our intensity threshold became too hard to reach.

I wasn't scared of him yet. I would poke and poke and poke him to get reactions and to see that side. And he would tell me straight up, "Bunnie, you don't want that side of me to come out." It only made me trigger him more. Call me crazy—I wouldn't blame you. But maybe that kind of terror felt like home. Or love. That kind of chaos felt exciting, and the intensity made it feel important. Maybe the fact that I could drive him to the edge gave me some kind of control, and it made me feel safe. Maybe that death wish was still alive inside me, and I wanted to see just how close I could take us to the darkness.

With the exception of that first rib hit, he held it together pretty well—until one night when I went too far.

XO

I STILL LIVED IN THAT house I'd kicked Paulie and his family out of. Karma had begged me to move in with Cindy and him, but I wanted my own space. Their relationship didn't bother me, but it still weirded me out. If I piss on a patch of grass, that patch of grass is mine.

I used his lying and the cracked rib as excuses to create distance between us when I need to catch my breath from the smothering romance. By then, I knew how to trigger him. He had a list a mile long of things I could and couldn't do, and sometimes I just wanted to rebel for the hell of it. I wanted space.

I'd run off to my house and disappear for a few days until I missed him. Then I'd resurface, which only triggered his abandonment issues. This particular night, I was on the phone with a friend of Karma's, and I was fucking mad. I was texting Karma all kinds of shit: *Fuck you. You're a bitch. Fuck you.* I was at my house, and he was at his. I didn't think anything of it. I sure didn't think he'd come over to my house. I didn't think he'd be able to break in.

I was getting heated on the phone, listening to his friend tell me all the shit that Karma had been doing behind my back. It was all gossip and definitely breaking the guy code, but he told me anyway. Next thing you know Karma kicked in my bedroom door. He had been sitting outside my bedroom door for God knows how long, listening to his friend's voice on speakerphone telling me everything. He grabbed my phone and started screaming.

"You're a fucking bitch. You're over here talking to my girl. I'm going to fuck you up when I see you."

He hung up the phone and threw me on the bed—not in a sexy way. He tossed me like a rag doll. Then he climbed on top of me so my arms were pinned to the bed with his knees, and stuck his gun in my mouth. I looked up at him, trying to figure out what the hell to do. He jammed the gun farther into my mouth, so hard he split my lip.

"I should fucking kill you right now, you stupid bitch. You want to fucking disrespect me?"

I couldn't say a word. I was just sitting there with his gun in my mouth, afraid my head was about to get blown off. All I could do was whimper in fear. One wrong move and I knew I'd be gone.

He finally stopped screaming, got off me, and walked downstairs. I lay in bed sobbing and scared out of my fucking mind. I wanted to run, to go anywhere but my house. I heard him walk toward the front door and then stop.

"Bunnie. Are you fucking coming with me or not?" he yelled.

I sat up in bed, wiped the tears from my eyes, and realized that I *did* want to go with him. I wanted his approval and to make him not mad at me. As insane as that sounds.

I got up and followed him out the door like the lost puppy I was. That night back at his house, he loved me down—again. It was almost like a reward for letting him take his frustrations out on me. I was allowing him to treat me this way. I had never been so mindfucked before, and I couldn't stop myself from allowing him to treat me like I was nothing. I know now that abuse changes your brain and your nervous system. That I'd started to see myself as making some kind of fair trade—the intensity of his love and attraction in exchange for broken bones and broken dignity. Being wanted and needed like that created some kind of chemical high in me that I'd keep on chasing, no matter what the crash felt like.

And what's more: It gave me some kind of purpose to try to save him. For years, improving the men I loved had given me some kind of direction. Karma wasn't any different, just more extreme.

Dr. Jekyll and Mr. Hyde, and all I wanted to do was help him.

XO

AFTER THAT NIGHT WITH THE gun, Karma wanted to be able to keep an eye on me, so he told me he wanted to live together. With Cindy. It still sounded fucking weird to me, but he told me it was now nonnegotiable.

"We'll just give her her own room in the new place," he said. Why not? It wasn't too different from our current arrangement, and I was willing to try—and I could keep even more of an eye on the two of them.

So we moved into a big house together: Karma and me in the master bedroom, Cindy down the hall, and now Karma's daughter, too, when she came to visit. I'm still close with his daughter and her mom to this day—they're the sweetest angels and the biggest blessing to come out of that relationship—besides all the lessons I needed to learn.

We were like Three's Company except he was no Jack

Tripper—and this arrangement went on for *three* years. Let me tell you, the minute we moved in together is when the sitcom ended. I was still working as a call girl for a service off and on, and by then, Karma didn't like me going to the casino bars to fish unless he was there gambling and could keep an eye on me. When working girls are fishing, you have to have complete focus to suss out undercover cops. And with Karma staring my way, I couldn't keep my head in the game.

I'd go up to the hotel room, cash out, and come back down, exhausted and wanting a shower more than anything in the world. But that's when the real work would start, because I then had to withstand Karma's guilt trips.

"I can't believe you just fucking did that," he'd yell from the driver's seat. "You fucking liked it, didn't you?" I was so mentally drained from the fight or flight I felt in the hotel room, never knowing if the john was an undercover cop or a hooker killer—these were just the kinds of things any of us working girls juggled all the time. The fear was so commonplace, it was basically invisible. Then I'd have to come down and talk him off a ledge.

But I told him the same thing I told all the men I was with: *I will never give up my independence for you.* It was our biggest conflict, but I held my ground. Sure, we had other money coming in. It turned out that my gangster boss was more small-time than he claimed. Cindy would give Karma her dad's money to buy drugs and flip them—weed, molly, and cocaine. But any money he did make as a half-assed drug dealer went fast—he was out spending hand over fist on strippers, bottles, and club life. No fucking way I was about to stop working.

But I wasn't about to leave him either. Something kept me with Karma. As with all abusive relationships, most of the time things weren't bad. We fought all the time, but back then, fighting was still my love language. I'd grown up watching my parents argue all the time. It was love.

And I *wanted* to see his darkness. I wanted to experience his demons, because I thought they played well with mine. But they say that if you play with fire, you're going to get burned. And I charged straight into the flames anytime I talked back and stood up to him, just to feel the pain.

One night, I was ready to fight. I was coming off a bender and was in a mood, so I started sending pissed-off texts to him while he was at the gym. Before he could reply, I turned my cell off. I figured when he got home, we'd probably fuck and call it a day.

I accidentally fell asleep with the bedroom door locked—but Karma came home and walked through the door like the Kool-Aid man. He yanked me off the bed and got behind me in UFC fighter pose, locking his arms around my neck. I was screaming and kicking and fighting as hard as I could. I knew what was about to come next.

He choked me until my body went numb and everything went black. I came to with him slapping my face and yelling at me to wake up. I started screaming, which only set him off again. He climbed behind me and choked me unconscious again.

The third time I woke up, I couldn't scream. I could feel my throat crack. Instead of running from him, I froze.

I hadn't resented him until that moment. *You fucking choked me out like I'm a grown-ass man and fucked my voice up?* I'd finally seen the depths of his darkness—the darkness I'd drawn out in some hope I could control it. Maybe I was a glutton for punishment. Or maybe part of me was hoping what I knew about him wasn't true. But I finally accepted that I couldn't keep lying to myself: This man could kill me. He would kill me. If I stayed, I would die.

I had to start plotting an escape. The next day I woke up with my throat on fire. He made sure to stay by my side for a couple of weeks so I wouldn't go to the hospital—and when he couldn't watch me himself, he made sure Cindy was there keeping tabs and reporting back at all times. I didn't care. I knew I was leaving, I just didn't know how. And all the anger and rage I felt inside—I just let it keep festering. I had gotten myself into this shit. I was going to get myself out.

I knew something was wrong with my throat and vocal cords, but he would laugh and tell me I was crazy. I could feel it and hear it, and to this day, I still can't scream, and I can't hit certain notes when I sing. Years out of the relationship, I finally saw a doctor who told me my larynx was cracked and my vocal cords were damaged because of that night of abuse.

But if you ask him, he'll say he never did a thing.

XO

I'D GOTTEN VERY GOOD AT pretending I wasn't living in hell by a few years in. By then, the abuse was constant and everyone around us knew. The passion we once had was gone. I hated Karma. I was becoming a shell of the person I once was. I was quiet. I was in fight-or-flight mode at all times. I wanted to get away, anywhere where he wasn't. He could feel how distant I was becoming.

If I looked at a bartender the wrong way, Karma would take me to the car to scream at me and then slam my face down into the gear shift to leave me with a black eye. When I would show him the next day, he would simply say, "I didn't do that." It wasn't even worth arguing.

But one night changed everything—and scared me into the spiritual awakening I now live by.

We were in a taxi together after another night out drinking when we pulled up at Spearmint Rhino.

"Why the fuck are we here?" Karma had fucked every single girl in that strip club. He was a big old fucking trick—not the boss he pretended to be, and the resentment grew more and more as time went on. Add it to the list, actually.

"I want to be here," he said.

"I don't want to be at a club on Christmas Eve with a bunch of girls you've fu—"

Before I could get the words out, he coldcocked me right in my eye. It instantly swelled up, but he kept hitting. He told the cabdriver to take us home and went on beating the shit out of me. He sat on top of me and beat me like I was a man. I went in and out of consciousness, blacking out and coming to and blacking out when he punched again.

To this day if you ask him about this incident, he will tell you he "never hit me with a closed fist." Does that even matter?

One thing I'll never forget is the two people in the taxi with us: some massive dude in the front seat—he was so big his head reached the roof of the car—and the driver. I just kept looking up at them as I was being hit and choked and thinking, *Why aren't they helping me?*

But they just looked straight ahead. I could see the pain on the passenger's face, but he didn't make a move to help. We pulled up in front of my house and Karma got out.

"Please take off," I begged the driver. "He's going to kill me. Go, go, go." I was crying and scared for my life, but the driver forced me out of the car, and the passenger had disappeared. I guess the driver was afraid of what Karma would do to them. But still, I couldn't believe he hadn't locked his doors and sped off with me.

Karma grabbed me by my hair and dragged me into the house like a caveman. He threw me on the pool table and started strangling me. I'd black out, and then he'd slap me awake.

"Wake up, you stupid fucking bitch," he'd yell, and then he'd strangle me some more, over and over again. Finally, after what felt like hours, I heard, "Leave her alone!"

It was Cindy, running down the stairs and screaming. I honestly couldn't believe what was happening, but she saw he was going to kill me. So he dropped me and went to chase after her. This is how it usually went. If she interrupted him beating me up, he'd beat the shit out of her, and vice versa. That night, I lay there on the pool table in shock, waiting for everything to end.

Eventually, we ended up going to sleep together. All I knew was he wasn't hitting me or strangling me, and I just needed to rest so I could wake up and make a plan.

About a half hour later, there was a pounding on the door. The cabdriver who had abandoned me for dead had called the police—thanks, you fucking asshole—and Cindy let them in. Any down-ass bitch would know you don't answer the fucking door when cops come knocking.

They took one look at me and immediately arrested Karma. When they asked what had happened, I told them I got jumped at the strip club. I didn't want Karma to go to jail. It was my job to protect him—and if I didn't protect him, he'd beat my ass when he got out of jail anyway. I was so deep in rationalization. This was all a nightmare.

They hauled Karma off to jail, and I lay in bed for two days while he was gone, trying to pull myself together. I couldn't even go make money if I wanted to. My face was mangled. Every blood vessel in my eyes had burst from being strangled. One eye was completely swollen shut, and the black rings around them were the deepest and darkest I'd ever had. It looked like my nose was broken. I didn't have a dollar to my name.

Looking in the mirror was devastating. Karma had stolen the one thing I had relied on my entire life, which was my looks.

When I stared back at myself, I didn't know who I was anymore. I didn't know if my face would ever return to the face I loved. All I knew was that Karma was not going to hurt me again. I couldn't. I wouldn't survive.

Later, when the dust had settled, I asked Karma about the huge dude in the passenger seat of the taxi.

"It was just three of us, Bunnie," he said. "You, me, and the driver."

I racked my brain. To this day I can see him clearly, and one day it just came to me. He had to be my guardian angel. He showed up in that car to let me know I was going to be okay. He didn't step between me and Karma, but when I'd felt so alone and afraid, he was there to comfort me. He didn't do anything to help me not because God was abandoning me, but because he knew I could help myself, and it was his way of telling me that I was worthy of protecting—and that I could protect myself. He was going to give me the strength I needed.

Then I knew for sure: The spiritual world is only separated from ours by a thin veil. You just gotta believe.

19

LIGHT THROUGH THE CRACKS

I'D BEEN TALKING TO MY MOM ONLINE FOR YEARS, BUT I hadn't seen her physically since I was three months old and she left me on a stranger's doorstep. But given everything I was going through with Karma, I needed my mother. I needed someone to just hug me. And Karma actually agreed that I needed to meet her—as long as he could come along.

Of course we were still together. Everything that guardian angel had come to tell me—that I was worth a damn, that I could protect myself and help myself and *live*—those realizations were years away. Abuse creates a set of chains around us, and even if I was screaming on the inside, my body just wouldn't move. I couldn't get free of him, not yet. And so he came along with me to Indiana, picking fights every step of the way, and drove me to her house.

I wore a cute little flowered skirt with a black top when we pulled up to a rundown shack in an alley, smack-dab in the middle of small-town Indiana. When the door opened and I saw my mom, I got teary-eyed right away. The little girl in me sobbed on the inside, but I mostly kept my composure on the outside. She was just the tiniest little thing, with big, bright blue eyes and auburn hair. I hugged her and just held on. We didn't let go for a long while, and eventually we were both crying. I'd waited thirty-six years to finally hug my mama. It was everything I could have ever dreamed of.

Inside, her house was run-down beyond belief. She didn't have gas. She didn't even have a stove. I didn't know it at the time, but there was no running water in the house either, so she'd shit in the bathtub or a bucket. Vanessa was a total hermit who never left the house, her anxiety so severe that it kept her confined to this tiny hellhole. I know how crippling anxiety can be—I've had it since the night I took that X pill laced with heroin. But I've had to learn to fight against mine and not let it control me. My mom just wasn't that strong, and I could just see the anxiety consuming her.

It made her an addict. And the truth about Vanessa is that she didn't aspire to be anything more than an addict. She dated biker dudes who treated her like shit. Her life was a dark mess. It infuriated me as I got to know her. Why didn't she want better for herself?

I was so disgusted by her house that first day, and I knew even then that it would eventually kill her. And it did—she developed COPD later in life. In those early days when we reconnected, she had pneumonia all the time. I left that day panicked and disgusted by how my mother was living, so I took my mom under my financial wing and started providing for her as best I could. But I couldn't save her, not with Karma hovering around, grimacing in disgust at my mom and at me too. I wasn't even in a position to save myself.

XO

GRACE, MY BEAUTIFUL SOUTHERN BELLE love, was still by my side no matter what—even if she had pressed charges against me for harassment back in the day. After that night when Karma went too far, I moved out of our throuple mansion and into a house with my girl.

I even tried to get a restraining order to keep Karma away from me. I just didn't trust that he wouldn't try to kill me if he got close enough. I was finally afraid of him, and poking and instigating was no longer on my to-do list. I'd already fucked around and I sure as hell found out.

As with all toxic love affairs, it's like you get addicted to the pain and can't stay away for long. Of course, we saw each other. We would fuck and he would promise not to put hands on me. It was *I love you and I can't be without you.*

But Karma was exactly who he was, and when he drank he affectionately called himself "the Werewolf." Once liquor hit his system, everything he did was destructive. One evening, we were getting shit-faced at the bar across the street from my house like we always did, and he left with an older lady. He'd just outright disrespected me and left me at a bar to go home with some fucking sixty-year-old lady because she had drugs. So I told him to go fuck himself. He fed me some lie and left, and I ordered another round. Hours later, I went home and started getting ready for bed. The sun was up, and I needed sleep. *I'll deal with him when I wake up.*

I didn't hear from him until six in the morning the next day. He started banging on my front door, and I wouldn't let him in the house. He was begging, but I stuck to my guns. Grace wasn't home, and I knew if he found out I was alone, there would be trouble.

Without hesitation, he threw a brick through my window, crawled through the broken glass, and grabbed a handful of my hair to start dragging me around the house. I ended up on all fours while he kicked me in the face and stomach like a dog. I didn't scream—it was just second nature to keep quiet by then. I knew if I screamed it would only make him hurt me more, and I didn't want him to kick my teeth out.

I also knew this man so well by then that I knew I could tame that monster. As he kicked my stomach, chest, and face, I looked up at him and pleaded as quietly as I could.

"Karma, I love you. Don't do this. You don't have to do this," I whispered. "I love you so much. Let's calm down."

He slowly moved away from me. His shark eyes came into focus as he realized just how badly he'd hurt me—again. I still get the chills thinking about how he looked at me, like a little hurt boy. He grabbed my phone, ran out of the house, threw it in the neighbors' pool so I couldn't call the cops, and left.

It didn't matter how many times I involved the police—there was no help coming from the justice system for me. There were so many other times when Karma hurt me, I've lost count. Eventually, I knew I had to change my entire life.

But no matter how much grace I have shown him, Karma is still trying to make my life hell. The difference is that now he has no power over me.

XO

ONE NIGHT IN 2015, KARMA and I met up with some friends at a Moonshine Bandit concert. The path for the rest of my life was set that night.

While we were at the bar, I heard a thick Southern accent.

"Y'all wanna get a drink?"

First of all: Y'all? Who the hell is that?

I looked over at this tall, chunky boy with the brightest smile and tattoos all over his face.

"Hi. My name's Jelly," he said, reaching out to shake my hand.

"Hey, I'm Bunnie," I said. I was—dare I say—mesmerized? This man was *not* my type. But shaking his hand felt like every star in the sky collided. My soul recognized his. It was as if I'd been looking for him my entire life.

Jelly had opened for the Bandits, and to be honest, I didn't even pay attention to his performance. Nor did I really care for his music. I was there with Karma, and we were barely hanging on by a thread. If you let Karma tell the story, he will say he "gave" me to Jelly—an outright lie. He will also tell you he performed with J—another lie. That night, we both met J for the first time. Karma didn't have a clue I was crushing on the Nashville boy.

It's strange, but I shot tons of videos of J on my phone that night—tell me why I filmed a man I barely even knew. He was sipping out of a plastic cup, and I just kept on filming him moving around and being, well, Jelly. I wanted to study him—the way he moved and the way he talked. I was never a sucker for a Southern drawl until that night. I do remember thinking to myself, "This boy is going to be a star one day." I even said it out loud to one of his friends one night when he played J's song "Cocaine in California" for Karma and me in some parking garage. I always knew he had that *it* factor.

Who the fuck are you? I thought to myself. But just as soon as the stars in my eyes started shining, Karma made sure to make his presence known and I was back to being the obedient girlfriend.

Still, that sweet, Southern boy's smile lingered in the back of my mind for weeks to come.

XO

LIVING WITH GRACE WAS MY escape, even when I couldn't get off the merry-go-round from hell with Karma. We'd lie out together or go swimming in our pool, and everything felt calm with her. We would laugh until we cried—no one could ever make me laugh the way Gracey did.

But Grace was a mystery. I could never understand how someone so reckless and without a care in the world could just float through life, until February 26, 2016—the day it all finally made sense.

A few months earlier, we had been out in the pool drinking and carrying on. Grace was a skin cancer survivor after having a piece of her back cut out years before. She'd been cancer-free for years. She swam over to me and pulled me close.

"Bunnie, look at this lump on my leg," she said. "What is it?" I looked and felt her skin with my fingers. It was a decent-size hard nodule. It didn't move when I touched it, but I couldn't imagine it was anything serious.

"Damn, girl. We need to get that checked out," I said, just to be safe. "I'll find you a doctor." But in true Grace fashion, she didn't wait for me to find her a real doctor. Instead, she called up an old trick of ours who ran a pill mill. He was a full-on medical doctor—but shady. Grace always had these back-alley doctors on call.

If I had known she was going to go to him I would have stopped her, but Grace never listened to anyone. Dr. Feelgood cut into the lump on her leg, didn't biopsy it, and didn't follow protocol—he just straight up cut. He started pulling black gunk out of her, and nothing about it sounded right when she came home and told me. I always remembered what Bill said: *Once they start cutting on you, you're never the same.*

It didn't take long for cancer to spread all over her body, and overnight, Grace was sick. It was like he opened Pandora's box in her body when he cut her open that day. One minute, we were hanging by the pool, and the next, she was sick as a dog and moved out to Arizona for cancer treatments so she could be closer to family.

I was stuck in that big house all on my own, afraid of losing my best friend, and afraid of my violent boyfriend.

XO

A SUGAR DADDY HAD JUST paid for me to have surgery, and I was laid up trying to recover. Just to be a dick, Karma went through my phone and found videos of this dude and me together. I would fuck him whenever Karma and I were on the outs. He knew about him—I never hid it, but it was an excuse to get angry. Of course, I had found a video of him fucking another girl once when we were fighting. We were tit for tat.

I was fresh out of surgery, completely helpless with tubes hanging out of me, sitting on a donut pillow so the fat transfer to my ass would settle, and this man just kept screaming in my face. He didn't hit me that day, at least—I was already a wounded soldier—but I remember sitting thinking to myself, *As soon as I'm able to walk, I'm moving out of here.* With Grace gone, there was no protection for me in my house.

I needed to be around people. I figured that if I lived in a high-rise condo with neighbors, at least someone would hear me scream if Karma tried to put his hands on me. So I moved. I was trying like hell to shake him, but of course, the codependency mixed with fear just kept me in the same cycle. He'd try to talk sweet to me to keep me, but he couldn't stay sweet for long. Neither of us knew how to let the other one go.

Luckily, God intervened—he knew I would never have left Karma had something not come between us. And I'm not talking about another man.

One afternoon, I was hanging with my girl Emily at my condo when a jail number started blowing up my phone. Dude was in *fucking jail.*

"You fucking did this, didn't you?" he yelled. "You set me up."

"What the fuck are you talking about? How the fuck would I set you up? Try calling your other fucking girlfriend," I said.

He was being held in Nevada while the law was trying to extradite him to Oklahoma City. I visited him a few times with my eyes still black and blue from the last time he hit me. It took years for those bruises to fully fade. When I finally did go to the hospital for my eyes because I was so scared I was going to go blind, the doctor told me he had only seen injuries like mine in women who had died from strangulation, and that I had a cracked orbital bone. He wanted to run more tests but because Cindy was there reporting everything back to Karma, I declined.

Even so, I felt I needed to be there for Karma while we figured out this prison shit. I don't want to see *anyone* go to prison, and I felt bad for him. I'd told his ass so many times he was a sloppy dealer. Plus I knew that if he got out and I didn't have his back, there would be hell to pay. So Cindy and I tried to find a lawyer to get him out.

Apparently, the feds had been investigating Karma for five years. They had so much proof *and* even associates who turned on him. He was transferred to Oklahoma and indicted on money laundering, ghost weed, and trafficking drugs across state lines.

I found out that Cindy had snitched on him and put the nail in his proverbial coffin. I fucking *knew* she was a snitch. She testified against him in exchange for immunity—on Valentine's Day of all days—behind his back while he was still free, years before he was indicted, and never told him. She went about life with him like everything was fine, and it was her dirty little secret. When I told him, he didn't believe me, but court records don't lie. And when he was shown the proof, he *still* stayed with this woman even after he had promised me he wouldn't. He was placed under house arrest in Oklahoma City, and I stayed out there with him while he was waiting on his sentence. But even my loyalty to him couldn't keep him from his cash cow, Cindy, and when I found out, I went back to Vegas.

What part of the game is that? You preach so much about being an outlaw and a gangster but the woman you've been with for twenty-plus years snitches on you to the *feds* and you *stay with her?*

It might sound crazy, but *that* was the last straw. You beat me, you broke my spirit, you fucking damn near ruined my life. But you stay with a woman who snitched on you and still call yourself a gangster? I was done.

XO

WITH KARMA LOCKED UP, I finally started to feel free from him. Actually, I was running around like a wild banshee. It was like the shackles had been taken off me—even though Cindy was watching my every move online and reporting back to him. By then, Jelly had gotten wind that Karma was locked up and started poking his head around me online too. When I reached out to one of J's friends and told him to give J my number, we reconnected.

The last conversation I had with Karma while he was in prison, he told me I was "crossing lines" by talking to Jelly even though he and J were never friends.

"I'm going to cross lines from here to Nashville, baby. Fuck you," I gleefully replied. We didn't speak the rest of his five-year sentence.

Still, our trauma bond was the hardest one to break in my entire life. It took years for me to stop feeling bad for him, like I had abandoned him while he was in prison—even after all he did to me. People don't realize that abusive relationships warp your mind into a sick, twisted infatuation with the pain and the person.

I know now what I didn't know then: Love isn't supposed to hurt. Not physically, not emotionally, not spiritually. And us women just *know* when something isn't right. We *know* when we're trying to make the impossible work. But I'm telling you this right now: He will never change. It will never get better. It will only get worse.

Most abusive men are more in love with their own egos than they could ever be with you. If you start seeing the red flags gleaming, run. And it will be the hardest fight of your life, especially us women with daddy issues. If you're like me, you're drawn to the high-passion, low-emotion dynamic. But all that's going to do is drain your looks, finances, and soul. Don't wait until you're dead because you want to be a ride or die. Love yourself enough to walk away and never look back.

It's taken a long time to really let it all go. I don't ever want to hate anyone. I'm just not wired that way. But how he acted after prison is what has truly shown me who he's always been—and it's made it easier to close my heart to him.

To this day, Karma denies everything he did to me, even though I have police reports and pictures that would turn your stomach. I've got hospital records. I've got pictures of the whites of my eyes gone blood red from his fists and from strangling me. My eyes swollen so tight I couldn't open them for weeks. Cracked ribs, strangled vocal cords, and so many black eyes. You wouldn't believe the paper trail.

I've tried so hard to work through the damage that man

caused. I've forgiven him—and to this day, I am still friends with all my exes. Can you believe it? Hell, I still help the daughter of one of my exes financially. I still help Paulie. I help all my childhood friends. I try to give back to the people who stood by my side in my life, even if our relationships weren't always perfect. I thought I could do that with Karma when he got out of prison—but honestly, I don't owe that man anything.

He has messaged me for years saying he loves me and will win me back—I tell him there is no chance I'm leaving my husband for him. I've talked to him numerous times just to hear him out, and I've tried to be his friend—because in some sick way, I thought it would help me heal. I've even seen him, but it only triggered my nervous system and I ended up running away from him within minutes. I've also offered to help him financially, because when he went to prison, I gave away all his clothes in a fit of rage and have felt bad about that ever since. He refused the money but will still hold out for a payday from whatever tabloid will hear him out with a story about me.

I did all this because I felt bad about what had happened between us—and to get some closure for that chapter of my life. But I have learned that closure is a lie. I'll never get the apology or understanding I so desperately needed from him. And that has to be okay.

When he found out I was writing this book, Karma blew up. He gaslit the shit out of me and told me, once again, that he never touched me. He's told me I'm lying and embellishing the story of abuse when I'm simply stating facts. As if there aren't police records. And he's said he's dead set on clearing his name even though I've never told anyone who he is—Karma's not his real name. I'm smarter than that.

He's even gone so far as to try to sell sex tapes of us to news outlets. Random people message me and tell me how he'll be drunk in a bar showing sex videos of us. He goes online and trashes my husband and me almost weekly. He's even said publicly that he will sell our story to the highest bidder. Deep down, he's proud of what he's done. What he did. When my face was black and blue, he'd take me out and make sure his friends could see the evidence. I'm so sad I let him. Years later, I know that I can't help or save him. Some people are just pure evil. And this is my truth, and I'll never let someone silence me. This shit is my testimony, and like I've told him, he's only a chapter in my life.

That relationship was the most gut-wrenching, humbling, put-me-on-my-ass reality check I've ever had. It blew my ego to pieces. Before that relationship, I was an awful human. I hurt people, and I had no remorse. I sure as hell couldn't be told otherwise. You might not believe me, but I'm thankful for my time with Karma, even if I couldn't understand where it was leading me at the time. It truly set me on the path I'm on today. It brought me to my knees.

I'm telling this story so women in my situation can say, *Damn, she went through all that—Karma and everything before. She had nothing to show for her life or herself but heartache, loss, and scars. She was locked in addiction. She was a terrible human. She used people. She let herself be used.*

And she changed.

She rose like a phoenix from the ashes and I can too.

Remember, if you keep carrying old bricks, you'll keep building the same house.

Drop that brick.

Build something stunning.

20

WHAT'S YOUR FIVE-YEAR PLAN?

WITH KARMA LOCKED UP, I DIDN'T EVEN KNOW HOW TO function. I had been controlled and living in fight-or-flight for so long that being able to do as I pleased was foreign to me. My life looked sparkly: I was living in my penthouse and driving my sports car—all paid for by my sugar daddies. But I couldn't help but feel sad and broken.

I was never one to wallow in misery—or, should I say, I was never one to deal with my trauma. So I went on a wild streak. I'd had a man every year of my life since I was in high school, and I just wanted to be single and have some time to myself. But that didn't mean I couldn't dip my toe in the dating waters.

I just wanted to smile again. I had my squad of girls around me, and we'd go barhopping every night. Having fun was my main priority. I earned it.

But I was also spending more and more time talking to Jelly, that sweet, Southern charmer I'd met the night of the Moonshine Bandits show.

He'd call and I'd have one of my boy toys lying in bed naked next to me. I'd get up to take the call in the other room, and he'd ask me questions about his daughter. He'd tell me about trying to be a better dad, and I loved hearing about it. Maybe it's because of Bill, but I've always had a soft spot for single dads.

I felt drawn to J in a way I'd never felt in my life. I was heels over head in love with a man I barely even knew. I picked out a bed for his daughter, and we bonded over decorating a room for her so he'd be ready when he got full custody. The first time I ever saw Bailee was actually an accident—her dad's phone and her iPad had the same login so when I Face-Timed him, it went to Bailee's iPad. That little girl appeared on the screen, looking at me with the biggest smile I'd ever seen.

Talking to J was easy. There were no expectations, and conversation flowed energetically. It was like my body could finally exhale and relax. And of course, never to stray far from my type, he was a tattooed felon and ex–drug dealer. But this one was trying to get his life together and take a different path—kinda like me. By then, I wanted out of the streets and to figure out how to be a better human all around.

J was different from anyone I'd ever met. Yet somehow also familiar, like we'd spent lifetimes together.

XO

I HAD VISITED GRACE IN Arizona when she was getting cancer treatments, but I could only go once. Karma had made it a nightmare for me to leave town without him, even if it was to see my sick best friend. Eventually, Grace went back to Texas to pursue healing and treatments out there, and we texted and talked all the time. In my heart, she was never going to die and this was all a part of her journey. She would go back into remission and would be cancer-free one day.

Now that I was free from Karma, I could fly to Texas to be with Grace and help her heal. I was so, so excited.

Gracey! I love you! I'm finally free to come visit you. Text me back so I can plan when I'm coming.

She never replied.

XO

KARMA WENT TO PRISON THE first week of February 2016. I got the phone call on February 26 that Grace had passed.

The cancer treatment hadn't worked, and my beautiful Southern belle was gone. I never got to say goodbye in person. We'd said our goodbyes over the phone, but I just thought she was acting the dramatic Gemini that she was.

Grace's death hit me hard. Very hard. It was just the icing on the cake of the hell I'd been through the past few years. I never thought I'd lose my best friend too—my sister from another mister. Her funeral was planned for the beginning of April, and I knew I had to go to Texas to say goodbye.

My life was about as dark as it had ever been. I'd just gone through the most vile, abusive relationship I'd ever had and lost my best friend at the same time. I couldn't get my head straight to figure out why any of it was happening, and I definitely didn't know shit about healing. I needed some kind of escape. It just so happened that J was on tour with Cypress Hill. I had an off-

and-on hookup with someone in that crew—I'd even set J up with the gig by putting in a good word for him—and they were playing an hour from Grace's funeral. *Fuck it.* I decided to stay in town and see J—and my down-low hookup too.

Grace's funeral was beautiful, just like her. She was sent off in a church, covered with her favorite flowers and surrounded by the people who loved her. There wasn't a dry eye in the place. I hadn't broken down, but seeing the casket with her picture beside it broke me. How do you say goodbye to a person who was so full of life? It just wasn't fair.

I still miss her laugh. I have so much to tell her and so much I know would make her proud. A decade with her wasn't long enough. Even writing this, I can't help but smile thinking about all the crazy shit we did together. What a wild ride, Sis.

After the funeral, I met up with J and hopped on tour briefly with the crew. I was starting to catch the vibe from J that he liked me—and I liked him too. But I was there with my down-low hookup—plus I had my boy toys in Vegas. But I tried to flirt anyway—why not? He was adorable.

I'd missed J's set, so we stood together backstage and watched Cypress Hill perform. Eventually, he leaned close.

"You wanna go up on the roof and smoke a joint?" he asked.

"Yeah," I said, batting my eyelashes. "Absolutely." We headed upstairs, and on the way, he somehow accumulated two other girls, who I didn't know. I'd thought we were finally about to get some alone time, but here he was, inviting two random chicks. *Absolutely not.*

Up on the roof, the girls and J smoked—and since the attention wasn't 100 percent on me, I dipped the hell out. I just left him there on the roof with ride-alongs. I wasn't being a hater, but I *was* exerting my alpha. Pay attention *to me* and *only me, sir.*

But I could tell there was something starting. I just didn't know what the hell it would be.

XO

J WASN'T THE MAN HE is today back in 2015 when we met, and a year later, he was still bouncing couch to couch and living in his brown van, Bertha. I'll never forget the first time J invited Karma and me outside to this heap of shit to smoke a joint. Full of pride, he slid the door open and revealed the dirtiest vehicle I had ever seen. And to top it off, it had a mattress lying on the floor inside. There were used condoms, crumbs, and trash everywhere. My OCD was pinging the Richter scale when he invited us in to sit down. I declined and went and sat in my car because it was so disgusting. But that van was his pride and joy.

But dirty van and all, our connection felt spiritual and like it would transcend the red flags of how we first met: me under Karma's thumb in that bar where J played a show to no one.

Back in Vegas, J and I kept talking on the phone. He'd watch my stories and see all the other guys I was partying with and nights out with my girls, but we kept getting closer and closer. He was becoming my buddy. One day, J hit me up and said he was coming to Vegas for a video shoot. I was excited—even though I'd never tell him that.

"Just drive all night," I said, "and you can crash with me." Forty-eight hours later, after a long drive from Tennessee, he showed up on my doorstep with some of his friends. My penthouse had plenty of room.

J wasn't my type—I love tough guys, or goth, emo boys in eyeliner. I wasn't his type either. So why the hell was my soul telling me *there he is* the minute we met? I couldn't explain it. And I didn't know how he thought about me at all. I had a hunch, but I wasn't sure. He'd had a chance, and he blew it.

He walked in to find me hungover and lying in bed with my girl Victoria. I didn't have a lick of makeup on, and I hid my face. I *always* had makeup on, and you had to be super-inner circle to see me without it.

"Hi," I said, staying in bed and as far away as possible. "You made it."

To this day, that man will not let me forget that I didn't get up and hug and kiss him when he arrived. After he drove forty-eight hours to get to me.

"You're not even gonna hug me?" he asked, his feelings hurt.

Reluctantly, I got up and gave him a hug, still trying to hide my face. It didn't take long for this man to come into my space and get comfortable. As soon as he walked in, he dropped his jeans in the middle of the kitchen and left them there. In fact, he started dropping stuff everywhere, and my OCD was triggered. I picked up the pair of pants and folded them neatly and laid them on the breakfast bar.

"Make yourself at home, why don't ya," I snapped. *Already cleaning up after him. Story of my life.*

XO

AFTER THE LONG DRIVE AND ego bruise of me not being elated when he pulled up, J popped a Xanny and passed out in my guest room. When he finally woke his ass up, we decided to go out and get shit-faced. Jay loves a honky-tonk, and the MGM Grand had just opened their very own, Losers.

We had a blast that night, laughing and giggling and just learning about each other—and we killed a whole bottle of vodka between us. It just felt so right. I sat in his lap and flirted. I kissed him right there in the bar while our friends whistled around us. Our chemistry was insane—we couldn't keep our hands off each other. I whispered in his ear.

"Let's go home."

XO

I STRIPPED NAKED AND CALLED J into my room. He walked in, hammered, took one look at me, and just about hit the floor. He was *so* shy! I sauntered over and sat him down and then got onto his lap. I kissed him and started to take off his clothes.

And that man absolutely would not bang me.

"Hang on, Bunnie," he said, pulling away and taking a breath. He grabbed at my hands and held them in place. "Let's just talk for a second."

What the fuck is there to talk about, my guy?

"Ummm . . . talk?" I was drunk and totally lost. I'd never been naked and ready to fuck to have a man want to talk.

"I just gotta know what we're doing," he said. "What's your five-year plan?"

My fucking what?

"I don't know what I'm doing tomorrow. I sure as shit don't know what I'm doing in five years."

All I knew was the room was spinning and I couldn't form two thoughts, let alone make a plan.

He explained that we were friends. He was fine if it was just a onetime fuck, but he didn't want us to regret it in the morning—and we needed to be on the same page. Plus, how casual could it be? I'd decorated his daughter's future room. We were so, so connected. He didn't want to ruin everything. And he was buying time, too, until his whiskey dick would start working again. I did see that part of his game.

"I really like you," he said.

"I really like you too," I said.

"So let's figure out what we're doing."

Frustrated but intrigued, I unstraddled him and lay next to him, wrapping my arm around him. I started to tell him about all the dreams I had. I wanted to be with him. I wanted my own talk show, I wanted to build a brand, I wanted to buy a house with the man I married, I wanted to raise a family.

He told me about getting custody of Bailee and how his life would change once she was home with him. He told me he wanted to buy a house and what he wanted for his music career. And he wanted to be with me.

For hours, we lay there together, dreaming out a future and how we could be part of it for each other. We didn't hold back anything. It was the most honest conversation I'd ever had. And I told him that no matter what happened with us, I'd help him get his little girl.

By seven a.m., we'd landed on the same page and sobered up.

"Pinky promise we're going to make these dreams come true?" he asked, holding out his little finger. I hooked mine around his.

"Pinky promise," I said.

21
THE WHORE TOUR

THE NEXT DAY, I MADE BREAKFAST FOR J AND HIS crew, and then they headed out on tour.

Now, remember, I was a call girl. Men promising me the moon and the stars was an everyday occurrence. So as much as I wanted to believe everything J had said the night before was real, I wasn't going to hang my hat on that. To me, it was a sweet moment I'd always remember—even if that's all it was.

But after a few weeks on the road, J and I were talking every day. He seemed to have meant what he said. One night, he called and told me he was missing me. A lot.

"Get on a flight and come hop on tour with me. There's no better way to tell if this is going to work than if we're out here together," he chuckled, drawling out each word in his sweet little accent.

"Are you sure?" I was floored. Wasn't tour time for the guys, no girls allowed? Would I ruin it? He didn't seem to think so.

"You're *one* of the guys," he said. Still, I had a problem.

"But how will I make money?" I held the phone to my ear, trying to calm my panic. Making money for myself had always been the way I kept myself safe. I couldn't stop.

But then, a brilliant idea hit.

"Would you care if I saw clients on the road? I'd be on my own tour?"

"Not at all," he said, totally calm. "Whatever you gotta do, baby. Just get to me."

"Okay," I said, shaping up a plan. "I can book clients in every city you're in. It'll be my own little Whore Tour."

XO

CONFESSION: I MIGHT HAVE A slight obsession with clothes. And when I say slight, I mean terrible, *terrible* problem. I have multiple closets in my house—and I always have. I usually only wear my going-out outfits once, and I have to have new clothes on if I'm going out. Likely, it stems from being that fourteen-year-old runaway who had nothing but a few T-shirts in a trash bag. And even when I couldn't afford clothes, I stole them. My clothing accumulation must be the strangest habit I have.

I'd never been on any kind of tour before, and all I knew was that I wasn't going to be home for at least a few weeks and possibly months. So I loaded up every suitcase I had in that penthouse—which ended up totaling four. I figured this would get me started. And if I ran out, I could always buy more clothes on the road.

When I finally landed, J picked me up at the airport in the eighteen-passenger van they were using to tour. When he saw me, he lit up in excitement. And then he saw my bags, and boom—his face turned annoyed. But sweet man that he is, he didn't say a word.

"Okay, honey," he said. "There aren't any more bags, right?" He kept his voice steady, but I could read the room. I knew I'd fucked up. But how the hell was I supposed to know? I just wanted to look good for him.

But he couldn't stay annoyed long, and we kissed and snuggled all the way to the venue. Our tour had officially started.

XO

THAT NIGHT WE MADE OUR five-year plan, J had asked me point-blank how I made my money. I was honest with him—I was always honest about what I did for work. Hell, even my own father knew.

"I'm a call girl," I told him that night in my bedroom, "and I make a lot of fucking money. There are levels in this business, and I guess you'd consider me 'high class.'"

Usually, people are either intrigued or disgusted when I tell them, and I hurried through it to try to preempt any questions. Still, I broke the whole thing down for him: how I got clients, services I offered—every detail. I figured that if the shoe was on the other foot, I'd want to know.

"I won't even go to dinner with someone for less than a thousand dollars, and you can't touch me for way more than that, at least five thousand." J was listening so attentively, it was like he already understood. He even had a tiny smile cracking the corners of his mouth. He wasn't scared or put off in any way.

"I respect it," he said. "You're a fuckin' hustler, and I ain't got a problem with it." From day one, he never once made me feel bad for what I had to do to survive. He'd listen wide-eyed as I'd tell him stories, crazy things I've seen, big piles of money I'd made, wild tales of my high-profile clients. He'd grown up with girls like me in the streets, and he'd also hustled himself. By then he was slanging music, but back in the day in Antioch, he was slanging rocks in some desolate motel.

My main hustle in those days was a website called Eros, where I paid a hefty fee to place ads for my services and for them to designate me as one of their top girls for more exposure and more clients. Clients could log on, find a woman in their city, and book her. Some of the most beautiful women I'd ever seen were on that website—it was like the Louis Vuitton of hookers. A lot of girls were on Backpage, but that website scared me. There was no protection, and any- and everyone had access to you. I was always extremely selective with who I saw, because I'd been arrested for solicitation before by an undercover cop. I checked IDs, social media, and business cards before I'd see someone new. On Eros, clients were at least *somewhat* vetted and paid a membership fee to even speak to me. I've always fully believed that if you're good at something, never do it for free. Charge what you're worth—even if the prices are astronomical. People *will* pay it.

When I was in the lifestyle, I never did "in call" until I moved to Nashville—I was always "out call," meaning I would go to my clients and they would never come to me, unless they were a trusted regular. It was always business with me. Some clients liked the professionalism while others wished I were more affectionate or loving, but it was a transaction, and I treated it as such. Overnights were out of the question—the idea of sleeping next to a trick makes me want to crawl out of my skin. (I'm not saying I haven't done it—I did, with some of my big sugar daddies. But those were rare occasions—and very expensive. We're talking $20,000-plus.)

Before I packed up my four suitcases, I updated my profile to announce I was going on tour. Before the plane landed, I was fully booked.

XO

HERE I WAS, ON TOUR with my rapper boyfriend and doing my own tour myself. I never wanted J to worry about me while he was pouring his soul out onstage, so I decided I'd see my clients *before* his shows so I could be there for him. I created an efficient routine.

While J was at that night's venue doing sound check, I'd meet up with whoever had booked me for the hour. To be clear—no one ever lasted longer than ten to fifteen minutes, except for the occasional guy who wanted to use the whole time. We'd talk and talk to build up the suspense until the last few minutes, when he'd be eating out of the palm of my hand.

For the first time in my entire life, my boyfriend wasn't jealous of my clients or threatened by my work. J just didn't flinch—he trusted me and knew that what I did to make my money didn't have shit to do with us. I think he could see in my eyes when I'd work that I was a different person. Almost like an actress in a movie. And when it was over, I was right back to who he knew I was.

While this should have felt incredible, it scared the shit out of me—much more than the abusive and controlling relationship I'd recently escaped. Just as I'd learned from an early age that you love with violence and control, I learned from the men I loved that I was an object—and a possession. If J wasn't jealous of the other men I let touch me—even if I was charging—did that mean he didn't care about me at all? Did it mean he didn't love me?

J knew that my clients were a means to an end. He knew I was used to making my own money and that he wasn't going to take that from me—he wouldn't ever want to. It was the first relationship where my boyfriend didn't want to change me—and I didn't want to change him either. He's a Sagittarius and he doesn't like to be tied down—just try and tell that man what to do and see what happens. I'm an Aquarius, and I don't like to be tied down either. Neither of us wanted to control the other. We both so deeply understood each other exactly as we were, and we were committed to those versions of each other, not some version we could manipulate into someone else. He let me just be *me*. But at that point in my life, I wasn't even sure who I was.

XO

INSTEAD OF SHOVING MY BAGS and myself into the van full of dirty, smelly men, I figured out a solution: I rented my own vehicle. I didn't need his crew lugging my stuff around—and it gave me some of my own freedom and space. And if you've ever been stuck in an eighteen-passenger van with twelve men, are you really living? *Whew.* And with a little breathing room, we had an absolute blast every single night. J would play in these seedy bars that held three hundred or so people, and after each set, he'd make sure he shook everybody's hand and signed their merch. Some nights he would perform to thirty people or less, and he still played like it was a sold-out house.

I'd never gotten to experience anything like it. Being on the road was a totally different way of life. Once I got my own vehicle, J would drive with me for three, four, six, or even thirteen hours at a time—just us caravanning behind the van. Asking each other every question we could. Playing each other the music we grew up on. Comparing traumas. Laughing and giggling and learning each other. What better way to fall in love ?

XO

I WAS SO HAPPY WITH J. It was a feeling I had never felt before. Peaceful, safe, even loved? But I was wounded. I hadn't begun to heal. Not even close. I didn't realize then how deeply scarred I was from my relationship with Karma. It would take over a decade for those wounds to start to heal and for my body to just feel normal. As I've said, severe abuse rewires your brain and your nervous system: That kind of violence stays in your bones long after the bruises have healed. Back then, I didn't know shit about healing. I just knew I had to keep moving.

But the edges started to fray. Panic attacks came on me. I couldn't be in crowds. These attacks were so severe, they'd send me to the hospital. Sometimes, they would happen while I was driving, and I'd have to pull the car over on the side of the freeway and puke my brains out. I called 911 to a hotel room we were staying in—more than once—because I was sure I was having a heart attack. Panic attacks are like that: Your heart beats out of your chest until you're completely convinced you're about to die. You feel like you can't breathe.

I'd jolt out of bed in the middle of night vibrating with anxiety, and I'd throw my shoes on and jog around the hotel for hours until I calmed down. The anxiety was starting to overpower me. I couldn't outrun the trauma, no matter how hard I tried.

I started drinking more and more, and it was hitting different. One night at one of J's shows, I felt the panic closing in on me. I looked around at the people in the audience, jumping and screaming their heads off, and their faces started to melt. Their eyes turned demonic, and I was sure death was coming for me. I was stuck in severe fight-or-flight mode. Frozen in fear.

If your soul is shattering into a million tiny shards, you get the fuck up and keep going. It's what I had done my whole life, and for some reason, this time it wasn't working.

I'd told J from the very start what I'd been through with Karma—and everyone since Mindy.

"I love you," I told him. "But if I get weird, I'm sorry. Please don't get mad at me when I'm having an anxiety attack. Just love me through it and let me have space so I can calm myself down." And that's exactly what that man did. When I was panicky, I'd go off by myself to self-soothe, and he'd let me. If he followed me or tried to help, it sent me over the edge more—I'd spiral about how *he* was feeling. He never once got angry when I withdrew or judged me if I had go to the hospital because I was falling apart.

If I needed to leave a show because I couldn't handle the crowds, he'd give me a kiss goodbye.

"You okay, baby? You're not mad?" he'd ask, and I'd shake my head.

"No, not at all," I'd say, and tell him I was overwhelmed with anxiety.

"You go and I'll be at the hotel room as soon as I'm done here," he'd say. It was the first time I'd ever had a love like that—a love that was actions, not just words.

XO

I'D BEEN IN TOUCH WITH Vanessa since I finally met her in person. I sent her groceries and tried to help when I could. She never asked for much. Just milk and bread and dog food. She never bothered me for anything but the bare minimum.

She came and visited us on tour, and that night at the show, she just loved on me nonstop. To this day, I'm thankful that my mom wasn't in my life during the worst years of her addiction. The trauma from being abandoned was one thing, but growing up with her might have killed me. Instead, I got to spend time with her when I had my own life—and my own means to escape. It was on my terms.

But while my mom and I were watching J perform, she started getting antsy and withdrawn. I saw the signs. I knew what was happening. Not only did I resemble this woman in general, but it was like looking at myself as she started spiraling into a panic attack. I tried to comfort her, but she bolted. She just couldn't be there.

I understood exactly what she was feeling. I know she'd been abused her whole life. I never got full stories from her—she never talked about her trauma—but I did get bits and pieces. Her own father owned an escort agency and pimped her out to men when she was young. She was a stripper, in and out of abusive relationships, and her downfall was always men. Sound familiar?

The venue door slammed behind her. It was hard to see her so clearly when she couldn't see herself. Her addiction had taken so much from her, but in her eyes, she wasn't an addict. Her pills, morphine patches, and Dilaudid were all prescribed by a doctor, so she said she "needed" them to function. All poison.

I'm thankful that I didn't end up like her. Back then, I saw too much of myself when I looked at her and it scared the hell out of me.

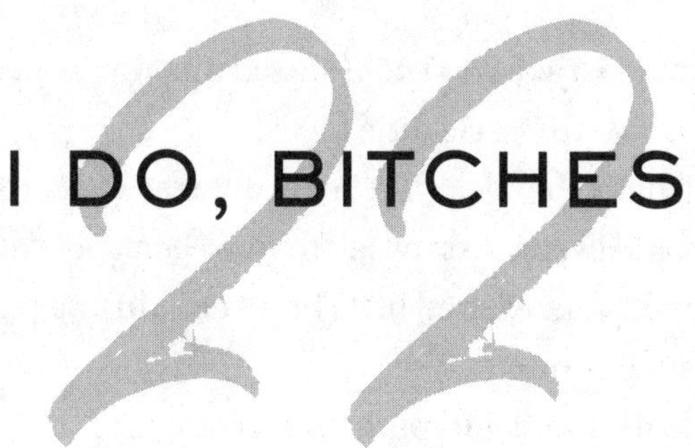

I DO, BITCHES

J AND I ROLLED BACK INTO VEGAS AFTER A MONTH TOgether on the road. It had been the most intense yet awesome way to begin a relationship. I always say if you want to get to know someone fast, lock yourself with them in a vehicle for thirty days. That's make or break, baby!

My divorce from Paulie was barely finalized, and I was what seemed like minutes into freedom from the last relationship. Today, I know I wasn't actually free at all yet—my whole body, mind, and spirit were wrecked from Karma's abuse. And I wasn't supposed to be in a relationship with anyone—especially not with the one who mattered most. I needed to be single and do things on my own. I needed to fall in love with myself and heal. But along came that sweet-talking country boy and I swooned.

Yelawolf was opening for Deftones—and J was performing with them. All my Vegas homies were in the audience—including a boy toy I'd been with on and off right before J entered the picture. I was excited to see J perform in my hometown for the first time, even if it was just one song with Yela.

But as always, J kept me on my toes. Backstage, he came barreling up to me with his big-ass smile and grabbed me by the arms.

"Let's get married. *Tonight.*" I stared him down and waited for him to say *Just kidding.* He didn't.

I didn't hate the idea. But with my track record, I worried whether I could even trust myself to make a responsible decision. J stood there like an excited little boy. I couldn't help but want to do whatever he wanted.

"Let's do it!" I said, jumping up and down.

Deep down, I was scared as fuck. I knew it felt different with him, but who was I to trust how I was feeling about a man back in those days? I barely had a functioning nervous system. But of course, I live for spontaneity. And it was exciting as hell, and I loved the passion. Would it end in disaster? *Absolutely*—but at least we could say it was a fun moment. *Hell, maybe I'll tell my grandkids about it one day. Or someone else's grandkids.*

"Start looking for a chapel," he called as he walked onstage. And like the Southern gentlemen he is, later he called me up in front of the audience to propose in front of everyone. I stood next to him as he got down on one knee.

"Will your fine ass marry my white trash ass tonight in Las Vegas?"

"Yeah, baby," I yelled into the mic, and the crowd erupted with screams. J and I ran offstage hand in hand, hearts racing on adrenaline, and stars in our eyes.

XO

WHEN I TELL YOU THAT neither J nor I remember our actual wedding date, I'm so serious. Backstage, J took one look at me and said, "Fuck it. Let's just go now."

I checked the time.

"The courthouse is open for about forty-four more minutes."

"Let's fucking roll."

The entire way to the courthouse we bumped "Let's Get Married" by Jagged Edge and "Gorilla" by Bruno Mars. We were so high on life—and other things.

J had specifically asked me *not* to do blow before the wedding, because he said he didn't want us to be on drugs while we got married. Unfortunately, I don't know how to take direction from authority and took his instruction as a challenge instead of something reasonable and sweet. So, consider me a coked-up bride.

Somehow, we got our marriage license and headed to a one-hour chapel. Outside, J grabbed my hand and twirled me around.

"Bunnie. I want you to know that you're not going to have to do what you do for work much longer. I promise you." Being drunk and high, I didn't want to get too serious—I'm never the one for a heavy conversation in a lighthearted situation. I giggled.

"Baby it's okay. You don't have to say—" But he cut me off.

"I'm serious. Look me in the eye. I promise you," he said. How could I not love this man? He was truly everything I had ever dreamed of but never thought I deserved.

"Okay," I said. "We'll figure it out." I wanted so desperately to believe him—but what the hell was I going to do for a living? Hustling was all I'd ever known. Standing outside that chapel, all I wanted was to become his wife. To be Mrs. DeFord and for him to be my ever after happily, if there was such a thing. We'd figure out the rest later.

The little stained-glass chapel in downtown Vegas was decorated with the most random decor, like ceramic urns and Greek columns, and the woman who married us was the tiniest, cutest little nugget. She had no idea what had exploded through those doors when we came in that night. I was in a shredded black dress.

At the altar, J said, "I wanna spend the rest of my life with you," looking at me with a big smile, and grabbing handfuls of my ass.

"I'm so in love with you," I said as I stroked his face. In the background, our friends started playing "Gangster" by Kehlani and our bodies swayed softly to the music as we exchanged vows between drunken giggles and kisses.

Did we think it was a happily ever after? I don't think either of us thought that far ahead. There was so much we hadn't thought about. We hadn't even decided where we were going to live—I lived in Vegas and he lived in Nashville. And that was the smallest item on the scale. He had kids.

Before me, J was a *player*. He had multiple women who he was with for multiple years at the same time. One of them was an off-and-on again relationship that resulted in a son together. This woman gave birth to his son a week before we were married—and today, there seems to be a lot of confusion when it comes to J's son, but honestly, it's pretty simple. They were together *before* him and me—off and on for about ten years to be exact. Their relationship was super toxic, but they decided to coparent their son as best they could. She was already eight or nine months pregnant when J and I decided to be together. And although my relationship with this baby mama was rough in the beginning, today I absolutely adore her and the woman and mother she is. And I'm so thankful to have someone in our equation who knows J just as well as I do.

And then there was his seven-year-old, that angel baby I saw staring back at me on FaceTime. I knew he was going to try to get custody of her soon, but stepping into a mother role didn't even cross my mind that night. All I knew was I loved this man, and I was willing to slay whatever dragons we faced together.

XO

THAT IS, UNTIL I WOKE up extremely hungover the next morning, reeling from the night before.

One thing about party girl me: I was a great time when I was riding that high. But boy, when I came crashing down, I caused destruction to anything in my path. That is the ugly side of addiction that many people don't want to admit.

I woke up in a booze, Xanax, coke hangover and meaner than a rattlesnake. J, on the other hand, woke up happier than a pig in shit. His happiness would be short-lived.

"J. Did we make a mistake last night?"

It was one of our first arguments. I lashed out. He didn't deserve it at all.

"I just think we shouldn't have gotten married. What the fuck was I thinking?" I didn't even feel real remorse. I was just hungover, and I wanted to bring him down, too. Or maybe I was subconsciously testing him to see if he would respond the same way. Because if we both thought we shouldn't have done it, then it would be a reason to sabotage the relationship, right?

I could see my words truly hurt his feelings, so I backed off a bit and we went to meet some friends for lunch. Two screwdrivers for breakfast, and I was back to my happy, chipper self and we moved past the fight.

Or did we? J let it go for the moment, but he sat in my words for a few days. Then we took a drive out to the Grand Canyon together to really hash it out and figure out if we were going to commit to each other. For real. The truth was that neither one of us had ever been capable of a committed relationship before. And my words scared him because he knew our limitations.

The drive up there was uncomfortable. We argued, we talked, and we were very raw with each other about our fears. I had never communicated with someone so openly, especially as new as we were as a couple. This was a different way of doing a relationship. I liked parts of it, but I also pushed back, because J forced me to identify my feelings *and* held me accountable for my words. That had never happened to me before—I was so used to throwing heart darts at the people I "loved"—including friends—when I was mad and then just moving on like nothing had happened. Not with J. He was going to make me own up to what I said. And he didn't say things he didn't mean. If he said something, he meant it. I wasn't like that. I had never known anyone like that.

As we looked over the Grand Canyon's edge, J was still hurt about how I acted the morning after our wedding. Still, he managed to say something that knocked some sense into me.

"I wouldn't have married you if I wasn't serious, Bunnie. This isn't a fuckin' game to me."

With one sentence, J had calmed every fear rattling around inside of me. For my whole life, nothing had been particularly serious—even marriages could be undone without too much trouble. No one was thinking about forever with me. But J saw me differently. He saw the long game. And I saw a man who really wanted to change his ways and learn to love truly. And with that, I straightened myself out and apologized.

It was just the beginning of all the things we as individuals and a couple would need to face head-on. But I've had several psychics tell me that J and I are soulmates—and twin flames. Twin flames are mirror images of each other, reflecting all the things that you need to work on. I had no idea that staring into his mirror would forever change the woman I was and make me into the woman I was destined to be. But thank you God for the gift.

COLD TURKEY

BUZZED BUNNIE WAS A GOOD TIME. I LOVED A BUMP of coke in a dirty bathroom stall, and I really loved my Lortabs, my preferred brand of hydrocodone. It was like a cup of coffee for me—I couldn't start my day without my cocktail of half a Lortab, a quarter of a Xanax, and a diet pill. Once I felt my hazel eyes go green, I knew the concoction had hit my bloodstream and I was ready for the day. I had been working up the right combination since I was twenty-one, and I could never imagine life sober. Nothing about that sounded fun to me.

I always told myself I wasn't an addict. If I were an addict, I'd be just like my mom. I wasn't. So I couldn't be addicted.

Plus, I was functioning just fine. I was always in control of how much I took, because heavy amounts of drugs made me sick. I wasn't like my friends who were taking eight to ten pills a day. Hell, no. I looked down from my high horse, thinking I wasn't anything like them. I was *better* than them.

But the truth is: Of course I was an addict. I couldn't function if these pills weren't in my system.

XO

J AND I HAD BEEN married and touring for a few months, and he was about to get custody of Bailee. We were working together with a lawyer by then to get her full time from her birth mom, who was deep into drugs. I hated the idea of a little girl finding my bottle of pills, or even worse, watching me wake up and need to take them every day. How would life with us be any different from the house she came from? How would I be any different from the woman she used to call her mom?

I wanted no part in adding to this kid's already traumatic life. At the very least, getting sober would keep me from inflicting *more* of that kind of trauma on her.

Bailee was a huge part of my decision to get sober—and she was part of a massive, swirling perfect storm of reasons why it was finally time to face my addiction. The truth is, I was falling apart on tour with J. The trauma of my past was rearing its ugly head and pulling me into the dark. I was taking anxiety medication but still having severe panic attacks. My Lortabs were making me so sick I couldn't keep them down, and the alcohol I was downing in increasing quantities only made my days horrific with anxiety and what I would soon come to realize was devastating depression. Eventually, I'd hit that point with all my vices: the dosage would go up, but the high wouldn't come. It would be all crashes.

I had always boasted that I'd never been depressed and *only* suffered from anxiety. I figured depression wasn't real. I figured it was something people used when they just wanted an excuse to be sad. Who has time to feel like that?

When I scoff at something or think I'm better than someone or something, God always finds a way to humble me. I believe wholeheartedly that God makes me go through situations so I know how the people I looked down upon felt, and boy, let me tell you. This was going to become one of the darkest times of my life—and it would be a five-year battle.

XO

I DECIDED ONE NIGHT WHILE we were on tour that the pills were doing the exact opposite of what I needed, and I could feel them polluting my blood. After all the years of being on them, something got a grip on me and I just didn't want this shit coursing through my veins another second.

"I don't want this in my system anymore. I don't want it in my blood," I said, looking over at J from the passenger seat of my rental car. "I'm not going to take it anymore."

"Okay, honey," he said, calm and gentle. "But you'll never be able to quit Xanax."

J had seen firsthand the severity of my panic attacks. The 911 calls, the emergency room visits, and the tears that followed from feeling like I had zero control of my body, mind, and emotions. And we both knew benzos alter your brain chemistry so you need them *fast*—and withdrawals can mean uncontrollable panic, hallucinations, body aches, brain zaps, depression, or feeling suicidal. Take it from me: Xanax is a bitch to quit. It kicks on the way out.

But my soul was desperate for a change. It knew what it needed. Just like I knew to leave home at fourteen and never look back to save myself, my soul knew it was time to quit.

And we were weeks away from getting Bailee. I told J that I wanted to be a better example for her. I just couldn't do that to her. Her coming into our home was a monumental catalyst for both me and J to change our lives. His change would be gradual—it's something I'd grow to learn about him. My change was abrupt, like everything I do—I make a decision and off I fucking go.

For the first time ever, I felt my relationship was a safe place where I could heal. We had a clean slate, and he saw all my flaws and still kissed them ever so gently.

I went cold turkey. I was done with pills and cocaine, but it would be a while before I let go of the alcohol. Either way, nothing could have prepared me for sobriety. Not even Jesus Himself.

XO

THEY SAY IN ORDER TO see the light, you have to go through the darkness. A month into not taking pills, my brain was flooded with all the feelings I had numbed out my entire life. Being numb to the world, you could walk through World War III and not even flinch. Being sober—not so much. You jump at every sound, and the overstimulation of the world weighs heavy on you. I was scared of everything.

BAILEE ANN

J HAD TOLD ME FROM THE START OF OUR RELATIONSHIP that he was trying to get custody of his daughter, Bailee. I'd dated men with kids before but this was a whole different animal. I was signing up to be some kind of parental figure to this kid.

After J and I got married, the first conversation Bailee and I had was in a Burger King in the middle of bumfuck Tennessee. Bailee is a take-charge, tell-it-like-it-is, bossy, rebel soul. Even as a young kid, she would fearlessly say how she felt. I always look back fondly on our first meeting because it was like I was staring Baby Lis right in the face—even if she didn't look like me.

So there we were, in the middle of nowhere at some random Burger King, and this child was staring through me into my soul. In dead silence. By ourselves. J was outside explaining to her mom's parents that he'd run off and gotten married in Vegas. It felt like sitting across from a mini Godfather—she even had her hands folded on the table in front of her as she inspected me.

Her big blue eyes focused on mine.

"What are your intentions with my dad?" she asked straight-faced. This kid didn't come to play.

"I love him," I said. The last thing I wanted to do was get defensive. All I could think about was when I'd found out my dad was marrying Mindy. How trapped and abandoned I'd felt. How invisible.

"I want to be with him. That's all—nothing else."

"Okay," she said, seemingly satisfied with that answer.

XO

SHE SEEMED SO MUCH LIKE me—she'd already been through so much trauma. She'd never felt heard or cared for. If I was going to give this child a chance to thrive, I would have to do everything differently than how it was done with me. I wasn't going to say "I'm your new mom," like Mindy had to a confused and scared five-year-old. I wasn't going to make her feel like she didn't have a place in the family J and I were making together. If anything, *I* was the intruder. This was *her* family I was joining. I wasn't going to give her the heartache I lived with my whole damn life.

I knew I needed to make her feel comfortable. If I was going to be in her life, I'd tread lightly and let our relationship develop organically. With this little girl, I was going to be honest and gentle. And I was going to do my best to pass whatever tests she threw at me. I'd answer whatever questions she asked.

The second test was her Burger King order.

"What should I get?" she asked, looking over at the menu on the wall. I didn't know what a picky eater she was—still is.

"You gotta get the Oreo shake," I said.

"*Ew*," she said, scrunching up her nose. "I've never had an Oreo shake and I'm never going to ever have one. Ever."

"Well, if you don't like it, you can throw it on the floor," I said as we both giggled. *Score!* I got the Godfather to crack a smile. "But I promise you'll love it."

Her eyes got wide. She pondered and finally gave me a nod. I ordered her an Oreo shake and put it in front of her, nervously awaiting her first slurp. *If this goes badly, she'll never trust me again.*

She took a sip and grinned. She absolutely loved it. *Whew.*

It wouldn't be the last test with Bailee. She didn't trust women—and as matter of fact, she still tests me to this day. But I can't blame her: Her mother and stepmom were both addicts, using heavy drugs that made it impossible for them to parent her.

After that day at Burger King, J and I started talking over what would be best for Bailee. No one ever wants to take a child away from their mother. Neither of us at that time wanted to be full-time parents, and we were messed up ourselves. We doubted we were stable enough to run a household that included a child.

My entire life was still in Vegas. But I hopped in the car with J and we drove the forty-eight hours together from Vegas to Nashville so I could see if it was somewhere I could live full time. Being a Vegas girl through and through, the thought of moving to the country terrified me. I lived a *very* fast life in bars and casinos every night. But I loved J so much, I was willing to try whatever I needed to be with him. I didn't want to leave his side.

We were about to make the hardest decision ever as a couple.

XO

WE DECIDED TO GO FOR full custody when we went to visit Bailee at her grandparents' house, where her own mom was in and out. We'd heard terrible things about their life—and when we saw it for ourselves, we had to act. There was no other choice.

I remember pulling up to the house and thinking how different the houses in Vegas looked from the ones in Nashville.

We showed up unannounced, wanting to see what Bailee's life was really like. We pulled the screen door back and walked into the living room. I couldn't believe what I was seeing. It looked like a Vegas trap house—dirty and cluttered, like it hadn't been cleaned in years. There were piles of trash and clothes everywhere. You couldn't sit on any of the furniture because it was all covered in shit. J and I glanced at each other in concern and kept walking.

When we entered the kitchen, Bailee was standing in front of the stove on a little stool, making dinner for her two cousins and herself. She was making toast with peanut butter, stirring noodles boiling on the stove. She was seven years old, taking care of two other children. My heart sank as I watched her serving the food, telling her cousins to come eat.

"Do you cook a lot, baby?" I asked in disbelief.

"Oh yeah. Every day," she said as she slapped some noodles on a plate with a heaping pile of butter.

My heart broke. I suddenly understood why she was so grown for her age. She wasn't allowed to be a kid. She was the adult of the house.

"Where's your room?" I asked, trying to sift my way through all the trash on the floor.

"I don't have one," she said. "Mom took it over so I sleep in that chair." She pointed to a torn-down La-Z-Boy with a pile of clothes next to it. The chair had a perfect indent from where her little body slept. Her mom wasn't there. Apparently, she would leave for days on end. Some days Bailee didn't even make it to school.

Choking back tears, I looked at J and whispered, "Baby we can't leave her here like this." He nodded, but he couldn't speak. He was in total shock at how his daughter had been living. He couldn't process how bad it had gotten without him knowing.

We kept looking around that house of horrors. There was a registered sex offender living in a basement with three baby girls living upstairs. Out back, the grass was so high it towered over Bailee's head. They had a sad dog, chained to a post outside, that looked like he hadn't been groomed in years. So much anger welled up inside of me. I could see it in J too.

It was damn near impossible to leave her, and we sat in the car in silence. I know our minds were sharing the same thought: *How had it gotten this bad for Bailee's mom? What had all those girls been through?* I desperately wish we could have saved them all.

We stayed silent as we pulled away. We both knew in our hearts what was going to come next. We'd been married just a few weeks, and real life had settled in on us fast and furious.

When we finally got back to the hotel, we both agreed it was time to lawyer up. I had a small amount of money to my name and I put it in J's hand.

"This should be enough for a retainer. I'll make more in the next few days. Let's just lock down a lawyer now."

And he did. Within an hour, he found one of the best family lawyers in Nashville and hired her.

XO

WE WERE STAKED OUT IN a hotel, but we knew the next thing that needed to happen was getting a stable home. The only problem was both of us had zero credit. I made money easily, so that wasn't a problem, but this was about being able to get a place in a neighborhood nice enough to raise this baby. So, while I worked out of another room in that hotel, J hustled playing shows. In a few weeks, we put enough money together to lock down an apartment in West Nashville. We needed someone to cosign for us, but we got that money together ourselves.

I was *so* excited. Not only was this going to be a home for J's daughter, but it was our first place together. We were really going to do this. Unsurprisingly, I kept my penthouse in Vegas. I didn't want to put all my eggs in one basket just yet.

We started collecting furniture for our new little condo and decorating a room for Bailee. We filled it with all the things for little girls that we could afford and hoped she'd like it.

Bailee would sometimes come over and visit, but she would never stay for long. She was very attached to her life at her house—even if it was piled high with trash and neglect, it was all she ever knew. Sometimes when she was supposed to stay the night, she would end up calling one of her grandparents to come get her. I didn't realize it then: That baby girl wasn't used to sleeping in a bed. She wanted to sleep in the chair in the clutter. It had become her comfort.

During the next few months, we dealt with lawyers to present our case as to why we were filing for full custody. Taking her away from her mother was not something we wanted to do, but for the sake of Bailee having a real chance at life, it was absolutely necessary. Things were getting worse and worse at home. But getting a court date was impossible.

Until the day we got the phone call. Bailee's mom and stepmom had been arrested for robbing their own next-door neighbor.

XO

WE FILED FOR AN EMERGENCY ex parte order to get full custody. That little girl had suffered enough.

The transition wasn't easy, to say the least.

Bailee felt betrayed by us. She hated us. She felt like we'd taken her from her mom, and at eight years old, her mind couldn't comprehend why. To her, we were the bad guys—and her mom did a great job of manipulating her every chance she got. Even though we were granted full custody, we never wanted Bailee to lose her relationship with her mother. So even though her mom was trapped in her addiction, she was still allowed access to Bailee anytime she wanted. She could call from jail and they bonded as she served her time.

Some people have negative reactions when I talk about Bailee publicly. But everything I say, she has said herself or has given me approval to mention. And I think it's imperative to talk about her childhood honestly—this is her reality and our family's reality. And I want the whole damn world to know how hard she's fought to become the little star she is. That child is a warrior.

Back then, Bailee's health was awful. She was fully malnourished, and she didn't know anything about proper nutrition. She didn't know how to brush her hair. She didn't know how to shower. It was a fight to get her to eat anything but sugar, instant mashed potatoes, or mac and cheese. She kept getting sick—over and over and over—and finally, doctors decided that removing her tonsils might help.

By the time she had surgery, we'd lived together for a couple of months, and I was full-time mom-ing. I wasn't sure that I liked it. It was triggering me every day: *What if I cause this kid trauma? Will she hate me like I hate Mindy?*

I was daydreaming and romanticizing about my old life back in Vegas. I was homesick. My life had been flipped upside down in a matter of months—and it was chock-full of responsibility and monotony—the two things I had managed to avoid completely since I left home at fourteen. Cracks were forming in our marriage.

Women from J's past were resurfacing. Other women in his circle in Nashville hated that he'd gone and gotten married, and they decided to make my life miserable as the new girl in town.

When I say I had to fight for my spot among the females in Nashville, I mean it. Online was a war, too, with people trying to dig up my past and use it against me. One of his baby mamas and her friend showed up to a show to try to fight me. His "best girlfriend" snubbed me. I'll never forget him pulling into the driveway one night and introducing me to a girl he called his best friend. I smiled at her and said hi, and she completely ignored me. To this day, that girl still DMs me, trying to be my friend, and I'll never give her the time of day. When someone shows you who they are the first time, pay attention.

J was going through a battle with one of his ex "managers"—I use that term loosely, because all the guy did was steal from J and make poor business decisions. And in a full-circle moment: that dude used to be best friends with none other than Karma. Dude was also posting my Eros ads and telling everyone J married a prostitute. In those days, I kept my private life private. My online following was growing, but some things still had to be mine.

It was all enough to cause major strain on our relationship. He could feel my mind was elsewhere. He knew I was getting ready to bolt. The pressure was too much.

When the doctor came in after Bailee's tonsil surgery, his words sent shivers down my spine.

"We experienced some complications during surgery. She is so malnourished that her tissues wouldn't clot. She just kept bleeding, so we had to do extra work to cauterize the tissues. She needs better nutrition." He was looking at J and me, judging us profusely. He thought we were the reason this kid was neglected.

"Thank you, sir. We're working on it," J said, embarrassed. "We just got full custody of her."

When we got her home, the recovery was rough. Her little body was fighting with all it had, but she couldn't talk, so she would write out her wants on paper. And sitting there with that sick baby and her father, I started to feel closed in.

And this part of the story still brings me to tears. It probably always will.

XO

J AND I WERE ARGUING more than we ever had, and I was scared of falling into another relationship like all the ones I had been in so many times before.

I woke up a few mornings after her surgery and packed all my stuff. I told J I was leaving, and he didn't try to stop me. I didn't realize then that he'd dealt with so much loss in his life, that he didn't chase things, even if it hurt him to let things go.

I was so overwhelmed. I just couldn't do this life of being a mom and a wife while fighting for a spot in the life of the man I loved against all the people who had an opinion about me and us—all on top of newfound sobriety.

Today I know that to my core, I'll never abandon my family. But that day, I did.

I could make up a million excuses for why I left, but it just boils down to fear. I was scared out of my damn mind.

I left J in that apartment with his daughter and drove for two days by myself back to Vegas. I didn't know what I was doing. I didn't have a plan. By the time I got to Memphis J had sent a text.

please don't go

It was too late. I wanted to see the neon lights.

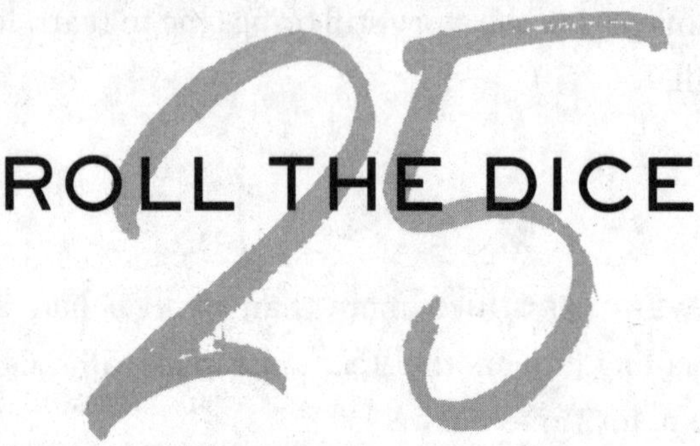

ROLL THE DICE

Finally, back in Vegas, I walked into my apartment and collapsed on the couch. I was exhausted from the drive, but I couldn't shake the feeling that I'd made the wrong decision. Part of me felt like I gave up my independence and changed my life so quickly for a man that it made me run away, but another part of me felt like I fulfilled my promise to J and helped him get his daughter and create a safe place for them to live together, and that I owed it to him to be there. Plus, the quiet in that penthouse was eerie. And for the first time in my life, I felt like I didn't belong there.

I took a couple of days to sit in silence and really sift through my thoughts about what I wanted out of life. J and I were still talking, and he understood where all my anxieties were coming from. He, too, was feeling exactly how I felt—the pressure of being a husband and dad and the noise of everyone around us. If I had just communicated with him back in Nashville, we probably could have worked through it. I owned that.

Neither one of us knew how to be parents, or spouses. We had no fucking clue what we were doing and we both were scared shitless. So we decided to raise Bailee in Vegas, to get away from all the bullshit and gossip. Bailee could still talk to her mom on the phone every day, and we could have a fresh start without the Nashville baggage.

But I knew we needed space. My two-bedroom penthouse would have us climbing the walls. I found a mini mansion with five bedrooms—Bailee even had her own living room *and* bedroom. J flew out to Vegas to meet me, and we went and looked at this huge house together.

"Baby, we can't afford this," he said, looking around in disbelief.

"I got us, I promise," I said. "I'll work and make the move-in, and then we can just split the rent. There's a private school right up the street for Bailee."

We were flying by the seat of our pants and living above our means. It was written all over his face. But it only made me want to work harder and prove to him that no matter what, I had him. It was my way of apologizing for abandoning Bailee and him. It was my way of saying *I'm in this for good now.* Actions, not words.

Reluctantly, J agreed, and we signed the lease. As promised, I came up with the move-in fees. Before we flew Bailee out, I made sure to go all out for her living room and bedroom to make her comfortable in her own space. Her little area was so fly, *I* wanted to hang there.

We had a friend fly with Bailee after the house was furnished. When Bailee walked in, her mouth dropped.

"This place is huge!" she yelped, and J and I smiled like proud parents. We ushered her upstairs to her area to show her what was hers. She shrieked with glee and went through everything in awe.

That night, we started getting her ready to sleep in her new bed, but she wanted to sleep on the couch. This is when I finally realized that she wasn't comfortable sleeping in a bed—she wanted her chair. Needless to say, it was a fight to get her to sleep in a bed, but she eventually learned. Nowadays, we can't get that teenager out of bed.

XO

NEXT, WE GOT BAILEE INTO that private school and tried to start getting her on a regular schedule. I was raised in a house that was nothing but rules and schedules, and J was raised in a house where there was no responsibility and no schedule. I could see early on that Bailee craved structure and routine, so I got her on a strict schedule. Everything was timed down to a tee. Bailee and J bucked and fought me on it a lot, but because of how I was raised, I thought this was the only way. It would take years of this parenting adventure to learn my biggest lesson: compromise.

I signed Bailee up for everything. Piano, guitar, theater, dance team. I was one of *those* moms. I just wanted her to thrive and have a chance to find something she liked and was good at. I didn't realize I was doing what Bill and Mindy had done to me by not giving her any free will or control over her life. Granted, parents are supposed to guide and help children find their purpose, but how can they find their purpose when they're under their parents' thumb 24-7?

Bailee and I have parallel stories. Both of our moms were drug addicted, both moms abandoned us, both dads did the best they could but also had to work through their own issues, and we were both forced to grow up too quickly.

If there is anyone in this life besides J that I have to thank for helping me heal, it's this little girl. Seeing so much of myself in her made me want to be a better "mom" for her. A better person for her. Bailee has helped us both learn how to be parents and sometimes I feel bad because she had to grow up with us.

XO

ONCE WE GOT BAILEE SETTLED, we had to get back to work—which meant touring and doing shows for J and seeing clients for me. We hired a nanny who was close to the family. Leaving wasn't for months at a time anymore. We were parents, and there was someone else we had to think about.

The first *Waylon & Willie* album—the album J and his best friend, Struggle, first released—was written in our Vegas house. Struggle and the crew would come down and stay in the house for weeks at a time. J was surrounded by his friends so he wouldn't get too homesick. And then we would venture out on tour and come straight back. This was our new norm, or so I thought.

All of a sudden J decided to pull the plug.

I never saw it coming.

XO

WHILE WE WERE GETTING SETTLED, one of J's ex-flings came back around. She was hanging with Struggle's daughter. I couldn't wrap my head around why she was welcome in our circle, and everyone was fine with it. I didn't want my insecurities to overshadow our relationship and the family we were working so hard to build, so I pushed them to the back of my mind and focused on family life. I had let my past trauma from Karma seep too much into our relationship already. Even if J and I argued a lot, it was nothing like my past relationships. I didn't think I had anything to worry about. I should have known with his supposed "best friend" around, it was about to be some bullshit. But instead of bashing Struggle, I'll just simply say my husband has been the *best* friend to that man, that man has *never* been a best friend to my husband. I'll leave it at that—until later on in the story.

So imagine my shock when J told me he had decided to take Bailee and move back to Nashville. We had been together in Vegas for only five months. When I asked him why, he gave me every excuse except for the real one: He was talking to his ex behind my back. Not a baby mama, but this young girl he was seeing briefly before he and I hooked up. I'd felt it but couldn't prove it. But I'd also felt his pain. The wounds that were deep inside him, left to fester, unhealed, and I could see how neither of us had really learned how to love.

"You can come, too, if you want," he said, but it was clear that he didn't really want that. By then, I was committed to J and willing to work through anything. I told myself he was just homesick. I'd left, too, partially because I was homesick. I understood it. I wasn't going to abandon our little family ever again.

So I started packing up our Vegas house and trying to find a home in Nashville in the area where J wanted to raise Bailee. After everything, I was going to have to be a Nashville girl after all, whether I wanted to or not. But I didn't care. This was my family, and whatever we had to do, I would do.

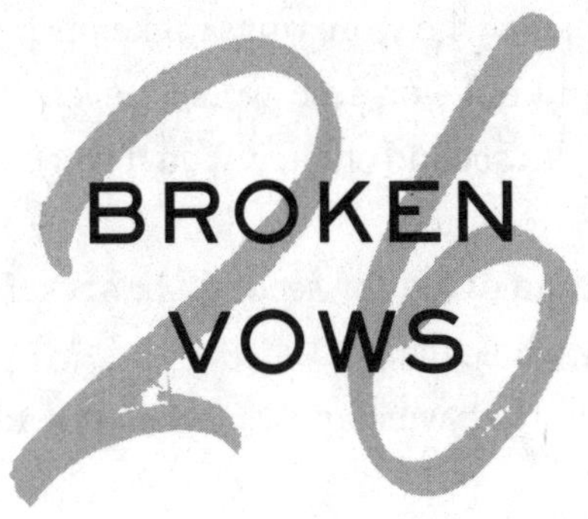

26 BROKEN VOWS

NOW BEFORE I GET INTO THIS CHAPTER, I WANT TO say that it's not in this book for any other reason than to show y'all how hard we have worked to be together—and all the things we've overcome. Will some people judge me for going back? Sure. But I don't give a fuck. It doesn't mean I'm weak, and it doesn't mean he is a horrible person. It means that we were two people who fell in love but didn't know how to maintain love in healthy ways.

We were two strangers who rushed to the altar in 2016 and became parents of a traumatized seven-year-old in 2017. Fully sober in 2018. It's enough to make anyone's head spin. We both were still carrying lifetimes of trauma on our backs.

Is it an excuse for his behavior? Absolutely not. But I do pride myself on being able to see both sides of the coin and put myself in another person's shoes. I'm also pretty fuckin' self-aware and can admit to my own faults in the beginning of our marriage. And I do believe that in some way, it was my karma for all the homes I contributed to wrecking in my previous career. The amount of my clients who wore rings make my heart hurt for the women who found out—or even worse, never did. Bottom line: Everyone deserves a second chance. And if you don't believe that, that's your story. Not mine.

But man, I thank God for second chances. Lord knows I've needed them my whole life.

Mmkay, now that we've gotten that out of the way, let's carry on.

J hadn't had a healthy relationship in his whole life, and I sure as hell hadn't. In those years, J, Bailee, and I were just three strangers, all trying to figure out how to be a family together.

Part of healing is figuring out what's in our control and what's not—and that almost always we create relationship dynamics and drama *together*. And I know now what I couldn't see then: The breakdown J and I were hurtling toward at this point wasn't a simple story of a villain and a victim. I brought all my baggage into our relationship—my bruises and the weight of getting sober and learning to regulate my own nervous system. I can't begin to tell you what J was feeling about me then—and how hard we were struggling to fight through his own individual trauma.

If we're far from perfect now, we were even farther then. But we both deserved grace with each other, and I thank God for our castles burning to the ground. It brought us so much closer and led us to healing. It made me realize that we can go through hell and still come out with our halos unscathed.

XO

THE TRIP BACK TO NASHVILLE with all our shit in the back was absolute hell. J was so mean to me the entire way. He made it clear that he did not want me with him. I couldn't figure out why, and it only made me cling to him more. When we finally made it back to Nashville, we tried to settle down after the chaos of the move.

But I knew something was off. You know how we women are—our gut instincts never let us down. And for the most part, I'm no square. I love to have fun with my husband in the bedroom, and inviting other women into our bed was never an issue. I thought my openness and willingness to have third parties would save me from all the other cheating I'd experienced in my life—even Bill, who couldn't stay faithful. Men want variety, right? When J and I first got together, I was a hooker who saw nothing but men cheating on their wives. Pastors, lawyers, celebrities—anyone with a penis was unfaithful. J was used to having multiple relationships at the same time with different women. So when we first got together, we both frowned upon monogamy. That's not to say that we agreed to go fuck whoever we wanted whenever we wanted—to me that's what an open relationship is, and we aren't in one. But if a girl wanted to come home with us, we more than likely wouldn't turn her down. Now, here comes the part that might surprise you. J has always told me that I can sleep with other men if I want to. At first, that hurt me, because I felt like he didn't really love me if he wasn't possessive and jealous. We argued about it many times until I finally just accepted the fact that that's who he is. I'm not going to try to change him into something he's not—and I started to agree with him. We both live by the motto that we aren't each other's possessions and consider our relationship to be free, not open. Free will. Which means: I'll give you the world sexually, but don't fucking lie to me or ever let me be the last to know something.

Glad we got that out. Now back to the story.

His ex was still hanging around Struggle's family—and it was now suspicious. I knew in my heart something was going on, but

I didn't want to admit it. Cheating has been a constant in every relationship I've had, and I truly wanted to believe J was different. Again, just don't lie.

For a year, this girl tormented me online. She would quote his song lyrics, she would post pictures wearing his merch, she would take cheap shots at me in her captions because she knew I was onto her. I just couldn't prove it.

J and I had moved into a cute house in an upscale part of Nashville to give Bailee a fresh start. Again. And I swore to myself this time that I wouldn't move out of Nashville until she graduated high school. I was fully committed to her father and—more important—to her. But the fights between us were getting so bad. I could *feel* his attention elsewhere, and anytime I'd bring up that girl's posts, he would gaslight the shit out of me and make me feel crazy for doubting him.

He would also leave and disappear for days on end whenever we had fights. He'd go stay at Struggle's house. *Insert long, dramatic eye roll here.* Can you tell I don't care for him in the slightest?

I was so desperate to figure out what was going on with us that I talked J into couples' therapy—which turned out to be a fucking nightmare. We went to a husband-and-wife duo. J and I thought it would be perfect: a male and a female opinion. Those poor people. They had no idea what kind of shitstorm came barreling into their office that day.

J and I sat next to each other, explaining the issues we were having, and at some point, a screaming match broke out between us. Nobody else could get a word in edgewise because we were at each other's throat, screaming at the top of our lungs. When the lady finally did calm us down, we both just walked out of the therapy session and went our separate ways. It was probably one of the lowest points in our relationship.

The fighting and suspicion went on for ten months until shit finally hit the proverbial fan and splattered all over the place.

XO

I GOT MY HANDS ON J's phone, and I wouldn't give it back to him during another one of our heated arguments. He had a total meltdown—and right then, I knew something was up. We screamed until he left—with Bailee. I was left alone in a house in the middle of a city I had just moved to for him.

I lay in bed for two weeks. I couldn't even shower. Then, after being depressed for weeks, I had to fly out to San Diego to see one of my sugar daddies and make some money. All so I could afford another cross-country move.

But when I walked through the front door on the night I got back from that trip, my heart sank. The house was all packed up, with J and Bailee's stuff moved out. No explanation. No goodbye. Just gone. I was furious at what he'd done to Bailee—uprooting her again. That child just needed some stability, and he and I couldn't get it right, and she'd bear the consequences.

I dropped to my knees and bawled. I couldn't figure out what I had done wrong. Didn't I deserve a conversation face-to-face? To be treated like a human being?

XO

ONE NIGHT WHILE I WAS lying there trying to piece everything together, I saw J was playing a show locally and decided to show up just to see him and hopefully talk. I wanted so badly to be near him. He would call me every other day from a blocked number, and we would speak, but the conversations always ended with him hanging up on me or me getting mad because I was just so frustrated with being lied to.

When I showed up, he was irate. He didn't want me there and was mad I would think it was okay to show up unannounced. I found out later that it was because he had his ex-fling waiting for him in a hotel room down the street.

Standing there without J, I told Struggle's wife how hurt I was.

"If he's cheating on me, I wish he'd just tell me go back to Vegas," I said.

She looked me in my eyes and spoke as calmly as she could.

"Bunnie, you need to go back to Vegas." I guess being honest with me is the least she could do after letting my husband have an affair under her roof. She'd confirmed all the suspicions and fears I'd felt for the past ten months. I left that bar immediately, went home, called my best friend, Monica, to fly out and help me drive cross-country again, with two vehicles, a twenty-six-foot U-Haul, and two dogs.

That night I contemplated taking my life. The pain was so intense that I genuinely just wanted to end it all. I went into my bathroom and grabbed a bottle of pills I had stashed in case of an emergency and held them in my hand. I stared at the bottle, wondering what it would feel like to die from an overdose. Would it hurt? Would I just fall asleep? What if it didn't work and I woke up in a hospital? Would J even care if I was dead?

I took a deep breath.

Tomorrow is a new day. Time to get the fuck out of here. Lights out.

XO

IN ONE OF OUR CONVERSATIONS, J and I agreed to do a three-month separation before announcing anything, but most importantly, before telling Bailee. That's all that really mattered to me. She had already been through so much with us in such a short time.

I didn't tell J I was moving back to Vegas. I knew he was cheating—I just couldn't prove it. It was hard to just pack up and leave, but at that point, I felt so unwanted and disrespected, all I could think to do was run.

As I drove down the highway toward Vegas, my cell started blowing up with messages.

I'm sorry sis

Are you ok

Bunnie I'm praying for you

What the fuck was happening? *Why are people texting me this all at once?* And then it hit me like a punch to the gut. I logged into Instagram and saw a post where J announced our breakup.

Are you fucking kidding me? We had an agreement. After all the confusion, all the arguments, all the heartbreak—that was the last straw for me with J. I vowed never to speak to him again.

I didn't know why we'd broken up. I knew I was a nightmare to deal with because of all the shit I brought into the relationship, but I knew in my heart I didn't deserve any of this. At least a heads-up would have been nice. I posted the Joker clapping in my story to say *You're a fucking clown.* And I left it at that.

I was fucking *mad.* And when I get mad, I get motivated.

XO

THE NEON LIGHTS OF VEGAS never looked prettier than after driving for days with two dogs and living in and out of motels and on gas-station food. I was genuinely sick. Lovesick. Heartbroken. It was so bad, I would probably have snorted an eight ball of lidocaine to just numb the pain.

I wanted to forget it all and put it behind me. Folks started DMing on social media telling me that J was with his ex-fling. The pieces started fitting together, and it made it much easier to disconnect from him.

I started looking for houses in Vegas to create my new bachelorette pad, all while making sure to make any twinge of heartache I'd feel turn into hatred. I had gone completely silent on everything and didn't attempt to reach out to J or answer any calls. Word got back to him that I left town. Deep down inside, he didn't think I'd really go.

So at night when he would drink, he would text me—finally using his real number. I didn't reply. What was the point? I didn't want to argue. I didn't want to cry. So I just ignored him.

He recorded and dropped his album *Waylon & Willie 2*—have you ever listened to those songs? Go give it a listen, and you'll clearly hear a man smack-dab in the middle of an affair, pouring his guilt into lyrics. Try having to sit side stage while listening to the man you love sing these songs night after night. To this day, I still hate most of the songs on that album, and I can't listen all the way through. We'll get there, though.

But after a few days of me not responding to his drunken nighttime messages, he finally texted something that got my attention.

I'll tell you everything. I just want my wife and my family back

My ears perked up. I texted him back immediately.

When and where. I wanted to puke.

I'll come to you, whatever I have to do

We agreed to meet in Vail. It was a place we loved, and it was full of beautiful memories for us.

My nerves were a mess as I stepped off the plane. The drive from the airport was a blur. And when I saw him—I was just so happy. I still loved this man with all my heart, and I just knew no matter what, we would get through it.

We reconnected over the next few days. We laughed, we cried, we talked like the best friends we were. I asked questions, and he was vague. He actually made up a story about a drug dealer's daughter he met at a bar, never admitting it was his ex-fling. So still lying. And I believed him. But he said he was sorry, and that was a start.

XO

AFTER OUR RECONNECTION IN VAIL, J wanted me back in Nashville, and I wanted to be back there too, with my little family. I immediately started looking for a new house for us—because no way in hell was I going back to the old one.

By the time we were back in Nashville, it was Father's Day. We headed out to his father, Buddy's, house.

I absolutely love J's father. He was so accepting of me the minute he met me—even when others weren't. I will cherish that man for as long as I live. Buddy might have had his flaws raising J, but the man I met left such an impact on me. Sadly, this was the last Father's Day that we would spend with Buddy alive, and it tears me up anytime I think about it.

As we walked into Buddy's house, we said hello and hugged everyone. J set his phone down on a table and went to the bathroom. Almost immediately, his phone started blowing up with a random California number. *Who is blowing my husband up?* I took a picture of the phone number, walked outside, and called it.

Ring ring ring.

"Bitch. Why the fuck are you calling my phone?" the girl said. I was shocked.

"Who is this? You're calling my husband."

Click. The girl hung up.

It all hit me. I was filled with rage and hurt—and every other feeling. I'd thought we'd reconnected. I thought he'd been honest. *You got me back to Nashville and you're still talking to this girl? I don't even know who it is.* Trying to contain my pain, I walked into Buddy's house, trying to hold back tears. I ran right into J coming out of the bathroom.

"I just talked to the girl who's been calling your phone," I said.

He turned white and told me not to do this in front of his family. But how could I not? I tried to pull myself together and stay quiet.

"Who is—" And then it hit me. It was *her.* The ex-fling was still in the damn picture, even if he'd sworn up and down that they were done.

Everything I'd gone through with him over the past ten months now made sense. It flashed in front of my eyes: the months of arguing, her posts, him denying anything was happening, her hanging out with his best friend's family—all of the lies.

J was buckling. He told me to hold it together until he could tell his dad goodbye and get Bailee to another family member so we could face it head-on. I was totally dazed, but I finally had proof. I had answers.

From that day on, I didn't want information from him anymore. He had his chance and he squandered it. So I talked to her.

She sent me videos, screenshots, timelines, and told me everything about their ten-month affair. She told me about how he got a house for them to live in and he wanted her to stay at home and take care of Bailee.

And out of everything, that's what made me sick. It wasn't about him fucking this broad—it was about emotionally cheating and then wanting her to play mommy to a little girl I'd fallen in love with. She was *my* baby.

As mad as I was at the girl, I'm thankful she at least had the balls to tell me her truth—even if J says she embellished. But honestly, how could I even really trust that when he told me she was a drug dealer's daughter? How could I trust his best friends? They were all in on it. They covered it up. They had me in their wedding—knowing my husband was fucking this girl on their daughter's bedroom floor the night before. She actually reached out last year, scared that I'd reveal her identity. In that moment, I truly felt for her and promised I'd never let that happen. Promising to protect someone who shattered me? The lessons are never-ending from this shock-wave fiasco.

There were so many times the salt was rubbed deeper into the wound. I had to see those people all the time and be constantly reminded of the shit humans they were then—and even now. I had to watch songs performed onstage that were written about another woman. I had to smile and hug people who lied through their teeth to me and stabbed me in the back. I had to watch these people literally use my husband for years and be told to fuck off anytime I tried to defend him or stand up to them. It was fucking brutal. The betrayal I felt in a new city, new relationship—that's something I don't wish on anyone.

Going through *this* sober was brutal. I truly don't know how I stayed off pills. It's almost like I wanted to feel every ounce of pain so that he could never hurt me that badly again. I wanted to remember how shattered I felt so that it would force me to level up.

When a man puts you through something like that, you

never stop loving them, you just love them differently. Your heart is more guarded. Less trusting. Cracked.

The next few years would prove to be the hardest for me. They say in order to appreciate the light you have to explore the darkness. I never understood that term until I came face-to-face with my own darkness.

You ever shook the hand of a smiling devil?

I was about to.

LOVE LOST, LOVE FOUND

WE SETTLED INTO A QUIET NEIGHBORHOOD IN A suburb outside of Nashville and started getting our lives back on track.

Quiet neighborhood or not, I'm not going to pretend that we just went back to normal. We absolutely did not.

There were many fights and arguments—and they even went to the point of me putting my hands on him. I'm not proud of that—not at all.

We were in the kitchen arguing, and he looked me in the eye and said, "I don't regret it." To my face. And it made me feel homicidal. The only thing I could think of was to throw the dish in my hand at him. The rage was pouring out of me, and I closed-fist punched him on his back, screaming like a wild banshee.

It's ugly, but it's honest. It would take years for me to put the affair aside. It would take years to actually feel like this man loved me—that I wasn't disposable.

I was never big into therapy—especially after the shrinks my parents forced me to see and my *Girl, Interrupted* stay in the mental hospital. I learned at a young age how to manipulate therapists, and I truly never valued any of their advice. That couple's counselor duo. Jackasses. Obviously, there were skeletons in their closets too. I could just feel it on them.

But after everything that had happened—the affair, the abuse, the trauma, addiction, all of it—I went on a quest for knowledge. I wanted to be a better person than I'd ever been. I didn't want to be the girl I was in Vegas. I needed to shed my skin and change. But I had no idea where to start. Therapy was the only tool that I knew might give me some sort of life-coping skills.

I needed them more than ever. We were raising Bailee full time, trying to rebuild our marriage, and make a family together. I wanted to be better for her.

So I started going to counseling. I started to really look back at my life. My husband and I dug deep into the generational toxic traits we'd grown up with. And we talked so many times about how we don't want to just do what we were taught. Now, we were in this *together.* It finally felt so good to have my best friend back and be on this journey to be better humans. When I think back on it, we just made a vow to change. And we did. No matter how hard it got. No matter what the other person said in therapy, we were finally both fully committed to working on ourselves together and separately.

I learned so much in counseling that saved my life. I learned that you have to feel to heal. I learned that when you stop running from your demons is when they stop chasing you. I learned to cry when I needed to cry—that one is still hard for me, but boy when I cry, I sob. It's so cleansing.

I also learned that my anger was really sadness turned outward. I learned how to decipher and untangle the two as they come up. I learned that I didn't need to make everyone around me miserable as a punishment for how I felt.

But most importantly, I learned my feelings were valid. In therapy and in my marriage, I was finally being seen and heard. Funny thing is when you *do* feel seen and heard after never having that feeling your whole life, you become softer, quieter, and less triggered.

J began focusing on his music heavily, and we rented a house down the street that he turned into a studio he could go to anytime. Songwriting was a cathartic way for him to work through his pain, and he threw himself into it. Little did we know that that house would become the birthplace of many of his future hits.

I was still seeing clients and trying to figure out what direction in life I wanted to go. All I've ever known my entire life was how to hustle in the streets, so trying to get out of the adult industry and become a "square"—as I like to call all the normies—just wasn't something I could ever see happening.

J and I started reconnecting as best friends and trying to date each other. We never went through that stage—we'd just hopped on tour with each other and gotten married a month after meeting. We didn't actually know each other. We were strangers who'd made the conscious decision to do life together but didn't know how the other person lived.

It was chaos and healing all at once. And then Buddy fell ill—and it was one of the hardest things I've ever had to watch my husband go through. One day, Buddy was okay, and the next we were getting a phone call that he could not get out of bed.

I'll never forget where we were when that call came. We were on the freeway, driving home after a date day, when Buddy called and said something was wrong. We turned around and hightailed it to his house. When we got there, we walked into a guest room and there he was, poor, sweet Buddy. He was covered in sweat and tears, frustrated because he couldn't sit up by himself or stand.

As J and I scrambled around the house to get him clothes and load him up to get him to a hospital, my heart sank. This was my husband's hero. Buddy had always been a constant figure in J's life.

Donna, J's mom, and Buddy had J later on in life. He was the baby of the siblings and his family lovingly calls him "Baby Jason." His mom struggled with addiction and mental-health issues, and Buddy had his own set of difficulties. But he remained a stable source of male energy J's entire life. Buddy was a special man. I loved him from the start, and I like to think he loved me too. J has always told me his dad stuck up for me numerous times during our arguments, and despite my past, always told J I was a good woman for him. One thing about the Budster: He was a man of few words, but when he spoke, it always meant something.

We finally got him to the hospital and they rushed him back because his vitals were so terrible. Hours went by, and they ran every test. Finally, the doctors came back with a diagnosis. Leukemia. I watched my husband's whole world crumble right there in that hospital room. He didn't cry, but his eyes told me everything. From that moment on, J didn't leave his father's side.

XO

FOR MONTHS, WE WERE IN and out of hospitals and nursing homes. It was a slow, torturous decline. If his dad was in the hospital, J was right there. He would bring a pen and pad and write songs. "Crosses and Crossroads" was written in a hospital waiting room as the one man he idolized was slowly leaving him.

J and I became so much closer during these months. I just wanted to take his pain away and let him know it was okay to hurt. J has never been good at showing emotion, and he buries things deep down inside. It's why he's such a phenomenal writer and musician—everything he writes about contains the emotions he couldn't let himself feel.

I'll never forget when they moved Buddy to hospice. J and his brothers would rotate time with him around the clock. And toward the end, it became so unbearable for J that he would wait in the courtyard outside his dad's window. One day my husband will tell this story when he writes a book, so I've left out a lot. In the end, it's his story to tell.

Buddy left me with the biggest blessing before he passed. I visited him at the hospice facility. That day, he'd been in and out of consciousness and hadn't spoken a word to anyone. But when I walked in, he opened his eyes and lit up. He started chatting away. Of course, it was near the end, so nothing made any sense. But he was *so* happy, and I could feel his spirit trying to tell me something.

I leaned down and I put my hand in his, and when my hand touched his, I was overcome by this beautiful, peaceful feeling. It brought tears to my eyes. And as he held my hand, I saw space and a pink galaxy filled with stars. It was like he was telling me, *Tell my son I'm okay. This is where I'm going.*

I told him I loved him as I pulled myself together enough to run to the parking lot with J behind me. I lost it—out there in the parking lot, I sobbed my eyes out. I told J the feeling and the vision, and he sobbed with me.

It was the last time I saw Buddy, and in March, my husband lost his best friend. To this day, my sweet husband can't talk about losing his dad without crying. I don't think he will ever be able to come to terms with the loss of his father. I'm just thankful that I was able to be by his side. We love and miss you, Buddy, but I always know you're never too far from us. I see you smiling proudly at every milestone you watch your son achieve.

And like the amazing soul you brought into this world, he never lets your memory fade.

28

HELLO, YOU SEXY MOTHERFUCKERS

DO YOU REMEMBER DELILAH? I THINK ALL '90S KIDS had parents who listened to her. Her voice is soft as silk, and her advice is always on point. To this day she takes calls and doles out sweet advice and support to folks who are hurting, playing love songs. She was the first woman on the radio to inspire my journey—way before I even knew what a radio DJ *was*.

When I was a kid, I'd sit in my front yard in Vegas with my battery-operated yellow boom box for hours, scouring the radio for music, listening to how DJs set the tone for their shows, and sometimes, I'd emulate the sounds. I was always locked outside anyway, and the radio became my escape from reality.

When I was older, I entered the era of Bob Larson, a radical evangelist my dad was obsessed with. Bob took calls from anyone dealing with darkness and evil. For hours, I'd listen to him cast demons out of those who called in to be soothed by his prayers and then sent on their way in their newfound glory. Was it fake? Sure—I know that now. But as a little girl, I was rapt.

But of all the radio shows Bill listened to, the one that always held my attention most was the man, the self-appointed king of all media: Howard Stern. Now I know people nowadays have their views on Howard, but the Howard I grew up on was hilarious, cutting edge, and captivating. Of course, I wasn't supposed to listen to him with my parents—but that didn't mean I couldn't eavesdrop from my bedroom.

Back in the day, Howard would go on for hours on end. His interviews with celebrities were always eventful—all the porn stars and his particular blend of crass and hilarious would make your jaw drop. My little-girl self decided I wanted to do what he was doing. I would be Howard Stern mixed with Delilah. Raunchy yet soft. There had to be a way to balance them, right?

When Howard got his own show on the E! Network, it was game over for me. I never missed an episode. I studied him, and I studied his guests. I watched what made them uncomfortable—and I also saw what brought them out of their shells. Paying such close attention showed me that deep down, Howard is a genuinely soft man, but for the cameras, he had to bring out that shock factor. It's what got him the big ratings.

I knew I could do that myself.

XO

BY 2018, I WAS TIRED of the sex industry—and I was also tired of haters trying to "out me" online. People would publicly try to shame me by posting my escort ads from Eros—even posting fake ones on other websites. They would outright lie, and it would enrage me. I didn't have a voice or anything but a small online presence of my own to use to stick up for myself. And we were raising Bailee. *What the fuck am I doing raising this kid around this?* I asked myself. I would go to a call and then come home and play "Mommy"—and I knew that one day, she was going to learn the truth about where I was when I wasn't home.

I knew I would be honest with her when that day came. But I never wanted her to ask, "Why wasn't I good enough for you to stop?"

So I went to my husband with all my concerns, fears, and a plan for what I wanted to do. One thing I love about my husband is how he's always able to see the bigger picture—just like on our first night together. It doesn't matter if it's a picture for years in the future, he sees it.

In those years, a lot of girls like me had gone online as what we called "internet thots." This was way before OnlyFans—most girls were doing private Snapchat. I presented the idea to my husband that I needed to build my own audience—and what quicker way to do that than by getting the attention of men? It would be like my camming days but on a massive, more professional scale. It would be a brand, the start of something much, much bigger. I was nervous as hell. I'd never put myself out there online besides my Eros ads, and I kept my life off social media—as hard as that is to believe now. Sure, I'd been online, but I'd kept things vague and without context. I wasn't making any money from my social media either.

My husband looked me dead in the eye.

"Bunnie, you have the looks. You have the body. Go for it. Build that brand any way you need to, because in the end, it's all for a brighter, bigger future," he said. "You need to start doing sexy photo shoots, you need to start talking to the internet like you do to me, and people will fall in love with your personality." He told me to start a YouTube channel—and that if I was so worried about the people who were trying to shame me, I should get honest. I should tell my story in my own words.

And with my best friend's blessing, I was off and running. I started doing photo shoots. I started vlogging on YouTube, and I started building every social media platform that I could. I even started my own blog called *Confessions of a White Trash Wife*—which shockingly took off immediately.

By 2019, I had built a little bit of a following. I despise the term "influencer"—hell, it wasn't even a word back then. I wasn't an influencer then, and I'm not an influencer now.

I had assumed my following would be mostly male because I was so scantily clad, and, well, because of my previous professional experience. But no. My girls of the interwebs really showed up for me. I've been blessed with a following of mostly females—even when I was doing all my thotiness online. This makes me *so* happy—no offense, fellas, but I'm here for you *and* the girlies.

This was *way* before the big boom of podcasts—all we had was Joe Rogan and *Call Her Daddy* and maybe a handful of others. Nobody even knew how to monetize podcasts yet—that's how new the industry was. But I knew in my heart that I was going to try. No matter how hard I had to work at building my brand, I was going to have my own radio show. That little kid with her yellow boom box wasn't going to give up.

Everybody knows I'm obsessed with Dolly Parton, and her first big radio hit was called "Dumb Blonde." I'd been trying to launch my podcast with a friend of mine who happened to be blonde, so we were going to be the Dumb Blondes. Sadly, my girlfriend couldn't see the vision and she bowed out, leaving me to forge ahead without her. There was only one left, and that is how the *Dumb Blonde* podcast came about.

And it was time for me to speak my truth.

XO

I STARTED MY PODCAST AT my dining-room table. I connected with a platform named Podfly that was an absolute godsend. I had no idea how to set up microphones. I had no idea how to record, but I knew that I was gonna figure it out, and they taught me how to get everything just right so that I could launch my podcast.

I worked my ass off for years before I ever saw a dollar from that podcast. There were so many times that I felt so defeated and like nobody was listening, but it was the only thing that I had that wasn't sex work. I wanted to quit, but it became my baby and my motivation to shed the skin of the old me. I knew one day the hard work was going to pay off. I just didn't know when.

The way that I made money to support my podcast—to be able to travel and do interviews before I had a studio—was still through sex work. When J and I had settled back down to get our lives on track, I didn't have many sugar daddies, but I did have clients and regulars. I poured whatever money I made into building our family and building my brand. I was a one-man band and did it all myself. I would borrow my husband's videographer to video my podcast for me for a small fee so that I had visuals, but other than that, I didn't have a team. I was too scared to let anyone in to help me.

In 2020, the huge podcast boom happened and the market flooded, and I was scared that I would get lost in the shuffle. But if there's one thing I've learned in life, it's that you can't deny hard work. I put my head down and watched as many people started podcasts and ended them. I started to see a pattern—launch with a bang and go out with a whimper. But I knew that if I worked quietly and steadily, I would stand the test of time.

Eventually, I had somebody on my team who believed in the vision as much as I did, and that was my hairdresser, Meme. Well, she *started off* as my hairdresser and somehow morphed into my manager, camera girl, editor, and everything else I could've ever dreamed of. I remember when I looked at her and said, "Meme, I don't have money to pay you right now."

She looked back at me and she said, "It's okay. I got you."

"I promise you one day I'll be able to take care of you and thank you for all you've done," I told her. And I have.

It's rare to find somebody who sees your vision, and Meme was a beacon of light. I can't imagine not having her by my side in this journey. Through every up and down, through every roller-coaster ride, she has always stood by my side—no matter what. Even this book.

XO

ALONG WITH THE PODCAST BOOM, 2020 was also the year my husband's career started taking off, and OnlyFans came on the scene. I was hesitant to join at first—I also didn't know how much money I would make. But again, I sat J down to talk it over.

"I can try it for a month just to see how much money I can make," I said. And my husband—being the ever-gracious, supporting castmate—nodded.

"Go for it," he said. And with his blessing, I did several nude photo shoots and launched my OnlyFans. To my surprise—and *shock*—I made $50,000 the first month. I couldn't believe it. My mind was blown and I wasn't sure I would ever top it. But as the months went by, the money kept growing. I ended up making my first million online on OnlyFans. It later grew to another million and another—and so on.

That success meant I could finally—after a few decades in the lifestyle—retire from taking clients and doing sex work in the streets. Now I could just work online and make a shitload of money—and nobody ever had to touch me.

I funneled that OnlyFans money into my Dumb Blonde empire, secured our own studio, and was finally able to put Meme on a salary. The podcast wasn't making any money yet, but things were finally looking up.

XO

THERE'S BEEN NOTHING BUT BLOOD, sweat, and tears poured into my podcast. I've earned the trust of my guests, and I finally started monetizing the whole thing about four years in. It wasn't a lot at first. But it grew, and I have now turned it into a multimillion-dollar business. In 2022, I was making so much money from the podcast that I was finally able to retire 100 percent from *all* sex work entirely and shut down my OnlyFans.

This was one of the hardest decisions I ever had to make, and I leaned on God. I know that sounds odd. But I had to have faith that the Big Guy wouldn't let me fall on my face. He'd had my back many times before. I had to trust He'd keep me off my back and on my two feet, doing this new career that I truly loved.

And God had me. The minute I got rid of my OnlyFans, my business more than tripled. God made sure to let me know that I made the right decision by no longer selling my body. I'm not shaming anybody who sells their body—not ever. But by the time I retired, I was just done. And for the first time, I was being seen and heard for what I had to say and not how I looked. And it felt damn good.

SUICIDAL

I KNOW IT IS HARD TO BELIEVE, BUT WHILE *DUMB BLONDE* was exploding upward, my mental health was still spiraling downward. I was sober from pills and cocaine, but I did continue to drink—even if it made me feel terrible. I still needed some sort of vice to get me through coming off pills. But drinking only made my hangxiety (the fucking killer anxiety/hangover combo) the next day that much worse. I didn't have Xanax to bring me back to baseline.

It wasn't until 2018 that I once again went cold turkey on the booze. The turning point was one night at my husband's show with four Belvederes on the rocks, getting completely annihilated—and everything that happened next.

By the time J got onstage, I was beyond drunk. It wasn't like me. I was a professional drinker, and alcohol didn't affect me like that. By the time my husband finished his set, I was totally gone. The lights were on, but nobody was home.

It was so bad, he decided it was time to get me home. The drive was a blur and I don't remember any of it. The memories start again when I got home and stripped off my clothes and climbed into bed *unshowered.* Anyone who knows me knows that I've got major OCD about such things—and that's a complete no-no. But clean or not, I next tried to slither my way all over the bed, being sexy for my husband. He watched in horror as I started puking all over our bed while crawling on all fours, butthole-in-the-air naked. Common sense me would have run to the bathroom, but not this sloshed-up orangutan. Nope, I happily relieved my nausea all over our pillows.

My husband somehow got me from the bed to our living-room couch, where he placed a trash can for me on the floor. Next thing I remember, I opened my eyes and found my husband sleeping on the living-room floor next to me. This was pretty unusual—he's a big dude, and sleeping on any floor is so uncomfortable for him. But when he finally woke me up the next morning, he told me why he'd slept down there. He said I was so messed up that he was scared I'd stop breathing in my sleep. He wanted to be right next to me in case anything happened during the night.

I truly believe I was drugged that night—it was so far beyond my usual drunkenness. And the sight of him on the floor, checking my breathing, on top of the image of me on all fours puking, was enough to make me swear off drinking alcohol forever. I was sick of myself. It was the last vice I needed to check off my list.

When I got sober from alcohol, the real battle of healing my brain and body began. I'd been pill-free, but alcohol is just as damaging. That newfound sobriety piled onto the existing stress—the affair and my father-in-law passing. And *those* stresses had been piled on top of what I was already dealing with: the intense anxiety I had battled with my whole life because of my childhood, and PTSD from my abusive relationship. The affair pushed me toward a nervous breakdown.

By the time I got fully sober, I was scared to drive. I was scared to leave my house, and I couldn't even meet a friend for dinner. I was a prisoner inside my own mind and body. So I started looking for answers.

Research on breast implant illness had started surfacing. Women were getting their breast implants removed to relieve pain of all kinds. My left implant was swollen and lumpy. It hurt like hell to the touch, and it was three times the size of my right breast. I knew something was wrong, and I desperately wanted to blame all my mental-health issues on my implants. I just wanted to feel better.

So that year, I had them both removed. Afterward, the surgeon told me that when he went in to remove my implants, he saw that my left implant—the swollen, painful one—had folded itself in half and caused scar tissue to form. I am certain that being kicked in my implants—and *all* the abuse I endured—played a part. Pictures showed the scar tissue was pretty much the same size as my 36 DD implant. That *had* to have contributed to how terrible my mental health was and how I was feeling, right? I could only hope.

As I was healing with my new Franken-titties, I started researching vitamin regimens and holistic wellness. I was trying to figure out how to heal my body from the inside out, but I could still see how broken I was. I'll never forget looking in the mirror after my ex-plant and being in shock at how mangled my breasts looked. But somehow, I just knew they'd heal. They did—they're beautiful, perky, natural Cs now.

In January 2020, I was about to turn forty. I was finally learning how to heal—spiritually, physically, and emotionally. J and I were rebuilding our marriage and our family. Therapy was giving me tools to cope with my past and create a different future. I was sober, experimenting with vitamins, and being better to my body.

But two weeks later, tragedy struck our house one more time.

XO

WE GOT A CALL ON the morning of January 16, 2020, and jumped into our car. By the time we found the hospital where my husband's best friend, Chizzle, had been taken, we were too late. He was gone. It was another moment of seeing the sadness fill my husband's eyes while he only offered a quiet reaction: "Oh." But he was in so much pain. We both were. We were devastated.

The whole way home, we sat next to each other in silence. This death would be another dark cloud we'd have to walk through unwillingly. Chizzle's funeral was scheduled a few days after my birthday, and we went hand in hand.

We approached the open casket. It would be the last time we ever saw Chizzle. Overcome with grief, I touched his lifeless body in the casket and just sobbed.

"Oh, Chizzle," I wailed. I stroked his chest. It was just automatic—I didn't think about it. I didn't realize the spiritual mistake I'd made.

XO

A FEW DAYS LATER, I woke up with a feeling of heaviness in my body—and a sadness like I'd never felt before. But sitting with my thoughts was so overwhelming, I made myself venture out of the house. I made an appointment to go tanning. It was worth a shot.

As I lay in the tanning bed, I was overcome with this feeling of eternal sadness. It was like I'd died and knew I'd never be able to come back. Lying under those lights, I saw myself in a vision. I put the barrel of a gun in my mouth. I pulled the trigger.

What I saw was so graphic and overwhelming that I jumped out of the tanning bed. I threw my clothes on as fast as I could. With tears in my eyes, the only thing I could think to do was drive to the nearest hospital. I knew that I was about to hurt myself—and if I didn't go to the hospital, my life would be over.

In the hospital lot, I parked and reached into my purse for my emergency bottle of Children's Benadryl. I took a sip and called the only person I knew wouldn't judge me. My mom.

I bawled and screamed to her in fear, and she calmly talked me down. She listened to me. And in that moment, I finally realized why girls say "I need my mom." For the first time, *finally,* she showed up as my mother. She calmed me down enough that I could drive home. I went straight to my bedroom and lay down in the dark. At some point, I'd called J to tell him what had happened, but I didn't know where he was or when I'd see him.

When he made it home, he quietly came into the room, lay down next to me in the dark, and held me. Just him, the silence, and our heartbeats. It was everything I needed, and I don't think he even realizes how much that meant to me. How much it *still* means to me. The two people I needed to show up for me in that moment did. And there's nothing more beautiful in life.

XO

I HAD NEVER EXPERIENCED DEPRESSION—only anxiety—so this was a new monster for me to meet. I had always prided myself on having anxiety and not knowing what depression felt like. I even thought maybe depression was fake—until the moment I felt that eternal sadness for myself.

At the same time, I began having excruciating pains during my period and blood clots just falling out of me, so I went to my gynecologist for an ultrasound. I lay on the table with my feet up, and when she looked at the screen, she raised her eyebrows.

"It looks like you're trying to pass a sac of some sort," she said, and instantly I just knew. I was having a miscarriage. At this point, nothing shocked me anymore.

Can I prove that touching Chizzle's lifeless body sent me on this downward spiral? No. But I do know that my depression didn't start until after I did—and given how spiritually in tune I am, it seems entirely logical that his body would have an impact on mine.

To this day, I refuse to touch an expired body for fear of having those same feelings come through me. But I also know that I've experienced enough trauma to lead me down the depressive path—I'm not delusional. Maybe Chizzle's death was the straw that broke the camel's back and sent me into a nervous breakdown.

The darkness stayed with me for years. It was so bad that I had to make sure we didn't have guns I could get to, because I was so scared of picking one up and blowing my brains out. To this day I still won't allow guns in our house unless they're carried by our security team.

I don't wish depression on my worst enemy, and I'll take a panic attack over depression any day. I'd rather be scared to die than scared to be alive. It took years and years of research, going to therapy, and taking vitamin cocktails to get my brain feeling better. I went on an extreme spiritual journey—but a truly rewarding one.

I've learned that bloodwork is the road map to health. So now every December and January, I do multiple bloodwork panels to check my hormones, vitamin deficiencies, and other things—so I can stay on top of my mental and physical health.

I also learned that the gut is your first brain and that depression starts there. If you're not feeding your body the correct foods your mind will feel like shit too. In my journey to understanding my body, I even found out that I have the MTFHR gene mutation—which means my body can't really process folate and

B vitamins. No wonder drugs always made me so damn sick. Because of the mutation, my body doesn't metabolize things properly, and my nutrient absorption is affected. Before I knew anything about my mutation, I went and overdosed on B_{12} and vitamin D trying to make myself whole. Don't say this journey didn't have wrong turns.

But most importantly, I spent a year working intensely with my current therapist, Glenn Cohen. I met with him weekly and he taught me how to meditate and redirect my thoughts. He guided me as I worked through much of the emotional pain I carried with me as a child, teenager, and adult. He also taught me how to create new neural pathways in my brain—which I desperately needed after the abuse.

That battle was long and hard won. It meant healing my body, my mind, and my spirit—and committing to healing for the long haul.

Remember: It doesn't matter how healthy you try to make yourself. If your soul isn't sitting right, everything else is null and void.

Through the years I've changed my mental health significantly and I praise Jesus every day that I don't feel that darkness like I once did. Not to say it doesn't show up occasionally here and there when I'm stressed or my hormones are out of whack. But the suicidal ideation has slowly turned to OCD and obsessive thoughts I've learned to control.

OCD has always been a part of my life. So it's like a second skin to me. But by accepting this about myself, I have learned to harness my thoughts and redirect them. This doesn't mean I've conquered them. I've done full-on meet and greets with gloves and masks on because of my fear of germs and sweaty hands. But I've slowly opened myself up more and more to things because I've learned that for me, the exposure helps me to change.

I cut out sugar almost two years ago and it's made a vast difference in my anxiety, depression, and OCD. Trust me, some days a big chewy brownie would make my day. But then the panic attack that ensues after would make it all a lesson learned. I'll leave you with this. I don't ever feel like I am fully healed. I feel like life is a journey of healing and undoing trauma that we never asked for. But the beautiful part is once we learn to harness our power and take back control of our emotions and thoughts, it's like a butterfly spreading its wings for the first time. You get addicted to the feeling of learning, applying, and achieving. I truly believe everyone deserves to feel this way in life.

30 EPIPHANIES

WHEN WE LEFT OFF WITH MY MADRE, I VISITED HER in Indiana when I was with what's-his-name. For years, we maintained our relationship over the phone and via social media. She called me and comforted me when I was suicidal. I didn't physically see my mom again until April 2022, when I got a call from a doctor in Indiana.

"Alisa? I'm your mother's doctor. She's alone and on a ventilator. If you want to say goodbye to her, now's the time." I knew she had been sick; my mom was prone to pneumonia, so her going to the hospital was never a big to-do.

But I was shocked when I heard she was on a ventilator and I needed to come say goodbye. I didn't even pause to think. I just knew I wasn't going to let my mom die alone—no matter what our relationship was like. She deserved someone there holding her hand. After all, in my darkest times since we reconnected, she'd been there for me.

I hopped in my car and drove four hours from Nashville to sit by her side. She was in a run-down hospital in a gloomy little town. I walked in and examined her hands. They were so swollen, but they looked just like mine. *So that's where I got these sausage fingers,* I giggled to myself. I stroked her gray hair and kissed her forehead and whispered softly.

"Hey, Mama. I'm here."

The next couple of days were a lot of her heart monitor beating, me talking to her, playing her classic rock, and talking to the nurses and doctors who came to check on her. Each one told me it wasn't looking good and she wasn't going to make it

I cried a few times to her and said things I'd held in forever about how my childhood had played out after she abandoned me and what it felt like not having my mom in my life.

But the next day, with odds stacked against her, the old bird woke up. The doctors decided to do a test to lower her medication to see if she could breathe on her own and wake up by herself. They did, and as I sat beside her, she started moving her fingers. Then her legs. I got so excited I jumped up.

"Mom!" I said, quiet but excited.

Her big beautiful blue eyes opened slowly. My mom had the prettiest, most piercing blue eyes I ever saw. She was too groggy to realize it was me beside her, and it took her a few hours to fully wake up, but eventually the ventilation tube came out of her throat. I sat at the end of her bed talking, but she just stared at me blankly. It was almost as if she had no idea who I was. I knew she was on heavy amounts of medication so I assumed she was confused.

My aunt—my mom's best friend—heard the good news and came right away. She walked in the room and my mom lit up and started chatting away like they hadn't missed a beat. In the middle of the chat, she leaned over to my aunt and pointed at me.

"Who is that?" she asked.

"That's your daughter, Alisa," my aunt chuckled.

"Aww, hell, honey! I didn't know that was you!" she yelped and held out her arms for a hug. Maybe I should have cried that she didn't recognize me after I'd tried so hard, but to be honest, I couldn't find any more pain in me. I'd let go of expectations with her. I just shook my head and laughed.

A few days passed, and things were looking up. I knew in my heart that her going back to that house was a no-go. I also knew that if I asked her to move to Nashville, it would be a fight. But this time, I wasn't going to take no for an answer. "Come to Nashville," I told her. "Let me take care of you."

Business was booming for Dumb Blonde, and I'd built a decent life for myself alongside my husband. A part of me felt like this was my chance to do more healing when it came to my relationship with her. And at this point in my life, bring it the fuck on. I wasn't scared of anything.

XO

TO MY SURPRISE SHE SAID yes. I'd get what I affectionately called "custody" of my mother—I became her POA (power of attorney) for all her medical care. After years of being rebellious and not accepting my offers of help, she was finally ready. Before she could change her mind, I arranged for her to be driven by ambulance from Indiana to Nashville and right into a glam nursing home with apartments for seniors. This place was *fancy*! Chefs, card-game nights, and karaoke. I had big dreams for Mom when she came to Nashville. Meme, her husband, and I all pitched in to make her apartment the cutest, coziest space. I wanted her to be happy and feel welcome.

Unfortunately, my mom had other plans. In true Vanessa fashion, she wasn't fully honest about how bad her health was and how much she had given up on life. She had become such a recluse that she'd been bedridden for a year already and entirely given up on walking. I didn't find out she couldn't walk until we got to Nashville. Her muscles just didn't work anymore. She needed oxygen full time for the COPD she battled.

When I asked why she hadn't walked in over a year, she told me she just didn't want to be alive anymore.

"Why?" I asked.

"I'm tired," she said.

I knew that feeling all too well. I had battled my way out of a depression not so long ago. All I could think of was how to get her motivated and happy again. I had brought in a therapist to help her walk. I visited at least three or four times a week. I pushed her to try the activities with the other residents and even eat dinner down in the restaurant—but she just wouldn't. She wanted to sit in her recliner in her room.

At first, I really tried to understand. And since I'd never eaten a meal with my mom I ordered take out and we sat on her couch for our first dinner together—ever—as mom and daughter. It was a special moment for me, and I hoped there would be many more.

As the days passed, I learned more about her side of the family, which was fascinating. I hadn't known anything about either side of my family because it's all just so broken. My dad never spoke of his parents, and Mom only spoke of hers one night.

She told me I was a product of white trash Kentucky witches. There were seven sisters, and one of them, my aunt Bunnie, always dressed in full glam, big fur coats, and fake eyelashes. My mom told me I reminded her of Bunnie so much. How had I never known about her? Bunnie was my entire brand—my whole persona. I'd never known she existed.

My mom told me how all the women on her side of the family had spiritual gifts. They all, including herself, were riddled with anxiety because they didn't know how to deal with the feelings of such powerful spirituality. This was the first time I understood my mom. She was speaking my language. She was describing feelings I had known my entire life.

As the weeks went on, I kept trying harder to push her out of her shell and get her walking again and feeling better. I just wanted her to have the best life she could now that we were finally connecting. It was the least I could do for her.

But old habits die hard. My mother refused to help herself in any way. I opened up, only to realize that I couldn't trust my mother fully. I was disappointed in the expectations I had of a woman I barely knew. It was heartbreaking, but it was reality.

XO

I GOT A CALL FROM the nursing home. My mom's oxygen had started slowly declining again, and an ambulance was needed. I went to the hospital, and immediately there was talk about intubation. This time, my mom refused. Who was I to force her to be intubated? I stood by her decision.

One of the doctors pulled me in the hallway and told me there was no way she could go back to the senior home. She needed to be in a 24-7 medical facility. She needed constant care. I transferred her to a facility that could give her the care she needed.

But she was miserable, bedridden, and done. Mentally, she had already checked out, and visiting her became tough for me. It was devastating to have so much hope for someone—and watch them not have hope for themselves. Soon, my mother began to stir the pot, wreaking havoc.

So I gave her an ultimatum.

"If you have time to gossip and be unproductive, then you have time to do therapy an hour a day and learn to walk again.

And until you start making progress, I won't come visit you." I was trying to give her a reason to want to be *better* at life.

We didn't speak for the last few weeks my mom was here on this earth.

I was just so frustrated with her. Why didn't she want more out of life? Why was she giving up? A part of me held a grudge with her—I was more her mother and she was more my child, and my inner child was distraught. Being around her triggered me so much. So I just removed myself and chose peace, thinking she would eventually come around.

Her nurses called with updates. She was doing better. I had hope.

XO

WHEN I VISITED MY MOM in April 2022 at the hospital where she was on her ventilator, she told me her favorite song was "November Rain." I was excited to play it right there in her hospital room and share a musical moment with her.

"Don't play it now," she said. "It's about someone dying."

To my surprise, on a cloudy day—November 3, 2022—I received the phone call that my mother had passed. Alone. In her hospital room. My biggest fear for her.

I didn't understand it. I had been told she was getting better. I was so angry. How was she dead?

J was boarding a flight when he got the call about my mom, and he immediately got off the plane and raced home to be with me—even though I told him not to. I could handle it myself, I told him. But he refused. He always shows up when I need him the most.

We raced down to the hospital and when I got there, they led me to her room. J stood outside so I could say my goodbye to her alone. When I walked in, the window was wide open. I knew it was so they could "let her spirit out," and I just gazed out the window for a moment before allowing my eyes to scan over to my mom's lifeless body. Lying in her hospital bed, she looked so peaceful. But her gray hair was tousled in a bun, which hurt my heart. She'd begged me to get her hair done. I'd agreed on one condition: if she would get up and just walk for me.

The tears started pouring and I wanted so badly to just drape myself across her body and be held by my mom like I had never been my entire life. But I was petrified after what happened when I touched Chizzle's body.

So I stood there, bawling my eyes out and telling her how sorry I was that I didn't realize how sick she truly was. That I loved her so much and thanked her for allowing me to be a part of her departure from Earth—even if I'd had no idea that's what I was a part of.

It was just her and me in silence. I never realized how loud silence really is. I just kept examining her face, knowing I'd never see it again.

Finally, I pulled myself together, wiped my face, and walked out to J. And I started questioning the doctors. I asked for medical records. I just couldn't help but feel like there was some sort of foul play.

I was in such disbelief that I immediately ordered her body to be picked up by the coroner's office for a private autopsy. There was no way she wasn't overdosed in the hospital—something had to be wrong. I couldn't live with the guilt of knowing I abandoned my mom in her final hours.

But when I got the autopsy results, the facts were clear. The years of hard drugs and beating her body up had just taken their toll. Her lungs were like cement, and her heart was so enlarged, the coroner said it was bigger than any grown man's he had ever seen. Her body was just tired. Just as she said.

I cried for days, mad at myself for forcing my wants on her when she clearly told me hers. As her daughter, was I just supposed to let her give up on life and sit by her side while she died? I couldn't accept that answer then. Now, my heart tells me yes.

She taught me more in her death than she ever did living. She taught me that forgiveness was for me, not for her, and that free will is what each of us has while we're here on Earth. What I may have wished and longed for our relationship is not what she wished and longed for.

I truly believe her gift to me was moving to Nashville to be close to me at the end. And I also truly believe that she stayed alive those extra seven months just for me.

I love you, Mom. Thank you.

Her life was a disappointment, but Vanessa was so full of love. She was not a good mom in the slightest, but she was *mine.* And when I needed her the most, she answered.

31

ONE LAST HEARTBREAK

YOU DIDN'T THINK IT WAS ALL BUTTERFLIES AND roses, did you? Ever after happily doesn't work like that—mine sure doesn't. I've learned that nothing in life is free and happy moments are fleeting. With every great high I've achieved, there's always been a low lurking around the corner to humble me, to remind me that even if you're on top of the world, it can all be taken in a matter of seconds. I really believe that's why I have such intense impostor syndrome. The universe constantly reminds me where I came from. As I've said before, my curse and blessing in life has been to give back to those who have helped me on my journey.

In 2022, J and I were riding high—dancing with the moon and chasing after our dreams. He had become one of the newest faces in country music and he was unstoppable. And me? My podcast is one of the top podcasts in America. We finally bought our first house together, and we were living the life we had dreamed about lying in bed that night we made our five-year plan.

Bill was always coming in and out of my life. That man and I couldn't get along for any real amount of time ever. But he was always a presence. And in classic Bill fashion, he wanted to make his presence known at the end. And go out with a bang. Boy, did he light shit up.

My dad was on wife number eight—I think I fucking stopped counting—and he'd married her behind our backs. Her name was Hagatha, and like all the women he had in his life, I did not trust her. When my dad told me he wanted me to be friends with her, the five-year-old me who was now allowed to stand up for herself did just that.

"I'll be cordial with her, but I will not be her friend. I'm tired of you forcing all these women on me," I told him. And with that, my dad cut me out of his life for another year. Oh well.

XO

I WAS IN THE MIDDLE of touring with J but decided to take a break at our house in Vegas when the call came. My dad had cancer, and he'd known about it for years but never told me. Now things were dire. As soon as I heard the news, I flew out to Houston to be with him.

As I walked into his house I saw him on his recliner, tiny, gray, and withering away. All I could do was cry. Cry because I hadn't had time to process and cry for the little girl who still so desperately loved him. Hagatha was there and kept reiterating how exhausted she was from waiting on him hand and foot. She had wanted him to tell us, she said, but he wouldn't.

We went to one last doctor's appointment and were told that

his diagnosis was prostate cancer that had spread to his bones. There was nothing more to be done. He had three months to live. The only thing I could think of was bringing him to Nashville to be with me, so we could try for some different opinions. At least we could put up a fight and see if we could keep him here longer. It didn't help that Bill truly refused to believe he was dying and therefore refused chemo. But he asked me to help him get better, and as his daughter, that's exactly what I was going to do.

XO

AT FIRST, BILL AND HAGATHA stayed with J and me, but eventually they wanted their own space, so I moved them to the same facility where my mom had stayed.

It didn't take long for me to see through Hagatha's facade. They fought like cats and dogs—but hey, that's my dad's love language, so I stayed out of it. I was smart enough to know that if I got in the middle, I'd lose my dad. He would always choose the women over me. It had been like that since I was five years old, and Bill's an old hound you can't teach new tricks.

I would even stick up for Hagatha sometimes, because honestly, Bill was a dick, and she was taking care of him. But I didn't realize how bad things were between Bill and Hagatha until they came to our house for Thanksgiving. We have a huge family shindig every year, and he was watching everyone sing their little hearts out on our karaoke machine. He seemed so happy and even a little at peace. I kept glancing over at him, because in my heart I knew it would be our last Thanksgiving together. But Hagatha wanted to leave, and she made it known. She wasn't whispering at him or hinting. She was screaming into his ear. For all the yelling and screaming I'd heard around my dad all my life, this felt different. More sinister. She was fucking losing it on him as he sat quietly in his wheelchair. It was hard to watch and even harder not to intervene. But I definitely made note of it. She didn't care that this was his last time with his family, Hagatha wanted her way. Bill eventually gave in and they left.

XO

DURING ONE OF OUR CONVERSATIONS, Hagatha confided in me that my dad had had cancer for twenty years and had never told anyone. She had found paperwork with the diagnosis and a treatment plan that he'd refused.

This man refused chemo because he had said he didn't want it to ruin his sex drive. Instead, he went through all kinds of crazy treatments. I can't imagine keeping such a dark secret to myself for so long, while also doing nothing to help myself. I'll never understand what he was thinking.

I tried my hardest to get right with his wife to make his last days peaceful. I put every feeling I had for her aside for the sake of Bill. I mean, Hagatha couldn't be all bad, right? She was taking care of him—allegedly, but I don't think it was out of the goodness of her heart.

The reality was that Bill had somehow acquired a bunch of dilapidated buildings and come into his own as a regular old slumlord. I didn't know how they got together. My dad had told me that Hagatha had been living with some other dude who couldn't take care of himself before she latched on to my dad. I couldn't ignore the fact that he had money now, and suddenly, there she was.

The hospital in Nashville exhausted all options for treatment. I even had a friend who owned a cancer center in Mexico give my dad treatments of vitamin C and various IVs to try to slow down the progress of the cancer, but nothing worked.

So I got the idea to make a bucket list for Bill—anything he wanted, I'd pay for it. I couldn't stand idly by while he just waited for life to leave him. And unlike my mom, he didn't want to die. He told me over and over. And he fought like hell to stay here. I wanted to make the last few months he had the best of his life. I couldn't help it. I hadn't forgiven him, and I'd never forget any of it. But some part of me was still that little girl who idolized her rocker dad, who ate little slices of hot dogs out of his shirt pocket. And that little girl wanted her dad to be okay. He was the first man I tried to fix, starting from day one. He was the last one too.

I put them into a cute little townhouse and moved them out of the senior nursing home. I figured that being out of the nursing home setting would help him flourish, and for the most part, it did. He surpassed the three-month mark that the Texas hospital had foreseen. He started putting on weight and getting some color back in his face. He used his scooter to get around. He was a shell of himself, but there was life in him still.

But no matter how perfect I wanted his days to be, the fighting continued. My heart kept breaking over and over—if I were on my deathbed, all I'd want is to be surrounded by love. I wouldn't want to go out like that.

I tried to stay out of it. I knew what would happen if I got too involved. When I showed up at the condo to check on my dad one afternoon, there was broken glass everywhere. I didn't ask questions not because I didn't want to—but because I knew I couldn't.

XO

"I CAN'T TAKE IT ANYMORE," Hagatha said by way of hello. "I'm leaving your dad for the night." Hell of a way to start a phone call.

Bill was in a wheelchair. He couldn't do anything for himself.

The man needed twenty-four-hour care. But as far as I understood, my dad was in the hospital that night, having tests done. And I know how overwhelming caregiving can be. I empathized. Bill was safe, so why not?

"I just need to reset."

"Okay, go take whatever you need," I told her. But then she started rambling.

"Bill doesn't need me. He just wants *her*." It took a little bit of negotiating to understand who the hell she was talking about, but it turned out to be some kind of health aide or nurse of Bill's that she was jealous of. Let the man live. Jesus Christ.

"Okay, Hagatha," I said. "Go do what you got to do."

I called Bill to try to figure out what was going on. One day, I'll listen to the recordings I have of all these calls. J told me to capture his voice so I could hear it after he passed. That day, Bill finally got honest with me—as honest as he'd ever get for the rest of his life.

"I never told you this because I didn't want you to have this on your shoulders," he said. "Hagatha was homeless when I met her, and I took her in off the street thinking that I could help her."

I tried to keep my cool, but I was already mad.

"Dad, you made her the executor of your will. You don't even really know her."

"Well, that's not going to happen," he said.

"What's not going to happen?"

"I'll take her out of the will." His voice cracked as he fought back tears.

"Are you at the hospital right now? Do you need me to come?" I asked.

"No, I'm at home," he said.

"Wait. You're at home? She left you?" Bill started crying, just big sobs over the phone. Bill was a fucking dick, but at that point, he was a sick man in a wheelchair, crying his eyes out alone. I thought about the broken glass, all the fights, the screaming at Thanksgiving, and it fell into place.

"Is she getting violent with you?" I asked.

"Yeah," he said, still crying. He told me she threw shit at him, broke things, screamed and screamed.

I raced over to get my father and I was going to move him into our house. No way in hell I was leaving him with that bitch one more second.

I walked in the door, and guess who was standing next to my dad?

XO

I WAS PISSED BEYOND BELIEF. My protective instincts were in overdrive. You don't kick a man when he's sick and dying, and you don't fucking hurt my family.

I wanted to say: *You're being violent with my dad, I will tear you limb from limb.* But I kept my cool.

"We need to have a conversation," I said to the two of them.

"I want to talk to you alone," Bill said, and Hagatha's jaw clenched.

"Bill, are you sure you want to talk to her alone?" she asked. You could just about see her pulling the strings. "Yes," he said, "but is there anything you want to say first?" Hagatha stood firm. She wasn't going to leave, because she knew that if we were alone, he'd go with me. But she wasn't moving, so I said my piece in front of her.

"Dad, if you don't want to be with Hagatha, I will send her back to fucking Texas right now and you can move in with us." Her face exploded and she started screaming so loudly I had to tell her to shut up. Unbothered, I kept on. "I'll move you right this very minute if you want."

Bill didn't answer for a second, and finally, he looked like he'd just given up.

"If we can work things out, I'd like to stay with Hagatha."

"But if she's fucking throwing shit and being violent with you—" I started, but Hagatha kept screaming the shrillest, loudest screeches I'd ever heard.

All my life, I've been around screaming, from my very earliest days. It stays with you—the way your body goes into fight or flight and your nervous system goes into overdrive.

"You're lying!" she screamed, running around the house like a crazy person. My dad looked after her and sighed.

"I'm sorry, honey. I shouldn't have said that. Come back in here and we'll talk," he said.

"Dad. Is she being violent or not?" And the way he looked at me was as familiar as my own face. He looked like a battered partner covering for his abuser. Hagatha kept screaming, and I lost my cool.

"Shut the fuck up and sit down. You two are acting like children," I said. They both looked at me in shock. I was tired of it all. The arguing, the manipulation, the drama.

Bill, you are dying. Why do you want to live like this?

Somehow, I wrangled us into fifteen minutes of calm. We made a plan to get them a counselor. We were going to work together. It was going to be okay.

That night, I texted Hagatha that I was sorry for yelling. I told her about the house I grew up in, and how nothing triggers me like screaming. I thanked her for taking care of my dad, and I told her I loved them both. She texted back that she was sorry and that she loved me too. All was well.

XO

I'D LEFT MY POPS AND Hagatha that night feeling great.

J had won an award, so we were set to fly to LA. I was going to be gone about five days, and I figured while I was away, they could reconnect and hopefully come to an agreement that they need to start being nice to each other instead of fighting. It was radio silence on their end the entire time I was gone, which I found unusual—but I figured I'd just give them space.

It was about five in the morning and we were getting ready to board a plane home after the awards week in LA. My phone buzzed with a text from my dad.

Hey, I moved back to Texas. Thanks for everything.

Wait. What? They packed up and moved back to Texas without a warning, a go fuck yourself, nothing??

I broke down. Bill had done some awful shit in his life, but this took the fucking cake. *You abandoned your daughter for another woman. Again. But wait, you abandoned her because she stood up for you after you told her your wife was abusive.*

It was genuinely hard for me to even grasp it.

That woman loaded up this dying man into a van and drove his ass from Nashville to Texas in a span of four days. In my heart, I feel she basically kidnapped a dying man.

"That's way too long to be in a car with his body like that," J said.

I had to leave home at fourteen because my father chose a woman over me. And even in the last months of his life, my dad had done the same. When was he going to stop hurting me? When would enough be enough?

I loved my dad so much—even when he was awful to me. But I'd reached the end of my rope, and it was time to call it.

Why? What did I do to you that I don't even deserve a proper goodbye?

I told my dad I was coming to get him—and he told me he'd have me arrested. Arrested for trying to help him.

I was done. All I ever wanted was his love, and I was tired. Tired of fighting for it. All I could do was just go silent on him. And him on me. Once again, we weren't speaking to each other.

EVER AFTER HAPPILY

A FAMILY MEMBER CALLED ME AND TOLD ME BILL WAS in the hospital in Texas for "treatment"—but she didn't elaborate. *Huh. The minute he leaves my side, he's back in the hospital.* Not too long ago, he'd been with me, putting on weight, scootering around, and showing signs of improvement.

But he was lying in a hospital bed, telling everyone not to leave me out of it. A week later, my family member called again—Bill had gotten worse.

I got mad. He was rotting in some hospital bed in Texas after being basically kidnapped in his wheelchair. So, I picked up my phone and texted his abductor/wife.

How dare you take my dad from me? And now he's sicker?

I was so furious. I didn't want our last conversation to be the fight we'd had over Hagatha—but it didn't look like I'd ever hear from him again. It was fucking heartbreaking.

Why don't you just call him? she texted back. As if I hadn't been calling, texting, letting the phone ring and ring and never getting an answer.

There's a special place in hell for women like you.

Shame on her for coming between a father and daughter. Shame on her for causing a huge rift while he was dying. Fuck her, honestly. It was like a repeat of Mindy—the beginning of my life and the end of his. Apparently, it was me versus all the women in his life, always. Until the end.

The tension between me and his wife thawed over the next couple of days, because I just needed facts. I tried to take the emotion out of everything and just get information. Was Bill alive or dead? Was he in pain? I just wanted to know if my dad was okay. I was willing to put everything aside—all the drama and anger and hurt—if I could just get information and hug my dad one last time.

She told me they were going home and that people should come visit Bill at some point or another. Nothing seemed urgent and it didn't look so bad anymore—I said I'd visit when they invited me. One thing about Bill: You do not fucking intrude when he's not feeling good. He'd tell you to get the fuck out. I knew that if he wanted me there, he'd reach out.

I'm not in communication with Baby Sis, and Bill wouldn't pick up the phone. So my only connection was Hagatha, and I tried to keep extracting any information I could.

We had just landed in Nashville from another award show in LA when she finally told me to come.

You need to see your dad today, she texted. It was like the world sped up from zero to one hundred. I dropped everything and started calling around to get on a flight. I'd rent a private jet—I didn't fucking care. I was going to get to Bill.

I was about to lock in a flight when Bill's wife called again. He was gone. The last words I ever spoke to my father were in anger. I was robbed of a chance to be by his side as he took his last breath. All because of a woman.

XO

MY POPS WASN'T AN ANGEL, but he was who I chose before I came here—and sometimes I still scratch my head and think maybe another soul ordered him and I somehow accidentally got him instead. I mean—what was I thinking?

My dad didn't have much to go on as far as models for relationships. His parents molded him to be the way he was—and he chose not to correct their mistakes in this life. His father never spoke to Bill again after he left for his other family, and even went as far as to cut my dad out of his will when he passed. Bill always said I reminded him of his mother. I'm not sure how—or if that was even a compliment—but it was probably because I didn't tolerate his shit. Either way, Bill never broke his generational curses and then left me with his crosses to bear.

My dad didn't have much, and before he died we went over his will together. He had decided to divide all his properties between me, Baby Sis, and my brother, Billy. At first I didn't want anything from him, but then I figured I could sell the properties and put a fund together for Bailee's college. Pass it from one generation to the next.

But in true Bill fashion, he had to give me one last slap in the face to make sure I knew how worthless I was to him. When they read the will out, he had cut me out just like his father did to him. To pour salt on the wound, he wrote, "I bequeath nothing to my daughter Alisa because she's well off and has reminded me numerous times."

I wasn't even mad about being cut out of the will, because I truly wanted nothing from him, but the words he wrote are what stung. Because none of that was true. If my taking care of him made him feel like I was throwing money in his face, then that was a him problem, not a me problem. Honestly, I expected nothing less from my dad. Just another cut on the heart he created.

XO

WHEN MY MOM DIED IN 2022, I felt an instant warmth that she sent me. She just wanted to send me all the love she could—more love than she could even show me while she was alive. She'd come to me in glowing, colorful lights. I'd wake up in the middle of the night not long after she died with my TV all lit up like the aurora borealis. She'd show herself through songs. I felt her with me all the time. Every time I speak to a psychic, she barrels her way to the front to let me know she's thriving and apologetic and learned her lesson in this life.

I think she wanted to thank me for taking care of her in the ways she couldn't take care of me. And I think she wanted to show me she'd made it to the other side—that she was okay, so I could let her go.

In those first years after she passed, I felt her all the time. It's died down now, but she still shows up from time to time, and I feel that same glowing warmth run through me.

But everything went cold when Bill died. It was almost like *no* feeling, and it freaked me the fuck out. I've always been so in tune with my spiritual side, and I've always been able to tap into the people I love. But the nothingness was so brutal. *Where the fuck is he? Where did he go?*

Back before Bill passed, I hit up a psychic back in Vegas. I sat across from her and asked what she sensed.

"Do you see any death around me?" I asked.

"Actually, I do," she said. "Your dad is going to be in the in-between and walk the Earth until you forgive him. He's not going to be able to go to the light until you forgive him."

It was way before Bill's last punch landed—so all her talk about forgiveness didn't make much sense to me. *What the hell is she talking about? I forgave my dad for who he was and for the life I had. Whatever. I'll talk to him in a couple of days.*

But when he passed, that cold didn't leave me. You remember that Bill went full Bible-thumper, and he was a devout Christian until the day he died. But he was also the world's biggest fucking hypocrite, and I don't know that he made it up to Heaven. Maybe he was still in the in-between, walking the Earth like that psychic predicted. Purgatory, if you will.

I also didn't want his spirit around me. I was so mad. So hurt. I cried for weeks. There was a moment when I sat down on my bed and just sobbed, drenching the blankets with tears. But after I allowed myself to grieve, I banished Bill from me—I walked through my house and cast out his energy. He wasn't welcome. *I don't want to see you. Don't you dare come visit me. No visions, no dreams. Stay the fuck away from me.*

But Bill started showing up all over the place. First, he showed my friends Amy and Sloan visions of himself on vacation, healthy and relaxing. If he couldn't get to me, I guess my people are as good an option as any.

But then he found me. Of course he did. Banished or not, Bill started showing himself to me as butterflies.

One day, a butterfly came and landed on my knee. Then another came the next day. Every day they were prettier and prettier, and I couldn't ignore them. One landed smack on top of J's nipple while we were out swimming. That's just like Bill's sense of humor.

Two beautiful does won't stop hanging around my home, and I've taken them in. My girl Tasha moved to Nashville, so now I get to see her all the time, and she caught eyes with one of those deer and looked like she'd seen a ghost. You can't tell me that all of this doesn't have something to do with Bill.

I think he's trying to make it up to me. I think he regrets what he did—or at least feels guilty, and he keeps showing up so he can make good. But I mean . . . if he really wanted to make it up to me, he should show himself as a crow. Just sayin'.

I haven't forgiven him, but I've found peace. I'm not mad at him anymore, but I don't like him right now either. It's obvious to me now that I'd put Bill on a pedestal. He could do no wrong in my eyes, even though he did me wrong over and over until his last breath. But I never realized until he died what a weak man he was. It took him dying to shatter the image of him I'd created my whole life and to really see him for what he was: everything I hate in a man.

Maybe seeing someone as they really are is a part of grief. I see that no dad should ever make a daughter feel the way my dad did his whole life.

I can't help thinking about my own daughter. I didn't give birth to Bailee or grow her in my body, but that child is mine. I'm her mama, and I love her with everything in me. And Bailee has been my way to find redemption and to break generational trauma. Bill was who he was, but his disgusting version of parenting stops with me.

I haven't been a perfect parent—or at times even a good parent. I've made so many mistakes trying to help raise her. Bailee went through some serious shit with us. She watched us both get sober. She watched us learn how to have a healthy marriage when we'd never seen one before. She has done so much work to heal herself, and parenting her healed me too. I'm really only able to look at my own life and see the trauma and abuse I survived when I see that sweet girl in front of me.

XO

THERE'S BEEN A LOT OF death the past few years—physically, emotionally, and spiritually. I'm not even the same girl I was in 2016 when J and I got married.

Mindy's sister, Andi—remember her? She died last summer from a fentanyl overdose. She was an addict her whole life. Another example of someone who wasn't willing to face the pain. She was one of those beautiful girls who never got it together—even if she was the most vile, abusive woman I'd ever known—besides her sister.

But alongside the death, there's been growth and new things too.

Bailee's sixteen now. She has a job and will be leaving for college soon. I could cry thinking about how she's so grown now. How much she reminds me of young me and how sad I'll be when she leaves home to become her own woman. I wish I could cocoon her and keep her here forever. We've had some pretty nasty fights—as do all teens and their moms—and I'm sure there are days when she hates me, and I know there are days when I don't like her. But in the end, we always know that we have each other. One thing she knows is that I'm protective of her because that's one thing I never felt as a child. I can only pray one day she realizes that's how I love her.

Now that we're finally stable financially and somewhat emotionally after all the healing we've done over this decade together, we're talking about the future—including growing our family. J and I have a surrogate, the sweetest woman ever, and soon I'll be starting my IVF stims. We have decided to use my own eggs with J's sperm—and we are trying for twins. I'm so nervous, because I've waited this long to have kids with someone I knew would be a great father—and to be able to make sure they have the best life. Some people frown upon our decision to bring babies into this world at our age, and I could give a fuck. We're going to raise these babies in love and give them everything we were never given. I can't wait to see a piece of me and him running around outside of our bodies.

I've accomplished so much in these forty-four years, and the next thing for me is to raise a baby or two and start my baby mama era. I want to garden and make a home and find a peaceful stride. A lot of people don't even know that J and I have been on this fertility journey since October 31, 2019—I can't help but giggle because a Halloween date is so fitting for us. I call us "the Addams family" of country music.

But back in 2019, we were nowhere near as stable as we are now. And I learned then that my Fallopian tubes were blocked and I would need surgery and that still wouldn't guarantee I'd be able to carry a baby. But with how much IVF has advanced over the years, and with the help of the most unselfish woman willing to carry twins for us, we'll be able to make our baby dreams come true.

After the surgery news in 2019 we paused. I'll never forget how nervous I was to ask J when I felt it in my heart that we should try the baby route again.

"How would you feel about having a baby?" I asked him. He didn't blink.

"I would love to have a baby with you." I honestly didn't expect him to be so certain. It felt so good to see how excited he was at the thought of growing our family.

And like I said, we're different people now. Our life is unrecognizable.

We got excited as hell and started our IVF journey. We'd decided to keep it off the internet, which has put us through the wringer more than once. Everyone has an opinion. I always say the internet loves to ruin beautiful things.

But leave it to my husband to accidentally drop the news on a podcast.

He came home from an interview with his tail between his legs.

"There's something we have to talk about," he said. I was *not* expecting him to say he blabbed to the world, but there we were.

"First of all, we should have done that on my fucking podcast," I joked. "And number two: We weren't supposed to tell anyone, babe." I giggled, because I just couldn't help but think it was so cute how excited he was.

How could I be mad? My husband is so happy to be having this baby or babies with me. Scream it from the mountaintops, baby. I posted the clip before the podcast episode dropped—shout-out to the *Bussin' with the Boys* dudes for letting me break the news myself. I needed to control the narrative for our future child. I had to protect them, even before they were born. I knew what was coming before anyone else did.

The amount of love we got back from our followers and supporters was beyond anything I ever could have imagined. There was hate too—talk that I was having babies for content or trying to get paid. As if I don't already have a lifetime's worth of content and I'm not already well off.

But that love we were shown meant the world. You can't understand this until you go through it, but anyone who's gone through infertility just wants people in their corner. The last thing we want is unwarranted opinions from naysayers. Sometimes all people have is hope, and it is so personal and fragile.

I didn't have another way besides IVF—you know how many babies I've lost and how pregnancy almost killed me. I know that my mental health couldn't take the hormonal changes. I'm in the best place I've ever been. I'm on an even keel and at peace with my own mind—and the best thing I can do for Bailee's future sibling(s) is to keep myself steady. I'm already so scared of the hormone shots, but it's the least I can do to bring the gifts of the universe to life.

XO

I'VE HAD EYES ON ME since I was in my twenties when I started escorting. Most of the time, it was me putting myself out there—the paparazzi didn't show up until a few years ago. Sharing my life online was lifesaving. It made me feel less alone. Not to mention I got to tell *my* story in the most raw and organic way I knew how.

Even then some people accuse me of lying about my past and to that I can only cackle. If I was going to make up a story, I definitely wouldn't have picked being a Las Vegas hooker. I would have lied and said I graduated from Harvard Medical School and become a neuroscientist.

But my life is crazy now: It's like a real-life *Pretty Woman*. A woman who grew up in the sex industry who pulled herself from the depths of hell and is now living on a higher frequency. How fucking beautiful is that?

Living life in the spotlight was always my dream as a little girl. I knew one day I'd make it. I manifested it my entire life, and it came to fruition. I'm so thankful for how kind the media has been to our family— not to mention all the other country stars and their wives who have welcomed us with open arms.

I've said things in the book that I've never told anyone—even for someone like me whose entire life is online. I can only hope and pray that my story encourages someone to chase their dreams—or even more importantly, discourages them from walking down the path of drugs and abusive relationships that I took. I'm no role model.

But I am an honest to God, Cinder-fucking-ella.

XO

I'VE LIVED ONE HELL OF a life—but it never made me hard. Rough around the edges, maybe, but I never stopped believing in myself or love. I am a hopeless romantic in all things. I try to see the beauty in the things most people run from.

J asking me about my five-year plan before he'd bang me back in 2016 was us manifesting our lives. And guess what? We made every single thing on our list happen—and then some. So, what's next, you ask?

I'm going to keep speaking up for the underdogs—like my husband and I always have—and to keep proving people wrong. That has *always* been fuel for my fire. I'm going to keep growing my production company and keep watching it expand beyond what I ever thought possible.

But most importantly, I'm creating a life for myself and my family where we can be safe and free. Where I can just *be*.

J and I are now the proud owners of five hundred acres and a mini farm sprinkled with the cutest mini cows, mini donkeys, and mini pigs. Being a farmer wasn't on my bingo card, but fuck it, I'm so ready. I have the love to give and want nothing more than to spread it.

We're going to watch Bailee graduate high school and go to college and become the doctor or lawyer she wants to be. I hope she finds love. Love for herself and love of someone who is deserving of her love. I hope she finds healing and understands her worth. All I know is I'm excited to see her grow into the beautiful woman she is.

And my husband—my dear, sweet, best friend who I've found over and over again in every lifetime—I can't wait to grow older with you on the front porch of our farm with babies crawling around the floor. Thank you for becoming the man I never thought I needed. And for being the safest of spaces.

My life has been a roller coaster of ups and downs and crazy fucking shit. But through it all, I never gave up. If I got knocked down, I stood right back up. One thing Bill did instill in me is resilience. And although worldly things are cool, the lessons I've learned are more important to me than diamonds.

I'll leave you with an Oscar Wilde quote that I've always loved—it couldn't explain my life more.

"You will always be fond of me. I represent to you all the sins you never had the courage to commit."

Go after what you want. Don't take no for an answer. Give 'em hell, kid.

Tell them I sent you.

ACKNOWLEDGMENTS

TO ALL THE LESSONS THIS LIFE HAS GIVEN ME, THANK you. Each one is woven into my patchwork soul.

To the little Vegas girl I used to be, I finally let you go, sweet child. You don't have to fight anymore. You can rest. You made it through the chaos so I could stand here today—sober, free—and become the woman you needed.

To my husband, Jelly, my best friend, my calm in the storm, and the man who saw *me* before the world ever did. Thank you for showing me that love doesn't fix you, it just makes you brave enough to fix yourself. You are my home, my safe space, my eternal flame.

To our daughter, Bailee, the heartbeat of my redemption story. You are the proof that even the most broken people can build something beautiful. Watching you grow is like watching God hand me a second chance in real time. You are everything I dreamed of being at your age. I'm so thankful to be a part of your journey.

To my team, my ride-or-dies, my coven. Every soul who's been in the trenches building this empire with me: Meme, you showed up when you didn't have to. For every harebrained idea at 1 a.m., you always made sure a spotlight was shown on it. Hailee, Jason, Momo, and Jaime, thank you for showing up when I didn't have the strength, the schedule, or the sanity. We built this from pure chaos and sheer determination, and, somehow, it's become so magical.

To my followers—you beautiful, wild, loyal humans—thank you for seeing and accepting me for the beautifully broken soul I was. You made a misfit girl feel like she belonged. Every download, every comment, every laugh, you've built this dream with me, one raw story at a time.

And to Jesus—I may have argued with You a few hundred times, but I see now You were never punishing me. . . . You were preparing me.

Sloane, my blonde bombshell agent. Thank you for clearing rooms for me and demanding people give me a chance. Haley and Margaret, thank you for seeing me before the world did, and fighting for my words, my story, and my voice. This book exists because you believed it could. And, Julia, thanks for being my partner and helping guide me through this unraveling of trauma.

Carrie Thornton at Dey Street, you saw a story that no one else did and made it come to life just like a real fairy tale. Thank you for bringing back my love of writing that I lost so long ago. To the rest of the Dey Street and HarperCollins teams—Drew Henry, Jennifer Eck, Rachel Meyers, Allison Carney, Heidi Richter—thank you for helping to make this dream come true.

For every woman who's ever been called too wild, too loud, too broken.

There was a time I thought my story was a warning. Turns out, it was a blueprint.

I didn't clean up for the world.

I rose up for myself.

And maybe that's the real miracle . . . that the girl who once lost everything could turn her scars into a sanctuary.

This book isn't a goodbye to who I was.

It's a love letter to the woman I fought like hell to become.